BETWEEN THE LINES

BETWEEN THE LINES

BY TOM FRAZIER
WITH DELPHINE FRAZIER

THE STORY OF A GERMAN BOY RAISED IN
NAZI TIMES WHO RETURNS TO HIS HOME-
LAND AS AN AMERICAN SOLDIER IN WWII—
PASSIONATELY FIGHTING FOR THE IDEALS OF
HIS ADOPTED COUNTRY WHILE SUFFERING
OVER WHAT HIS FATHERLAND HAD BECOME.

REGENT PRESS
2001

Library of Congress Cataloging-in-Publication Data

Frazier, Tom 1921-
    Between the lines : the story of a German boy raised in Nazi
times who returns to his homeland as an American soldier in WWII
... / by Tom Frazier with Delphine Frazier.
        p. cm.
    ISBN 1-58790-008-4
        1. Frazier, Tom, 1921- 2. World War, 1939-1945--Personal
narratives, American. 3. World War, 1939-1945--Campaigns--
Western Front. 4. Youth--Germany–Biography. 5. Soldiers
–United States--Biography. 6. World War, 1939-1945--Search
and rescue operations--Europe. 7. World War, 1939-1945--
Prisoners and prisons, German. I. Frazier, Delphine, 1924-
II. Title.

D811.F717 A3 2001
940.54'8173--dc21   2001019327

Front Cover: Tom with the American flag on his sleeve,
next to a small Alpine village that had just been destroyed
by the Germans. It had no military value.

Original Drawing by Rick, 1945

Manufactured in the United States of America
Regent Press
6020A Adeline
Oakland, CA 94608

DEDICATION

TO THE FUTURE

■

DYLAN

ERIC

ISABEL

ACKNOWLEDGEMENTS

It may seem strange and certainly immodest that I am sending my first thanks to myself. I am immensely grateful to the young man—the protagonist in this story—who typed up the events and his thoughts about them during these memorable years of his life while they were still fresh in his memory. Thanking myself as a youth seems scarcely immodest to me, since it is hard for me to believe that I am the same individual who originally wrote this story. So much has been forgotten . . . certainly the details. So much has changed in my attitude toward risk taking and adventure. Also, I have lost the naïveté—though I hope not the optimism—to believe that goodness can be achieved merely by working toward it. In addition, during the war years, the shock of the atrocities committed by the Germans shattered my feelings for them and led me into a useless anger. I hope this has changed into something deeper and more constructive. I have come to admire the intensity with which those Germans with whom I have worked in the last years are meeting the challenge of facing their past and using their history to recognize threats to democracy and to understand the need for constant effort to work toward a good society. I now realize this transformation is far more complicated than we ever imagined, and I want to thank all those who are struggling with this process and have taught me so much.

There are many who participated in the production of this book. First and foremost is my wife, Delphine, who in the last year worked at least as hard as I did with this manuscript. After more than 50 years of marriage, she not only can finish my sentences but she can often start them as well. To our good friend, K. Goff who labored tirelessly reviewing the manuscript with enthusiasm, interest and a real understanding. To Katherine Dieter, our editor who is a real professional in her love of the language and who invariably was able to translate what I said into exactly what I meant. She taught us so much about the fascinating world of writing.

My thanks to many who read this manuscript and who lived through their own voyages into a new world. I wish they would tell their stories. Thanks to my brother, Chris Heinicke, whose memory was a real help and to his English-born wife Sally, who shows through as a true writer. Our thanks to Fanita English and the Moores— Ursula and also Ernst. He and I compared our times at Camp Ritchie, the Intelligence camp in Maryland.

Thanks to my former commanding officer, Lieutenant Leonard Woods, whom I met again recently after 55 years. He participated in much of this story and was generous in his critique of the manuscript, and in allowing me to use his photos of our times in the High Alps.

Although it may not seem that I appreciated it, I thank all those, led by Christine Stusche, of the Odenwald Institut, who nagged me, encouraged me, pushed me, and argued with me, to get this book in print. Thanks for the support of Beth Gawain and Mary Goulding who have written their own books. Not least, thanks to Bob Cusick who led me through the important technicalities of KINKOS' copy machines while we reminisced about some of our similar experiences as G.I.'s. And thanks to our daughter, Delphine Mozlowski, who helped with the computer and word processor.

Also, thanks to Mark Weiman, owner of Regent Press, and Melinda Applegate, his graphic designer, who shared their love of the printed word, and who made the intricacies of publishing and distributing seem possible if not easy. The experience this last year of being involved in producing a book has been for us as much a joy as a learning experience.

And finally much gratitude to all those who have enough interest in the years of this story to read the book and ponder the meaning . . . and the ways we can use this history and what we have learned from it . . . to create the world we all truly want.

CONTENTS

Preface

For over 50 years I have been told, "You absolutely must write the story of your life." Now, finally, I have a great desire to organize in writing my experiences of the important times in which I lived. This book is the result.

The first part of this book is a personal story of my childhood in Germany as I remember it. It was not a typical childhood, and yet I feel that it was my ordinary day-to-day experiences that cast light on that fateful period. I have been inspired by other profound and moving stories written by Germans who were children in the 20s and 30s and who emigrated to the US. I believe these stories hold the answer to the question that continues to disturb Germans and those of us who love Germany and have many dear German friends: How could the people of that country, with their deep love of nature, music, and art, and their ability to enjoy life with great energy, have allowed and even embraced the evil of the Third Reich? There have been many intellectual answers, yet I have come to believe that it is the stories of that time which best bring about an understanding and an awareness that cannot be adequately analyzed and summarized in words. These stories explain how Nazi life and philosophy became an encompassing part of everyday life. The answer lies, I believe, "between the lines," beyond intellectual and reasoned explanations.

The rest of the book deals with my experience during World War II, a subject that still seems to be of great interest to others, perhaps because the great German question has not been fully answered even now. My story of the war tells of a unique experience of high adventure and spirited times as I worked with others—between and behind enemy lines—to liberate Allied soldiers and to search for important documents. Fortunately, in 1944 and 1945, I wrote copiously of my experiences, especially after I "liberated" a typewriter. Writing was one of the ways I would pass the time during long, boring periods of waiting, so often a feature of military life. It also was a way to begin to integrate many of the experiences that were overwhelming me. Telling the story on paper often allowed me to let go of the immediate pain and confusion of the war. When I returned home, Lloyd Reynolds, a creative writing professor at Reed College in Oregon, encouraged me, and helped me get my experiences into orderly form. The following year I wrote my remembrances of my childhood in Berlin and my reaction to coming to America. I then put the material away, where it lay dormant for over 50 years. When my wife and I recently read it again, we were amazed and fascinated.

Some of what I wrote I no longer recall in detail, so I have been careful not to add anything that might not be accurate. What I have added from the present perspective, I have usually placed in parentheses. Many of my ideas about the Germans or the French, or about politics, or other broad categories reflect the opinions of my youth, and as such, I think it is important to include them, even if they are not necessarily the opinions I hold today. They may help explain how most of us, as American soldiers in World War II, experienced our part in the war, and the fervor with which we served, whatever our role.

When my mother died in 1990, I found among her things a collection of all of my wartime letters home to her. This source provided another important perspective of my time in the army, and I have included the parts of them that did not deal with repeated requests for candy or instructions of what to do with money orders. At one point during the war, I also "liberated" a camera and was able to take many pictures of scenes that few others saw, and I have also included a few of these herein. The pictures often are of very poor quality but I felt many were very important.

As I reread my story today, it sounds as though I had one continuous adventure and plenty of great times socially. These are the parts on which I chose to focus at the time. I still vividly remember today the other realities —struggling with mud and snow, fighting a jeep engine that would not work well, surviving the general dreariness of GI life, or taking orders from superiors who did not always know the total situation with which I had to deal. There were frequent brushes with death, there were many painful scenes that I could not blot out, and they have deeply influenced the rest of my life. I believe they remained with many of the GIs. Whatever the problems, however, I was always grateful that I had the opportunity to do something that I thought was important, and I took great satisfaction from our successful liberation of many Allied soldiers and our retrieval of important German documents.

My trips through the cathedrals of Europe were also important for me and maintained me through difficult times.

For many GIs, the war experience was, and remains, a high point in their lives because of the dedication with which they undertook the task, and the closeness that arose between men in combat who were ready to give their lives for each other, and for their country. I firmly believe that the men in that war, particularly those of the infantry, are responsible for the lives of opportunity and freedom we have today, both in this country and in Europe, and I am grateful to them daily.

I am also deeply grateful to the partisans I knew in various countries in Europe—men, women, and whole families—who, despite tremendous odds, risked their lives daily to help individual Allied soldiers, and to fight the occupying Axis forces. Their strength, both physical and emotional, and their endurance and drive, have remained with me as a source of inspiration for service to the world.

Chapter 1

•

1921 - 1932

When I was born in Danzig (now Gdansk) in May of 1921, World War I had been over for two and a half years and Germany was still reeling. Like the Danish-Prussian war of 1864 and the Franco-Prussian war of 1870-71, WWI was largely begun by a government that was dominated by the military. The revolts of 1848 by the Berliners did not bring about a more democratic government. Instead, any movement toward more political and personal freedom was completely suppressed under the guidance of Bismarck and the Kaiser. The Germans respected and feared authority, and after a very punitive Versailles Peace Treaty at the end of WWI, the average German was not prepared to live in a democratic society. Although the Weimar Constitution was a very good instrument, the Germans were not ready for it. And the military held on to their power.

The terms of the Armistice had declared Danzig to be a free city, no longer ruled by Germany. Yet, as it gained its independence and freedom, it also found itself without any nation to support it in a time of economic and political turmoil. It had fallen into despair and became a place of great poverty and hunger.

The city had been founded in the fourteenth century by Teutonic knights who came from Germany to Christianize the Slavs. My mother's family had been there since that time. She often told me that every day as she walked to school, she passed the ancient Teutonic fortifications, branches of which still stand at Marienburg on the Vistula River. By the sixteenth century, Gdansk (Danzig) had become a center of learning, and with the nearby port of Gdinia, it was also one of the great capitals of commerce.

My Mother—Lottie

Charlotte Marie Luise Fuchs Heinicke Levy, my mother, was born July 5, 1900. She entered the world with the new century and took an active part in many of the great events in it.

Lottie, as my mother was called, and her brother Bernhard, who was four years older, were the beloved and pampered children of Frau and Herr Fuchs who operated the B.I. Fuchs firm, which manufactured all kinds of civilian uniforms, work clothes, and cheap garments. Her mother supervised the home plant and her father handled the administrative aspects. The family was prosperous and well regarded in their community, where they were known as a devoted couple. They lived on Dominick's Wall, a part of a new city development built on the walls and moats of the old fortification. The modern and stately city blocks had manicured lawns, small parks, and a wide boulevard.

While Lottie and her brother may have been pampered and loved, they did not see very much of their par-

ents who were busy with their firm.
Lottie's mother would disappear
into the factory each morning as
soon as she was dressed and had
her hair fixed by the maid.
Herr Fuchs took very little
interest in raising the children,
although he was obviously
devoted to Lottie (somewhat
to her mother's annoyance).
The children were actually
raised by Omachen, Lottie's
mother's stepmother, a warm, jolly
little woman who loved the children
and provided them with
warmth and caring. As was the

LOTTIE AND BERNARD

custom in such families, the children were brought in to
see their parents after dinner, to kiss them and say goodnight. Lottie would often ask her father to play the
piano and sing, and he would say, "Maybe after you are
in bed." Lottie would wait for
what she remembers as the
most magical and happy
times—those nights when he
did play and sing many
German lullabies.

Lottie's father, Bernhard
Johannes Fuchs, had been
born in a rural parsonage and
hence belonged to the "upper
class" of society, even though
his family's life was actually
very restricted and they had

MATERNAL GRANDFATHER
BERNARD FUCHS

few economic resources. His father had watched his parsonage burn to the ground during Napoleonic times. To Lottie's mother and brother, the family background always seemed important, and Lottie's brother tried to make connections and establish facts about the family tree when he joined the army. There had been "von Fuchs" in the eighteenth century—two musicians and a botanist—but it was too remote a connection, and ultimately too expensive, to get the authorities to return the "von".

Lottie's father had been sent to the university in hopes he would become a clergyman like his father, but he had run away and eventually found a sponsor who set him up in business.

Lottie herself learned to play the piano and sing, which gave her great pleasure throughout her life. She loved her father immensely, and a look of disappointment on his face was all the discipline she needed. Far from being the stereotypical Prussian autocrat, he was a loving and adoring father, though he took little part in raising the family. Lottie remembers that his face lit up whenever he saw her, and she ran to him as often as she could. Her mother, she remembers, smiled more often at her brother, Bernhard.

One fall, Lottie remembered, her father spent much time in bed with heart problems, a broken ankle, and other complications. The following spring he suddenly died. This happened when Lottie was not quite 11 years old, an over-protected, spoiled little girl by her own description, suddenly without a father. People tried to be nice to her, but she changed from a docile, dreaming child into a fierce, distrustful creature, especially toward her mother, and she would dissolve into crying fits at any mention of her father.

It was some time later that her uncle told her that her father had died of syphilis, contracted years before during his wild days at the university when dueling, drinking, and carousing were the mark of the aristocratic gentleman. According to the law he must have been in remission for at least 12 years before he would be allowed to marry.

When World War I began, Lottie's brother joined the Reitende Jaeger, a cavalry regiment not far from Danzig, and it was decided that Lottie must go to the university and embark on a profession. Medicine seemed to her the most interesting choice and there were many German women doctors at the time. She liked to read and study and this seemed to her the easiest way to be left alone.

She attended Pastor Dr. Kalweit's confirmation class. These classes were an opportunity to learn about the great thinkers, about philosophy, and cultural history, and also to explore an intellectual understanding of God, or what others throughout history had thought about the Divine. This was Lottie's first experience with intellectual efforts and she remained fascinated by the philosophy surrounding religion. To Lottie, religion was a means of inspiration to lead the best life possible and to help others attain what they could. The spiritual life for her included art and music, and often her ideas of democracy seemed the nearest expression of the spiritual life. Throughout her life she remained dedicated to social justice and to working for those she thought were treated poorly. Lottie often "rescued" others, and was inclined toward condescension. This attitude made living in a democratic society later in life difficult. She did remain dedicated to helping those who were unjustly treated, however, and often she did so at a time when it was not the acceptable thing to do. She writes:

> *"Kalweit's influence on me was as decisive as Niemoeller's was on you. [Niemoeller confirmed me in 1937.] He turned me away from tradition to more liberal thought. We studied Kierkegaard, Sibelius, and Eckhart. He read to us Matthias Claudius, and Tersteegen, and he said, "Doubting is searching." Through him I came to love Bach, and I never missed the vespers service, which consisted mainly of Renaissance music."*

During the years of World War I, Lottie suffered as everyone else did. She worked long hours helping refugees who arrived with all their belongings. Often she was without enough to eat and recalls walking two miles for some skimmed milk. She remembers working so hard that she fell asleep on her shovel. Due to these experiences, she later said, "Food and its preparation—thinking about it, planning for it, and serving it—became an important part of my life." She also developed a sense of frugality so that she was able to save for the comforts of life and the beautiful things that were so important to her. She continues her story:

> *"I met your father at my friend's place in the country. We fell in love and became engaged. My future study of medicine quietly collapsed."*
>
> *"Dr. Reinke, a friend of the family, claimed my brain was over-stimulated, and they should give me a rake instead of books. My mother stated (correctly)*

that I did not know how to cook an egg (neither did she) and that I do some kind of cramming in Home Economics. [Lottie's aunt] suggested sending me to Scherpingen. This was the district school for the "Education of the Daughters of the Landed Gentry." There I would learn everything a hausfrau should know. I did not care much where I was going. I was in the grip of love, of constant suspense and dreaming. I barely passed my last school exams."

Training at Schloss Scherpingen seemed to be planned in the spirit of the Prussian military academies. When the girls graduated, they received a gold pin "Maid," which stood for Mut, Ausdauer, Idealismus, Demut [Courage, Endurance, Idealism, Humility]. It stood mainly for unquestioned obedience. The constant stress of responsibility, of leadership and discipline, inflated our sense of duty extravagantly. As a by-product, it also developed a good amount of conceit, the Prussian Junker-arrogance. The mediocrity of these "Junker-Fräuleins" amazed me. They were mostly raw boned, graceless, and with poor schooling, while the daughters of the high government officials seemed to come from refined and cultured homes."

"The amount of hard work, classes, theory, and extra duties seemed monstrous, but at the end we emerged with the basic know-how of "everything": cooking, gardening, house cleaning, laundry, dairy, sewing, poultry-raising, and keeping books. This last item I unfortunately escaped. [She handled this

*lack much later in life, she said, by always being
certain she had an excellent stockbroker.]"*

Another lesson Lottie learned well at that time was
how to direct servants and how to demand her own way,
lessons that were to become a hallmark of her life.

ANNA ELIZABETH HEINICKE
1780-1825

H. SAMUEL HEINICKE 1773-1841

My Father—Max

My father, Felix Max
Heinicke, could trace his
genealogy in detail for several centuries. During the
Nazi times, his brother
Erich, who later was the
architect for the city of
Kassel, was expected to join
the Nazi party in order to
keep his job. To do so, he
traced his family tree back to
the early 1700s and hence
proved his Aryan (non-
Jewish) ancestry. Thus, Max
received a detailed account
of the Heinicke background.
Most family members ran
small businesses or owned
large farms, and since the
early 1700s, the Heinickes
had passed down, from
father to son, the trade of
posamentierer—fancy braid-
ing and ribbons or embroi-

dery that adorned women's skirts and men's uniforms. But the fame and the pride of the family rested with Samuel Heinicke (1727-1790) who founded the second "deaf-mute" school in Europe and invented a non-digital language for the deaf. His name is still quite well known for that.

SAMUEL HEINICKE 1727-1790

Most of my father's family came from the southeast-ern part of the Polish Corridor, and from Saxony. Max was born in 1894 and raised in Halle on the river Saale in Saxony where his father had a large

MAX'S FATHER AND MOTHER

commercial laundry. Max was the middle born of three children. Aside from an older brother, Erich, he had a younger sister, Hertha. His father died of an infection when Max was about 11 years old.

As a child, Max learned to play the violin, which he loved, and sometimes performed in cos-tume. He came from a large extend-ed family who kept in touch

FATHER MAX AS A BOY

with one another, and often he attended their get-togethers. Occasionally, in the 1920's, a distant relative, Marlene Dietrich, the actress-singer, came with her white gloves and what the rest of the family described as snobbish and fussy manners.

As a boy Max had been an enthusiastic member of the Wandervoegel (Hiking birds), a German youth organization like the Boy Scouts, that, if not quite counter-culture, at least represented the desire of young Germans to move away from adult materialism and Prussian authority and toward fellowship, singing, communing with nature, and appreciating the simpler things. Later, as a young man, he became active in Moral Rearmament, a worldwide movement that believed that if each individual attained the highest morality, a sort of global utopia without wars could be attained. This meant doing good deeds, having concern for others throughout the world, and it emphasized a faithful and devoted family life. The hope was that wars—the outcome of previous generations' mistakes, commercialism, selfishness, militarism, and nationalism—could be avoided. Such youth or student movements had long been important in the history of Germany. It was a seek-

ing of the idealistic, romantic alternative to rigid, authoritarian, selfish ways.

When World War I broke out, however, Max volun-

FATHER AND MOTHER 1920

teered for military service and after four months at the Russian front, a bullet pierced his left arm. He was sent to a military hospital for four months and when he recovered, his left arm was an inch shorter than it had been. He then went to Danzig where he studied civil engineering while earning his room, board, and tuition.

After Max finished school he married my mother, Charlotte Fuchs, in May of 1920, and she joined him in Danzig. There was hunger in the land, political unrest, and the beginnings of a terrible inflation. When Lottie became pregnant she had a relatively normal pregnancy despite the lack of food, but the delivery was very difficult. That was May 15, 1921. They lived in Langfuhr, outside of Danzig, but, fortunately, my mother was able to get to the hospital where I was born. She did not produce enough milk to breastfeed me, however, and although the pictures of me at that time depict a sturdy baby, my mother always insisted that there was not enough food for me at the time.

My parents named me Ulrich. This name was from the ancient epic titled, "The Edda," a sort of Norwegian-Icelandic "Ulysses." The hero of this saga was Ullr, an "incomparable and celebrated traveler." According to the legend he was an excellent archer and ski runner. Ulrich also meant Herr, which, as my mother explained, implied to her "independence, capable of determining your own life, and inclined to accept responsibilities." Thus, I was welcomed and well prepared for life with a good Teutonic name. No one could have imagined at that time that it would not last me my entire life.

Meanwhile, my father became a Diplom Engineer (licensed civil engineer), and, attesting to his competency, he was given a position as an assistant at the Institute

FAMILY TREE: *FRAZIER-HEINICKE*

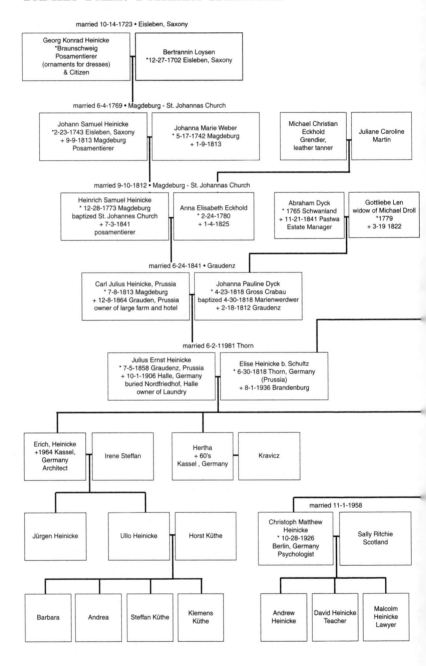

married 10-14-1723 • Eisleben, Saxony

Georg Konrad Heinicke
*Braunschweig
Posamentierer
(ornaments for dresses)
& Citizen

Bertrannin Loysen
*12-27-1702 Eisleben, Saxony

married 6-4-1769 • Magdeburg - St. Johannas Church

Johann Samuel Heinicke
*2-23-1743 Eisleben, Saxony
+ 9-9-1813 Magdeburg
Posamentierer

Johanna Marie Weber
* 5-17-1742 Magdeburg
+ 1-9-1813

Michael Christian
Eckhold
Grendier,
leather tanner

Juliane Caroline
Martin

married 9-10-1812 • Magdeburg - St. Johannas Church

Heinrich Samuel Heinicke
* 12-28-1773 Magdeburg
baptized St. Johannes Church
+ 7-3-1841
posamentierer

Anna Elisabeth Eckhold
* 2-24-1780
+ 1-4-1825

Abraham Dyck
* 1765 Schwanland
+ 11-21-1841 Pastwa
Estate Manager

Gottliebe Len
widow of Michael Droll
*1779
+ 3-19 1822

married 6-24-1841 • Graudenz

Carl Julius Heinicke, Prussia
* 7-8-1813 Magdeburg
+ 12-8-1864 Grauden, Prussia
owner of large farm and hotel

Johanna Pauline Dyck
* 4-23-1818 Gross Crabau
baptized 4-30-1818 Marienwerdwer
+ 2-18-1812 Graudenz

married 6-2-11981 Thorn

Julius Ernst Heinicke
* 7-5-1858 Graudenz, Prussia
+ 10-1-1906 Halle, Germany
buried Nordfriedhof, Halle
owner of Laundry

Elise Heinicke b. Schultz
* 6-30-1818 Thorn, Germany
(Prussia)
+ 8-1-1936 Brandenburg

Erich, Heinicke
+1964 Kassel,
Germany
Architect

Irene Steffan

Hertha
+ 60's
Kassel , Germany

Kravicz

married 11-1-1958

Jürgen Heinicke

Ullo Heinicke

Horst Küthe

Christoph Matthew
Heinicke
* 10-28-1926
Berlin, Germany
Psychologist

Sally Ritchie
Scotland

Barbara

Andrea

Steffan Küthe

Klemens
Küthe

Andrew
Heinicke

David Heinicke
Teacher

Malcolm
Heinicke
Lawyer

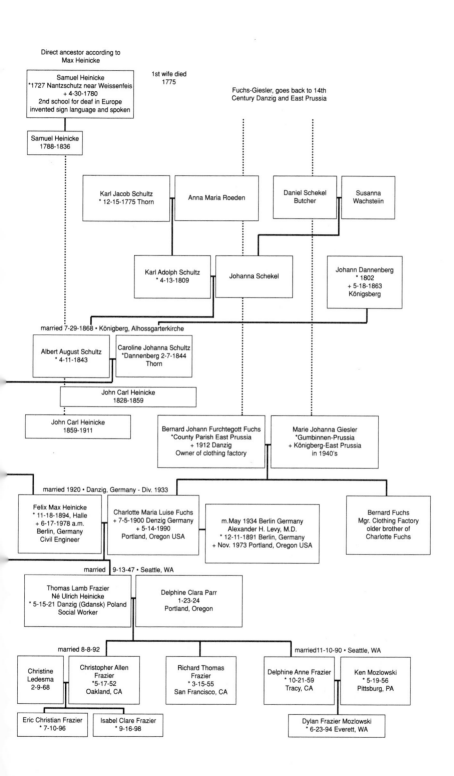

Direct ancestor according to
Max Heinicke

Samuel Heinicke
*1727 Nantzschutz near Weissenfeis
+ 4-30-1780
2nd school for deaf in Europe
invented sign language and spoken

1st wife died
1775

Fuchs-Giesler, goes back to 14th
Century Danzig and East Prussia

Samuel Heinicke
1788-1836

Karl Jacob Schultz
* 12-15-1775 Thorn

Anna Maria Roeden

Daniel Schekel
Butcher

Susanna
Wachsteiin

Karl Adolph Schultz
* 4-13-1809

Johanna Schekel

Johann Dannenberg
* 1802
+ 5-18-1863
Königsberg

married 7-29-1868 • Königberg, Alhossgarterkirche

Albert August Schultz
* 4-11-1843

Caroline Johanna Schultz
*Dannenberg 2-7-1844
Thorn

John Carl Heinicke
1828-1859

John Carl Heinicke
1859-1911

Bernard Johann Furchtegott Fuchs
*County Parish East Prussia
+ 1912 Danzig
Owner of clothing factory

Marie Johanna Giesler
*Gumbinnen-Prussia
+ Königberg-East Prussia
in 1940's

married 1920 • Danzig, Germany - Div. 1933

Felix Max Heinicke
* 11-18-1894, Halle
+ 6-17-1978 a.m.
Berlin, Germany
Civil Engineer

Charlotte Maria Luise Fuchs
+ 7-5-1900 Denzig Germany
+ 5-14-1990
Portland, Oregon USA

m.May 1934 Berlin Germany
Alexander H. Levy, M.D.
* 12-11-1891 Berlin, Germany
+ Nov. 1973 Portland, Oregon USA

Bernard Fuchs
Mgr. Clothing Factory
older brother of
Charlotte Fuchs

married 9-13-47 • Seattle, WA

Thomas Lamb Frazier
Né Ulrich Heinicke
* 5-15-21 Danzig (Gdansk) Poland
Social Worker

Delphine Clara Parr
1-23-24
Portland, Oregon

married 8-8-92

married11-10-90 • Seattle, WA

Christine
Ledesma
2-9-68

Christopher Allen
Frazier
*5-17-52
Oakland, CA

Richard Thomas
Frazier
* 3-15-55
San Francisco, CA

Delphine Anne Frazier
* 10-21-59
Tracy, CA

Ken Mozlowski
* 5-19-56
Pittsburg, PA

Eric Christian Frazier
* 7-10-96

Isabel Clare Frazier
* 9-16-98

Dylan Frazier Mozlowski
* 6-23-94 Everett, WA

ULLI AT 6 MONTHS

of Technology in Danzig. Living conditions in Danzig remained very poor (no milk, eggs, or butter were available), but the young couple stayed until 1922, when they decided they must move. Danzig had become a free city, no longer under German rule, and we could no longer keep our German citizenship if we remained there, so we moved to Berlin. After much searching, my parents found an apartment (two courtyards back from the street) that resembled a big pile of stones, with little fresh air and almost no sun. Inflation was increasing and money was rapidly losing its value.

ULLI (TOM)

Shortly after the move, Max became very ill with scarlet fever. The doctor had little hope he would survive and took him to the hospital to conceal his critical condition from my mother. He recovered, however, and soon afterward, he got a position with Siemens Bau Union, a big German engineering firm. His first assignment was to develop plans for and build a bridge across the Duna River in Riga, Latvia. As a result, we moved there in 1923, and finally got some decent food. My mother remembers it as the first time that she had eaten chocolate since the beginning of the war.

My first memories go back to that time: I had a two-year-old playmate who was sitting in a highchair and she suddenly spilled a glass of milk. I was deeply embarrassed for her. I also remember a particular afternoon when a huge pile of sand arrived that Father had sent from his construction site—just for me. I was in seventh heaven, and I made tunnels, sand castles, and slides for my marbles. I can still feel the moist sand, the collapsing bridges, and the marbles going down the slides.

When I was three, after a year in Riga, we returned to Berlin, and on the way back we stopped over in Danzig for a week to visit my mother's mother in her shirt factory. I remember one episode clearly. I had lost a button from my coat and one of the employees was told to sew it back on. I started to rebel and to scream, as a three-year-old can; whereupon an employee took some clothes off the wall, revealing a telephone rarely used, and he threatened to call the police. Soon two strange men appeared, supposedly to keep me in line. I was very frightened and I acquiesced, allowing the button to be sewn on, after which, my grandmother took me by the hand and we went home. Later, I found out this had been an elaborate trick. The telephone was out of order and the two "strange men" who appeared were only customers. For the first time, I felt deceived; I had learned something about German "jokes."

A German Boyhood

We returned to the same gloomy apartment in

Berlin we had left—Fritzschestrasse 70, the second courtyard in the rear, on the fifth floor. Dinner aromas from other kitchens crept into our rooms and it was my job to fan the air for ventilation by swinging the door open and shut. By this time, Father had thrown over the idealism and strict moral code that had meant so much to him in his youth when he was a staunch supporter of Moral Rearmament. He began drinking heavily and seeking out other women. I once witnessed a physical fight between my father and mother when he threw her onto the bed, hit her, and tore her stocking. I loved my father and I could not understand why he would do such a thing. The horror, fright, and helplessness I felt that such things could happen shocked me to the core, and it was all the more confusing to me because I loved my father and knew other sides of him. I knew he cared for me by the way he would play with me, pretending to be a clown, and always full of interesting bits of information that he loved to share with me. He had once come home from work with a piece of chocolate in his mouth, telling me to close my eyes and open my mouth; then, he slowly placed the candy in my mouth. Even though he smelled strongly of cigarettes, I was thrilled.

In 1925, when I was just over four years old, Mother enrolled me in kindergarten. Every morning twenty of us stood in line waiting for a cup of hot chocolate. Each child brought a cookie that was in the shape of a man, dog, chicken, or some other creature, and we gave it to the teacher. The one who had brought the nicest cookie was slightly favored by the teacher, it seemed. (In America, we polish apples!)

My clothes were not fancy but they were clean every day. I wore shorts and long tan cotton stockings that were held up by elastic straps attached to a leibchen, a vest-like kind of underwear. At the end of the straps were garters to hook on to the stockings. Unfortunately, the elastic often stretched or the garters disappeared, and the stockings and remaining garters would fall beneath the bottom of my shorts. For many years this became a major challenge for me; and probably was for an entire generation of German boys as well. The long stockings weren't necessary in the summer, and as I got older I could wear knee-high stockings and was released from this garter misery. (I also had a sailor suit with a wide collar and a dickey and tie, which my mother thought was very attractive. Unfortunately, this outfit too was worn with shorts, long stockings, and garters.)

Early in the morning on October 28, 1926 with the air full of excitement I was sent to my mother's friend, Christof Drexel, a well-known painter. I arrived and was holding an oatmeal cookie in my hand, when, around noon, the phone rang. Christof answered it, and was told that the stork had brought a little baby —my brother, Christoph Matthew. I felt I had gotten a big Christmas and birthday present all in one. I went home the next day and was allowed to glance over the edge of the clothes basket where Christoph lay screaming mightily.

1927 ULLI HOLDING CHRIS

In 1927, I entered first grade. We were placed on hard wooden school benches and told to be quiet, so we all sat there as if made out of stone. When the parents left, many children started to cry in spite of the teacher's efforts to make us smile. I was confident that my mother would come back, as she had always returned. Finally, all the parents arrived again, carrying large, colorfully decorated paper cones about two-and-a-half feet high and filled to the brim with all sorts of candies and fruit. This welcome gift to children for the first day of school is still a custom in German schools.

For many years I was in the rhythm of school, vacation, school, vacation, school, vacation. I was a happy child with wonderful playmates with whom I shared many adventures, and a brother I could play with at home. I tried to please my mother, although I had the feeling that whatever I did was never quite good enough. She was a strong, controlling person who expected to get what she wanted, and she had learned well how to do this. I was not an easy child for her. In order to establish my independence, I developed a stubbornness that remains to this day. It has often served me well, but has also kept me from exploring new things, and has probably hindered me throughout my life from learning as easily as I could.

I remember bedtime in those days as a particular treat. My father would come and kiss me goodnight and my mother would read to me and sometimes also sing to me. My love for music began to develop.

In those years I was full of many adventurous ideas that were not always well thought out, a beginning of a lifetime habit of unorthodox risk-taking. One morning I was playing in front of the house on Fritzschestrasse when a horse-drawn beer delivery wagon came by. I ran behind it, hung on the side, and suddenly fell onto the pavement. The wheels glanced me and I was catapulted into the street. Passers by carried my limp, unconscious body to my mother. Fortunately, nothing was broken, and after a quick trip to the doctor I recovered nicely and never chased beer wagons again.

Fritzschestrasse intersected Bismarckstrasse, a big avenue. One day in 1927, there was a great commotion and a large crowd lined the streets. A big parade passed by, and seated in the back of a huge open Mercedes was the German president and war hero, Field Marshall Paul von Hindenburg, hero of the battle of Tannenberg, bedecked with medals and wearing the familiar spiked helmet. Germans loved their heroes and their uniforms. I was very impressed with all the pomp and circumstance surrounding him.

That spring, when I was six, we moved to Dahlem, a suburb of Berlin and I was enrolled in elementary school, which involved a 45-minute walk each way, rain or snow. I particularly loved and respected a teacher named Herr Rothe. We lived near the "palaces" of the rich, and the nearby forest lured us for walks and bicycle rides. A block down the street was a huge complex of apartments occupied by army officers. They walked through the neighborhood resplendent in their uniforms with all sorts of medals. Some of them were picked up regularly by army chauffeurs. They were part of the Wehrmacht, and a whole culture and mystique surrounded them. This was only nine years after the end of WWI, and the Rhineland was still occupied by English and French troops. The ignominious defeat in the war, however, had not lessened the glamour and power of the

German army. As a small boy I was tremendously in awe of these officers, and yet, their stiffness, their isolation from the community, inspired considerable fear as well.

In Dahlem, I lived out the dreams of my childhood. We lived downstairs in a large old apartment of a five-story building, and the janitor-manager, who was hated by everyone, lived across the hall. One night we had to call the police because he was standing in his nightshirt, holding an old decrepit sword, ready to fight a tenant to the death. I played many tricks on him, like throwing a stink bomb through the mail slot of his door. Such bombs could be bought at the local variety store.

That was also the year I got my first bicycle for Christmas. Since training wheels didn't exist, my father taught me to ride it by running behind me. I caught on quickly and was thrilled with the freedom and chance for adventure the bicycle provided me.

Around the corner from our apartment was the brown field, which got its name from the brown fence around it. Inside this fence was a perfect wilderness with weeds high enough that we couldn't be seen from the outside. We were a group of boys and girls, most of whom were eight or nine years old, and we organized a club, choosing as our leader a smart and pretty girl of about 12. We decided to make the brown field our head-quarters, and we began to dig a cave that would hold 15 children. The "Boss" had a bag of candy, and for every foot the group dug, each member received a piece of candy. Finally the square pit was about five feet deep, five feet long, and wide enough to hold all of us. We then "organized" (stole) some boards for the roof. We put dirt and grass on the boards and built a trap door at one end of the hole so no one could recognize our "castle" from the outside.

That same week we inaugurated our cave by camping all day in the brown field. Someone brought a small stove so we could cook. Three people were commissioned to "organize" all kinds of fruit, and some had to stay near the stove to throw potatoes into the fire or see that the applesauce did not get burnt. Others went to their parents to collect a variety of coupons that they took to the grocer to exchange for sauerkraut, candy, pickles, and pipe cleaners. (I do not remember why we needed pipe cleaners.) One boy had brought cigarettes he had taken from his father.

At noon we all met and sat around the stove. Everyone was dressed as we imagined American Indians would be, brown pants with fringes on the sides, a brown shirt ornamented with false beads and what we thought was Indian embroidery. Such a costume was almost a necessity for many German children at that time. We had taken some corks, blackened them over a flame, and painted mustaches on each other (not knowing that Indians had no mustaches). On our heads were Indian caps with dyed seagull feathers. Everyone had to have a jack knife, of course, and a bow and arrow. There we sat—15 "Indians," digging through the burnt crusts of potatoes covered with applesauce and garnished with pickles. Our battle ax was buried under the dirt and we were smoking the pipe of peace. For dessert we had the stolen apples, which had the unique effect that only stolen apples have—especially when they are not quite ripe.

We got our ideas about the Indians from Karl May, a German author who had never been to America but who wrote about the American Indians—"Winnetoo" and "Old Shatterhand"—with intensity and drama, if not with accuracy. I had read and re-read him often with great enthusiasm because of the adventure and super-human abilities of the Indians. In addition to writing Indian tales, Karl May also spent some time in jail for forgery, but his stories deeply influenced several genera-tions of Germans with the romantic ideal of the natural man pitted against the forces of civilization, and with an idealized spiritual life somehow connected to nature. Karl May is still read in Germany, and the American Indian is still admired by Germans, despite the misinfor-mation planted by Karl May. People from all levels of German society, even now, often speak of their admira-tion for the Native American. The spiritual basis of their lives resonates to the desire of many Germans searching for ideals, and for something beyond the rational, espe-cially something connected to nature. (Since World War II, the mistreatment of the Native Americans by the U.S. government is often mentioned by Germans, in an effort to remind us that countries other than Germany also bear guilt for their treatment of minorities.)

Our interest in "organizing" continued. One after-noon I put on my Indian costume, painted my face with burnt cork, and with a small basket over my arm, climbed the neighbor's cherry tree. My basket was almost full when I noticed an old woman approaching. She had not yet seen me, so I held my breath. Unfortunately, she had come to see how the cherries were coming along, and she discovered a wild little boy in a strange costume sitting high up in the tree, stealing her cherries. I decided to jump out of the tree, landing right in front of her, then ran, hanging onto the basket of cherries. When I got home I told my mother a dear friend of mine had given me some cherries to bring home. Mother took these cherries and preserved them, unaware they had been stolen.

Once we entered the orchard of a very wealthy person. I was supposed to "organize" the apples while several others were on the lookout. My pockets and shirt were just stuffed full of apples when a servant came along the path opposite from the direction where my friends were keeping watch. I was so busy gathering apples that I did not notice him until he was only 40 feet away. I suddenly decided to run away, and first had to scale a high fence. I ran and ran with the servant close on my heels until finally I reached the nearby woods and lost him. No one was hurt, not even the apples.

Occasionally, a fight broke out between our gang and a group from Church Street. We used blackberry branches as weapons and often came home with bumps or bleeding wounds. But in times of peace we went to our clubhouse in the brown field, sat around the fire, passed the pipe of peace, and scraped the scabs from our wounds. We had heard that doing so left interesting scars.

Christmas was the most important holiday of the year with a ritual orchestrated by my mother. The whole family participated in the preparation, including the maid, who lived with us and took part in all the festivities. I still cannot understand how we could afford a maid when there was barely enough to eat, but one was always there, and was always included as a part of the family.

Winter in Dahlem in 1931, when I was 10 years old and my brother was five, was very cold, and Germany was deep in an economic depression and politically unsettled. There were 33 political parties. One was the

Vintner (wine growers) party, and another was a small, aggressive Nazi party that was elbowing itself into power in parliament. My parents and their friends thought the Nazi party consisted of crude and uneducated people, incapable of being effective. My father Max was unemployed, having lost his job as an engineer with Siemens, the big German firm. He found independent jobs, copying architectural drawings for architects, and I helped him deliver the drawings to various architectural offices.

On Dec. 24, 1931, we were all at home—Mother, Father, my brother Chris, the maid, and I. In spite of the depression, in spite of my father's unemployment, we had enough money to celebrate the birth of Jesus. At 5:00 p.m., as it was getting dark, Chris, the maid, and I were asked to step into the small room next to the dining room in preparation for the celebration. When the door closed it was pitch black and we were told to meditate and "tune in" to ourselves for a short while. We couldn't help but hear a lot of hustle and bustle through the door—chairs being moved, matches being lit, the lid of the piano being opened. We were all excited, and in the dark I reached for Chris and tickled him until he giggled, but I knew he didn't like it. The maid tried to calm me down and separate us, but I kept it up until just before Chris was ready to scream. Then I stopped. Suddenly there was piano music—Ihr Kinderlein Kommet (Oh Come All Ye Children)—and the door opened. There stood the Christmas tree all lit up with burning candles. To put the candles onto the branches, we held the eye of a sewing needle (held by a pair of pliers) over a gas flame until it was glowing hot, then poked this glowing eye into the bottom of the candle and stuck the other end of the needle through the branches of the tree so the attachment was hardly visible. This was undoubtedly very dangerous but it provided the whole room with a special atmosphere, unlike anything else. Small apples, candies, nuts, and paper cut-outs hung on the trees, and there were also small silver stars and metal balls (from Czechoslovakia), and lots of angel's hair. This tree, I knew, represented the spirit of Christmas. Chris, the maid, and I sat on the sofa with one eye on the white tablecloth that covered the presents under the tree and tried to guess what they were. My mother had made a crèche out of wax with Jesus in a small crib, Mary and Joseph standing next to the crib, and oxen and donkeys too. Mom had given her artistic creativity full reign. The stable was covered with real straw and the flickering candles cast dancing shadows all over the room while their sweet, pungent smell permeated the air. My brother and I sat in awe of this scene: the lights, the decorations, and always the big white tablecloth, which hid the presents. On the buffet were five Bunte Teller (colored plates full of goodies), one for each person. As part of a centuries-old German Christmas tradition, everyone in the family got a plate full of marzipan, apples, oranges, spice cake, chocolate, and whatever else was affordable or available on the market. There were sweets from Grandma Fuchs (Mother's mother) and always a piece of Lottie's honey cake. After we received this, my mother would read the story of the birth of Christ from the Bible, Luke 2:2.

We had learned some Christmas carols, so Mom sat at the piano, Father took up his violin, and we sang Christmas songs: "Lo, How a Rose is Blooming," "From Heaven Above," "Silent Night," "O Tannenbaum," and many others. We loved the ritual and the singing, and were in awe of the scene and the feelings about the miracle of the Christ's birth, but the whole experience was highly colored by the intensity of our eagerness to get at the presents. Finally, and much to my relief, we approached the tree. The candles were still burning, giving off heat. Father removed the white tablecloth to reveal many presents. Each person including the maid had to give a homemade present to other family members. Chris had made a picture of Baby Jesus in the manger; I had made Mother a pin cushion, because she loved to sew. We were then allowed to receive our gifts. Mine was a wind-up train with an engine and five cars, as well as a circle of tracks. Chris got building blocks. There was a real Indian tent. The spirit of excitement and joy, the harmony and love, set the tone for many Christmases to follow.

After opening the presents we sat at the table for a modest meal. We had neither money nor much food. I have forgotten what we had for the meal, but I do remember dessert—Lottie's honey cake, a recipe that became a tradition in our family. After all the Christmas festivities, I put on my Indian costume, erected my tent on my bed, and slept in it all night. In the years to come we lived through many separations, tragedies, many new experiences and much joy, particularly at Christmas time, but that special Christmas in 1931 stands out for me.

I helped my mother bake this cake at Christmas, and later baked it many, many times myself. My children learned to bake it, and as our children had children, they too are learning the tradition of baking Lottie's Honey Cake, particularly at Christmas.

Lottie's Honeycake

Preheat oven to 350°.
Butter and flour a glass pan, 9 x 13 or equivalent
(or several small pans for gifts)
Melt 1/4 pound of butter until it turns brown,
then cool.
Beat 1 cup eggs at high speed until foamy.
Add 1/2 cup brown sugar, 1 cup white sugar, 2/3
cup honey
Add by hand 1-1/2 tsp. cinnamon, 1/2 tsp.
cloves, 1/2 tsp. nutmeg, 1 tsp. almond extract, 3/4
tsp. salt.
Add by hand 2-1/4 cup unsifted flour, 1 tsp. baking powder, 1-1/2 tsp. anise seed.
Add cooled butter carefully.
Bake 45 minutes or until tester comes out clean.
Cool; and cut in half horizontally, spread with
tart jelly (current), or marzipan or liqueur.
Cover with semi-sweet chocolate melted over low
heat (or chocolate chips may be put on top of the
cake, and the cake placed in the oven at 150°
until they are melted).

ENJOY!

A Waldorf Education

At school the teachers said I was of above-average
intelligence, but they also said I was not "working up to
my capacity" in school; I was "too anxious," a "worry
wort." For years I suspected this was because I could
"never do anything right for my mother."

Perhaps hoping to get me to "work up to my capacity," or to mold me into a form more acceptable to her, my mother enrolled me in an Anthroposophical school (usually called Steiner or Waldorf school). Rudolf Steiner was an Austrian social philosopher-pedagogue (1861-1925) who founded the Anthroposophic Society in 1912. He believed in a method of self-discipline that made a connection between the cognitive (thinking) world and the spiritual world. My mother was intrigued by his ideas.

To go to school, I took my bike and rode it to the nearest rapid transit station where I left it at a local bar; then I took the train to the heart of the city. The school was in an old apartment building. It covered all 13 grades (in Germany, one goes to school until the age of 19), and the classes were small, about 15 students each. Although the subjects were fun, there was strict discipline. The teachers were friendly but they were definitely the authorities. One time I got sarcastic and the principal, a disciple of Rudolf Steiner, rapped me across the knuckles with a ruler. That taught me to keep my mouth shut, but it did not make me less of a worry wort. Most of the time I had fun at the Steiner school. At the age of ten I was learning four foreign languages: Greek (aget os Spartas oi andru), Latin (omnes gallia in partes tres divisa est), French (maître corbeau sur un arbre perché), and English (silver moon, floating in the sky, snow-covered mountains, palaces, and fountains). We learned foreign languages through poetry. The English may not have been very relevant when I later needed it, but the foundation for learning languages remained with me, and I continued to pick up new languages easily and quickly.

We also had a eurythmics class where we stood in a circle and manipulated a 2-1/2 foot copper bar to music, or we lay on bamboo sticks on the floor, creating a rhythm with our hands and feet. We also had a small school orchestra and I played a piccolo flute. The school was co-educational, and both sexes had to learn to "sew and saw"—the beginnings of gender equality. I carved a wooden cooking spoon that stayed in the family for years, and I sewed a stuffed camel (that did not). My buddy and I sat at our sewing machines with a long strip of cloth, and, at a signal, raced each other to see who could sew the fastest. We also learned to knit and I made a pair of gray wool socks. The top was knit two, purl two, and at the toe, we dropped a stitch after each row. The heels were beyond me so I went to Cornelia Auerbach, the mother of my recorder teacher, for help. She did both heels for me. I took those socks with me to the U.S. and wore them for many years, mending them again and again, as we did at that time.

Looking back on the Steiner school years, I became aware of how much I learned there—the Indian-Yoga philosophies, Nietzsche ("Thus Spake Zarathurstra"), the ancient Persian philosophies, the Greek gods, the Egyptian myths, and much of all this taught through poetry, painting, and sculpture. (As these topics became increasingly popular in the 1970s and 1980s, I realized the strong impression they had made upon me earlier.) In some sense, it was the beginning of a search for spiritual meaning in my life, but at the time, such ideas were overshadowed by my daily life: family resentments, Hitler, and the confusing political scene, and my parents' very rocky marriage.

The Steiner school did not give grades but instead

sent a poem written to reflect our strengths and call attention to areas for future development. An example of my report card upon entering sixth grade, follows:

Everywhere
all over the world
and rooted in the earth
there are wise
prescribed laws.
Only the fool
will withdraw from them.
Who recognizes the laws
is wise to fulfill
important things.
Only the fool
is satisfied
to brag.

As with much of my experience in the Steiner school, I did not quite understand how this applied to me, but I was honored by what I believed must have been the deep thoughtfulness that went into this report, and the time and effort given by my teacher.

The report card for the following year was more revealing, and considerably more to the point, but still showed the expectation that an 11 or 12-year-old should have deep philosophies and ideals:

"Ulli [my nickname] has become more independent, and is determining more and more his own direction.

I am happy to say that his inner being has become deeper, and that in turn has changed his attitude toward school work considerably

His attention has become more steadfast. He participates with more interest in classroom discussion and in activity— he is genuinely present. He does not express his inner thoughts sufficiently, but one can recognize their existence and maturity in his written assignments. He practices his thinking skills, especially in algebra where he does good work. His judgment becomes more calm and mature. His application to the work, which at first was wavering, has become more steadfast. His body is not as relaxed as could be and this shows up in his penmanship and in drawing. This will improve when he follows the power of his will in the direction he chooses.

Go into the world in many directions, and yet remain true to yourself."

Comments by the teachers in ten subjects followed, mainly stating that my interests were changeable. Their positive comments followed, apparently hoping to point the way toward growth.

During this period, my father landed a job with a large engineering firm, Gruen und Bilfinger. In the worst of the depression, Max was usually able to find a job if there was one to be found. He sometimes took on temporary assignments. He had a very good reputation, but there were often times when even Max could not find work.

Social Scene in Berlin Under the Weimar Republic

While I was busy sitting in cherry trees and struggling with the complications of knitting, my parents, despite their unhappiness, were busy living in the creative milieu of the late 20s and early 30s of Berlin, (a

time familiar to Americans because of the movie
Cabaret.) Berlin was a beautiful city with many woods,
and wide streets such as Unter den Linden or the
Kurfürstendamm, with lovely shops and sidewalk cafés
serving delicious cakes and whipped cream with coffee.
Berliners had a reputation for knowing how to enjoy
themselves, whether walking, singing, or socializing. The
restraints of the Bismarck era, akin to the English
Victorian period, were loosening. I heard without com-
prehending them the stories of "wild parties" or "wonderful times," and something about people climbing in
and out of hotel windows visiting their girlfriends. (Fifty
years later I met two women who had been young with
me and we began comparing some of the stories we had
heard. If some of the wild stories we heard were true,
these women may have been half-sisters without knowing it.)

In some ways my parents' lives were reflecting the
tenor of the times. I knew my father and many other
fathers were often without work, and hence also often
unable to provide enough food or other material needs
(strangely, there was always a maid). Yet, after WWI,
Berlin, beginning in the Roaring 20s, had an artistic and
Bohemian influence on a people who loved to socialize
and enjoy life. It was a largely apolitical scene, allowing
for the rise of many small and sometimes radical political parties that flourished without much concern.

My mother in particular was influenced by the artistic energy of the times. She came to know a number of
relatively famous artists who had been close to the very
well known German impressionists. One of these friends
was Christoph Drexel with whom I had stayed while my
brother was born. Christoph had lived and worked with

Paul Klee, and also collaborated with Carl Jung, and
he taught my mother a
great deal about modern art
and gave her a lasting love
and understanding of
design and beauty, and the
ways of looking at art.

LOTTIE

My father also had a
deep interest in design,
focused mainly on cathe-
drals. Max said he had little
use for religion, but went to
church for the music, the
architecture, and the feelings they inspired in him. He
talked to me a great deal about cathedrals, and explained
how the composition of the various architectural features
combined to produce an effect on people. The height,
the altars, and the spacing of the aisles, even the century
in which a cathedral was built and its style, was a part of
the total experience, as was the music and the colors of
the stained glass windows. Max truly appreciated and
was in awe of the genius of the designers of cathedrals,
and of the artisans and workmen who constructed them.
In our home we had many beautiful books with pictures
of cathedrals and we would study them together. This
instigated my fascination with cathedrals, and I would
later pour over these pictures myself. One of my fondest
dreams was to some day see such cathedrals in person.

Music was an important part of our lives. Lottie did
not approve of music on the radio unless we listened
carefully with great respect to the whole work, and she
felt the same about records. Father played the violin and

the piano, and Mother sang and played the piano. She took singing lessons and once took me to a rehearsal where she was a member of the chorus singing the B Minor Mass of Bach under Otto Klemperer, the famous conductor. I sat up in the balcony and felt the big chords go up and down my spine. Both parents loved music and loved to make music. Max was accurate and disciplined and a hard worker in his career, and he also could play the violin very well, but he often played with "schmaltz" and had a lack of regard for discipline when playing the piano or violin for fun. (He was a mix between Liberace and Victor Borge, as one of his grandsons said many years later.) He also lacked understanding or awareness of his musical partner's feeling, while Lottie demanded perfection in others and was quick to criticize. Often the two of them played together, but as with many aspects of their lives, their differing attitudes and self-righteousness resulted in disaster. Max used his bow with a vengeance in these instances, hitting the pages of the music to get his point across. Regardless, music continued to be a source of great joy and inspiration for the whole family, even though we developed it under conditions considerably less than harmonic.

My mother, by this time, found more and more satisfaction in the social scene. Her skills in cooking (or directing the maid to cook), and her knack for bringing interesting people together, made her a successful hostess. She had always considered herself a great beauty, and she enjoyed the effect she had upon men, who apparently also enjoyed her responses. She took great care of her face, often slathering it with her own particular white concoction, which contained a good deal of zinc oxide and borax. Several times she answered the door in this white-face makeup, frightening the trades people. She used this preparation throughout her entire life, telling women many decades younger

MAX, LOTTIE AND CHRIS

that their skin could be as lovely as hers if they would use this preparation. She also worked regularly to keep her figure, employing peculiar exercises mainly to maintain her bust, of which she was very proud even into her late eighties. She came of age before bras were common and often wore clinging, nearly transparent blouses, which shocked her friends in America in later years. She was also careful to "rest" a great deal, and, not to work too hard.

While we lived in Berlin-Dahlem, mother began to have gentlemen admirers. One was Walter, an engineer from Austria, who for many years would send her a cyclamen plant at Christmas. He was Jewish, and in those days (the early 30s), I didn't know anything about Jewish people or about prejudice. Some of my friends and many of my parent's friends were Jewish, and all I knew was that some of them went to a different sort of church, called a synagogue, but many did not even go there, and they had different beliefs, rituals and holidays.

In the public school I attended, we divided up for religion classes. Some were Catholic, some were Lutheran or Evangelical, and some were Jewish. In those

FRIEDL TREMMEL, HANS TREMMEL, LOTTIE, MAX
AND A PICTURE BY DREXEL ABOUT 1931.

classes, we learned about history and theology—the philosophy of the great thinkers of our own individual religions—and, of course, about ethics and morality.

LOTTIE AND ULLI

Hans Tremmel was another friend of my mother's, a cabinet-maker who later became a substitute father to me. Whenever I could, I visited him in his shop where he made furniture, including a living room table and chairs for Mr. Ley, a member of Hitler's cabinet. Hans took my family to Laubenheim, near Mainz on the Rhine where he was raised. We picked grapes and

LOTTIE

ULLI

I got to ride in the cab of his brother's steam engine. We followed the river. I rang the bell and just before each street crossing I blew the whistle.

Over the following years, Hans Tremmel and I became good friends. He had a kayak and on weekends I joined him on the Wannsee, part of the Havel River outside of Berlin. We had a special spot near the end of the lake. Father, Mother, Chris, and I, as well as Hans and his girlfriend Friedl, picnicked there. Lisa Weiss and her husband Hugo, both ardent Communists, sometimes joined us there. We brought food and made

1931 ULLI, FRIEDLTREMMEL AND HUGO WEISS

coffee in a gallon can that had a handle on it made out of a coat hanger. I heated the water over a gas flame and then put in coffee grounds. After everything was hot I took the coffee can by the handle and, in a centrifugal movement, swung it around so the grounds would settle on the bottom of the can. We swam, raced, jumped, and even spent the night in a pup tent where I was kept awake by the unfamiliar commotion in Hans's tent. It was no doubt a romantic night for Hans.

I went on many overnight trips with Hans Tremmel, and it was a happy time. On one of these trips years later, in 1935, we were in our kayak on the little Wannsee when we approached a large yacht. There on the railing high above us were many beautiful women in low-cut bathing suits, gyrating their hips, and surrounding a little man who had one heel elevated.

"Hans, that's Goebbles," I said. He was Hitler's propaganda minister, a man with seven children who later poisoned himself and his whole family in 1945 at the end of the war. I had heard frightening stories about Goebbles and his use of propaganda. I was scared to death of the man, and we paddled away as quickly as we could.

While there was the appearance of gaiety and good times, my mother later recalled it as the worst time of her life. She had two boys to care for and a marriage that was growing unbearable. There was no option for her to leave the marriage; she had no way of supporting herself if she did. She vowed at that point that somehow she would take care of her boys regardless of what their father did. It was at this time, in the depths of despair, that she met Al (pronounced Ahl)—Alexander Levy, M.D., head surgeon at the Berlin Charität (charity hospital). They met at one of many uproarious parties at the home of a doctor, who was also Jewish. He was married to a beautiful Peruvian woman. (I learned later from one of his daughters that he was quite a "skirt chaser.")

Al had two daughters, pretty little girls who were cared for by a nursemaid, Meta. I first met him in Dahlem when he drove up to our house in a black convertible Auburn Cord that had red stripes on both sides. He did not look particularly handsome to me, although both he and my mother thought he was extremely good looking. With his slick, glistening black hair, which he carefully maintained until the end of his life, and his dark olive complexion, I thought he looked like the Sheik of Araby. Al looked me directly in the eyes when we spoke to each other, and I was impressed with how friendly and supportive he was. He listened very carefully to me. It was clear to both my brother and me, however, that his interest was primarily in our mother. That day he wore an expensive, gray herringbone suit and gray suede gloves. The rim of his felt hat was tilted to one side. In our neighborhood he definitely stood out as someone special. A month after I met Al, our apartment manager, Mr. G., threw some acid on the Auburn Cord, presumably because Al was Jewish; and I threw more stink bombs through Mr. G's mail slot

AL AND HIS DAUGHTERS, HANNAH AND RUTH WITH CHRIS

in retaliation.

One day my family, including Father, was invited to the large and opulent estate of Al's father-in-law, the very wealthy founder and owner of a chain of shoe stores (that still exist today). His beliefs and practices were at the very least strange, and yet it was a time when many spiritual beliefs and ideas about the supernatural were being explored in Germany. He embraced a philosophy that was close to the Anthroposophic teachings I had been exposed to, and what seemed peculiar to others seemed natural to me after my experience at the Steiner school. Once he threw a whip far up into a large oak tree and ordered me to go and get it, and when I did, he rewarded me with a Deutschmark, which seemed an enormous reward at the time. Another time in the evening, we all followed him, walking slowly and reverently toward the moon, and standing and watching it with some kind of ceremony. It did not seem unusual to me at the time that Al had invited my father, my mother, and her family to a party with his wife present.

Although my father remained the most important man in my life, I also began to like Al, who was nice to me, and I had a wonderful friendship with Hans Tremmel, who gave me a respite from the growing tensions at home by inviting me to his cabinet-making shop. Mother had her friends and Father had his liaisons also. Neither talked to me about their difficulties. Both were very self-concerned and self-absorbed, so I never felt there was a possibility of them reaching a workable solution together. I also never felt I had their full attention or any solid reassurance that I was okay.

In 1931 the Heinicke family moved to Zehlendorf, a suburb further away from the center of Berlin. We moved into a small apartment on the ground floor at Spandauerstrasse 109 (now called Uncle Tom's Cabin Street). There was a large apartment complex, five stories tall and spanning several blocks, all built by a Mr. Sommerfeld, a Jewish contractor. It was two blocks away from the big forest, the Grunewald. I continued going to the Steiner school with a long daily commute.

The following year, I joined a group of boys in town called Technische Bereitshaft, (Technical Preparedness.) We learned how to lay telephone wires, work with combustion engines, use Morse code, and I learned how to cook, but above all, I enjoyed the fellowship. We learned many songs which we sang lustily, and went on overnight hikes, sleeping in tents. I was very happy in this group, and my mother and Al were happy about it and encouraged my participation. We had no uniforms and there were no lectures or any kind of political messages.

Yet, times were uncertain for me. My parents' marriage was faltering. I didn't realize how deeply this affected me until I once let my rage out on the maid. I hit her on the back with a wooden clothes hanger because she was singing "funny songs," and when Father came home, he took the hanger to my back until I was bouncing on the bed. I really hurt. I still hurt today. In despair, I spent time with the man at the newspaper kiosk down the street. He seemed to understand me and never discounted me. Every morning we watched the Crown Prince, the Kaiser's son, and his chauffeur drive by. The Kaiser was living in Holland where he had been banished in 1918.

In Zehlendorf, Mother met Cora Schröder, whose mother had taken me through the intricacies of knitting heels in socks. Cora had a doctorate in music and was an expert on the cembalo (an early piano). She had married Hanning Schröder, a relatively well-known German composer who was a Gentile, while Cora was Jewish. She taught me how to play the recorder, which I learned well, and she also taught me piano, which I did not learn with as much discipline, but did enjoy.

The recorder dates back to the willow pipe used by primitive tribes, but it appeared in today's form in the fourteenth and fifteenth centuries when it was 12 inches long (C-soprano). In Germany it was called the block flute, referring to the block in the fipple of the mouthpiece; in English, it's called the recorder (the bird "records" its sweet note); and, in French, it is known as flute douce (soft flute). In the sixteenth century the recorder became the most important woodwind instrument in any chamber ensemble, especially when secular music came to the fore. (Up until then, the Catholic Church had forbidden any secular music.) The instrument had a simple, pure and mellow tone, and was easy to play. It reached its height of popularity during Shakespeare's time when it was referred to simply as the "flute." As the number of instruments in the orchestra increased, the soft tone of the recorder was drowned out, and by the end of the eighteenth century it had almost disappeared. In the early 1920s, the instrument was revived by new recorder movements in Europe— Dolmetsch in England, and Herwiga and Harlan in Germany (Harlan was a colleague of Cora's).

The recorder was my main instrument and we played in a small group in the woods near Cora's home, on the radio, and in folk arts exhibits. By this time I had acquired an F-alto as well as a C-tenor recorder. I played the recorder in duet with my mother who sang. At Christmas my mother and I would go from house to house to play and sing carols. A recorder is not really a solo instrument so later I learned the guitar for group singing, or to play folksongs with others.

In Zehlendorf there were many difficult and uncertain times. One day my father went off with his bicycle, and Mother asked me to follow him quickly without being seen. She suspected he was seeing a girlfriend, and wanted me to verify this. In her despair, she loaded this problem onto my shoulders and in a conflict of loyalty, and bearing the pain of my mother's burden, I followed him at a respectful distance to the address of his girlfriend and reported it to my mother.

My mother was very close to my brother. Chris who provided her with the acceptance and affection she needed, and was an adaptable young boy. I was jealous of him and of my mother's attention to him, and began to give her a great deal of trouble, which only added to her despair. I wanted her love and support so much, and it seemed my brother got more than his share and I always managed to do something to drive her away. I was close to my father, and was sure that in his way he loved me, but he was sarcastic and condescending toward women. He had no long-term friends. Although he served as a strange role model, I am grateful for what I did take

ULLI AS A TEENAGER.

from him—his sense of humor, his clowning, his interest in fixing things, his music, and his hard work ethic and reliability.

Al was paying more and more attention to my mother, giving her many gifts. One day my mother announced casually that she was driving to St. Gallen, Switzerland with Al to have a hysterectomy. He drove up in his fancy Auburn Cord, and I went out on the street to wave goodbye. Mother looked happy as she waved back and they drove off. I stood by the newspaper kiosk and cried bitterly. I felt deserted. There was no one with whom I could share my pain. This is a scene that I replayed in my mind again and again.

Dawning of the Nazi Era

During the time of our family's disintegration, the political situation was changing drastically and there were now Brown Shirts all over Berlin. In the center of town they paraded, sang, and shouted, often holding burning torches. They fought with Communists on the streets, and I once witnessed such a fight near the Steiner school. A group of men, fighting on the side of the Communists, had the hammer and sickle emblems on their lapels. Eventually it became clear that the Nazis involved were about to overpower the others. At this point, the erstwhile Communists turned their collars around to expose their Nazi pins. They continued fighting, but this time on the side of the Nazis.

My mother had close Jewish friends, and I knew she thought a great deal about social justice and philosophy, and Father had no connection with or interest in politics. I could get no clarification from either of them about what all this meant. They just did not talk about it—at least not to me.

Chapter 2

•

1933 - 1937

s the political scene changed, my life also underwent an upheaval.

On January 30, 1933, Hitler was nominated to be Reichschancellor by President Hindenburg, the venerated but senile WWI hero. There was a big torch parade of storm troops in brown uniforms, many carrying swastika flags. All political resistance was quickly squelched and the press was censored. Communists who had not converted, officers from the army, homosexuals, and many others were put in prison or killed. On our street corner about 100 yards from our apartment, next to the U-Bahn station (the underground train), the Nazis put up a box with glass in front to hold the newspaper called the Stürmer (the Stormer), a purely anti-Semitic paper published by Julius Streicher, a dedicated and vicious anti-Semite, who hoped to be recognized by Hitler for his propaganda. The drawings or cartoons were very primitive and poorly drawn, showing Jews as very ugly with huge noses and lots of curly hair, grabbing blond "Aryan" women. There were always money bags lying around in the cartoons. The paper was saturated with hatred and lies, suggesting that the Jews were taking all the money and destroying the German culture. Hundreds of people passed this box every day as they came from the metro station. Some only glanced at it; a few stopped for a moment to read. As I watched them I wondered what they were thinking, but I was already aware that this was not a good thing to talk about. I could not understand why they would publish such a paper. It seemed so rude. The Jewish people I knew were not like that. Al certainly was not that kind of person. He was not ugly, and although he loved expensive things, he worked hard at a civil service position for his money, and was a very understanding and caring person. The only thing that pertained to him was that he was involved with an Aryan woman—my mother. I was sad and confused and became physically ill. The box stayed up, and every week a new edition was put behind the glass. I worried that Al might see it and wondered if he had, but no one in our family spoke about it.

One day Father returned from an out-of-town trip. My mother looked grim and they both went into the little room down the hall and closed the door. Before long I heard a heated argument. Mother told Father she wanted to get a divorce and Father tried to persuade her to change her mind. They argued for some time. I knew there was tension between them, but I never suspected they would end their marriage. Apparently my father didn't expect this either. In spite of his years of drinking and womanizing and his disregard for my mother's feelings and position, he seemed totally shocked that she would consider leaving him. When it became clear she was serious, he tried again and again to dissuade her. I was not supposed to be listening, so when I thought they were about to come out, I ran to my room and shut the door and cried and cried. I had never felt so alone.

My father wanted me to stay with him. I knew he loved me and I truly loved him, but I knew he would be unable to care for me, and I felt more secure with my mother and Al who definitely wanted me to stay with them. One day Al took me aside and told me I belonged with my mother, and he gave me a big silver coin. I was impressed, but I had already made up my mind. There was no question about Chris staying with our mother. He was eight years old and I was 13. A big part of me was hoping that somehow my parents would stay together, and despite all evidence to the contrary, I continued to hold on to the hope their relationship would be repaired. (In fact it took considerable therapy, and some 30 years, before I could truly let this hope go. Max remained shocked by the separation, and he too held on to the hope of reconciliation for the rest of his life.)

Al and Lottie married in the summer of 1934, just in time; for in the fall of that year the Nuremberg laws were passed, which prevented Jews and Gentiles from marrying each other. I remember no concern expressed by anyone because of the differing religions. It seemed perfectly normal. Only Lottie's brother, Bernhard, expressed his disapproval. He offered to help her get a divorce from Al, and told her she would never inherit money from the family if she were married to a Jew. Al's sister had some reservations, but mostly because she did not feel Lottie was up to the academic and social standards of their family. It was permissible for her beloved brother to have Lottie as a girlfriend, but it was not acceptable for him to marry her.

Lottie and Al found a downstairs apartment in a

two-family house in
which the owners, the
Steins, lived upstairs.
Mr. Stein was Jewish
with a Swiss citizen-
ship. Eichkamp (Oak
Camp), where we
lived, was an isolated

HOUSE IN EICHKAMP

little settlement of mostly one-family homes on the edge
of Charlottenburg near the Grunewald. It was also right
on the AVUS, a racetrack, where I later saw the Porsche
racing cars zooming by, one driven by Manfred von
Brauchitsch. Al and my mother had separate bedrooms,
and Chris and I shared a room. We now had a new maid
who had her own room. Hitler had issued an edict that
Jews could not have maids under 50—well past the
child-bearing age—so our maid was 63 years old and she
was often confused. One time she put salt instead of
sugar into the whipping cream, and to remedy the situation she emptied a whole bag of sugar into the bowl. She
was a sweet old lady but not as attractive or as playful as
the maids we had before her.

In Eichkamp, I passed the last days of my childhood.
Here I changed from a child to a young man. My voice
changed, I began to grow pubic hair, and I became interested in girls and all that that entailed.

Hitler Youth

The Technische Bereitshaft, which I had joined two
years earlier, continued to be an important part of my
life. I loved the overnight camping, the hikes, and the
chance to learn about all sorts of interesting technical

things. I made many good friends and deeply enjoyed all this group had to offer. Quite suddenly the year before, in 1933, we had heard that the group was being taken over by the Hitler Youth. I did not see any change at first, except that we had new uniforms consisting of a brown shirt and a black scarf (which already connoted an uncomfortable political message). Our corduroy shorts were cut so short that the pockets peeked out from under the pants, especially when they were loaded, as mine often were, with so many items of hardware and assorted tools that I thought were necessary for my survival. I was old enough to forego long stockings and as a result, my knees often suffered in the very cold weather bringing on physical problems that remain with me today.

Al continued to encourage me to remain in the organization because he thought it was a good social experience for me, and he knew how happy I was with it. He was confident that I would never become a Nazi, "Ulli wird nie ein Nazi werden." Perhaps he remembered one of the high points in his life—his Army days as surgeon in World War I in the Turkish campaign, when the comradeship and the feeling of doing something important for his country meant so much to him. Perhaps he also wanted me to maintain my social contacts, which seemed to keep me happy and got me out of the house and busy with something "worthwhile." My mother was somewhat less certain about the organization. After we moved in with Al, I would pedal my bike to Zehlendorf where my father lived, and change into the Hitler Youth uniform there. It was enough that Al allowed me to continue in the group; he should not have to live with someone wearing a brown shirt.

Aside from some very subtle political remarks, which I tried to ignore at first, or translate in my mind to something more acceptable, I saw very little change from the old Technical Bereitshaft, and I continued to enjoy much of what we did very much. We were sent to several farms to help harvest the potato crop. Often we sat around the campfire telling stories and singing the old folksongs that I loved so much. I made up my first joke: pointing to two telephone wires that were weaving in the wind I asked the group, "Do you know why they're weaving so? Well, it's two drunks talking to each other." I was very proud of my humor, and the uproarious laughter I received convinced me that I had a future as a great humorist.

In the Hitler Youth I learned to cook for 100-200 boys in a big portable field kitchen on wheels. I continued to learn more about telephones and car engines, and most important, I had lots of friends. With one friend especially, Albrecht, I established a blood relationship. We each pricked a finger, dipped the bleeding fingertips into a dish of water, and as the blood flowed together, we held hands and swore to an eternal friendship. I never saw him again after the Technical Bereitshaft, but the memory stuck.

A mass rally of adult Nazis and the Hitler Youth was planned for the fall of 1934 in Berlin. I was curious and decided to go to one of the streets that gave access to the big plaza where Hitler was to pass by. Both sides of the street were lined with storm troopers, their helmet straps tightened under their chins, all facing the sidewalk. There was a crowd on both sidewalks but no one was allowed to enter the street. Soon there was a commotion and I heard the engine of a single motor bike driven by a storm trooper who was scanning the crowd for any trouble spots. I had on my Jungvolk (Hitler Youth) uniform so I did not feel out of place, although I was apprehensive and scared. After the first motorcycle came two more mounted by non-commissioned storm troopers. After them, a V-shaped formation of about 15 high-ranking storm troopers on motorcycles passed by in a fear-inspiring crescendo. Then came a small military vehicle containing four high-ranking Nazis, and about 20 yards behind them, a black convertible Mercedes. The windows were down and after all the motorcycle noise, this fancy but quiet vehicle commanded attention. The chauffeur was wearing a storm trooper uniform, and all alone in the middle of the back seat sat Adolf Hitler. He had on a brown military jacket and a military hat, and he raised his right hand with a bent elbow to shoulder height to give the Hitler salute. I thought for a fleeting moment our eyes met and asked myself, Does he know that I am not totally dedicated to him? Can he tell that I have a Jewish stepfather? I stood there with my right arm stretched out before me, and was mesmerized. How could he not like Al? But I knew those were forbidden thoughts and truly wondered if he could read my mind. Soon he had passed, followed by a squadron of storm troopers on motorcycles, and I remained standing there in shock.

That year our whole troop of Jungvolk went to a big camp by the Baltic Sea. A Nazi flag had been planted on a hill and we took turns doing guard duty at the flag post for four hours at a time. We had to stand perfectly still, and some of the boys fainted in the hot sun.

In the evening we gathered around a big campfire and were told that a "special big Nazi" would speak to

us. Little did I realize that this was to be the beginning
for me of having to take responsibility for my personal
political decisions. The speaker started out by telling us
that someday we would have to be prepared to give up
our lives for a greater cause. For me this was a shocking
statement. I had certainly never considered giving up
my life for anything. While I was pondering this
thought, the speaker continued, saying that it was our
duty to give up our lives for Hitler, that we had a holy
allegiance to the Führer. At that moment, I knew in my
heart I did not agree with him. I could not accept what
he said. There was no way I could pretend I didn't hear,
or could twist this around to be more acceptable. To
give up my life for a great cause was one thing, and that
in itself required much thought. I was certain I would
not do it for Hitler. The speaker continued. He said
that if we saw Frenchmen coming over the hill of our
encampment, the Führer would expect us to kill every
one of them. I didn't even know any Frenchmen and
saw no reason to kill them. He went on, his voice rising,
"If you see Jews and you have guns, you must kill every
one of them even if you get killed in the process. Hitler
expects you to do it for the Fatherland." He ended by
raising his right hand, saying "Heil Hitler," and so we
all responded by screaming "Heil Hitler." Whether others were agreeing with him or simply thankful that the
speech was over, I could not tell. I looked around at the
other boys. They had all been dutifully listening, waiting for the speech to be over as we so often did when
adults spoke. As well-trained German youth, we were
accustomed to waiting patiently for adults to finish their
speeches so that we could continue with what we wanted to do. No one would have thought to comment or

question an edict from any authority. I could not imagine what the others were thinking, but I knew instinctively that this was not something we would talk about amongst ourselves. At this time the whole Nazi movement could be kept to one side or ignored a bit; we all knew that it would never be possible to raise any questions about it or be known for criticizing it.

That evening I felt very frightened and upset. I began to realize that something very terrible and evil was going on, and I was becoming a part of it by remaining in the Hitler Youth. I imagined the hill that the Nazi speaker had described and I saw Al coming over it. Why would I want to hurt him? And why would I want to kill Frenchmen? Why should I get killed for the Führer? I decided then and there that somehow, sooner or later, I would have to find a way to leave the group even though my parents were not pushing me to leave and I knew it would not be easy.

The following autumn, in 1935, I went on a bicycle trip with the Hitler Youth. We were camping in an old barn when suddenly at 3:00 in the morning, there was a great noise. Dirt and stones came flying through a window shattering the glass. Some village boys wanted to play a trick on us, and when we got to the door they were gone. At 7:00 a.m. we had to line up in front of the local pond and strip naked. Our leader counted to three and we jumped into the cold lake. After skinny-dipping we had to appear in clean uniforms and be inspected. Even our fingernails had to be clean. We were then dismissed and the whole troop climbed a huge nut tree and for an hour ate all the nuts we could. In the afternoon, the leader, one of the other boys, and I rode through the forest on our bikes. It was just getting dark when a man suddenly jumped out of the bushes and fired his gun into the air. He was the forest ranger, which in Germany is almost a military position. He was the boss in the forest. We apparently had wandered into territory where regular civilians were not allowed; so, when we got back to our camp in the village, we had quite a story to tell. Just as we were bedding down our leader came into the barn: "Pack your knapsacks, we are going on a night hike" he said, and we set out for a 17-mile march that we had to finish in six and a half hours.

Soon after that trip, some high-ranking officers from the Hitler Youth came to our group to teach us some more Nazi "ideals." For instance, they said it was a disgrace to look into the eyes of a Jew or even to shake hands with him, and they reminded us that our lives belonged to the Führer. It was Al, a Jew, who allowed me to stay in the Hitler Youth, who fed and protected me, and into whose eyes I looked every day. I knew that I had to find a way to get out of the organization soon. I had heard by this time that it would be very dangerous, if not impossible, to try to leave, and I had never heard of anyone who had. One just did not do anything so openly that opposed the Nazis. I didn't know exactly what would happen if I were to leave, I only knew it was not done. Already we knew that nothing that in any way could be seen as criticism of the Nazis was be permitted. I told my mother about my desire to leave and about some of the things that we were being taught, and she was upset and talked to me at length about it. She was very pleased that I had come to the decision to leave, but she had no suggestions as to how I should go about getting out. Al had no suggestions either, and my father seemed to have little interest in my problem. While my mother and Al had no solution for me, they were busy with plans to find ways of leaving Germany.

For some time I tried to figure out what I could do without getting into major trouble, and worried intensely about it. I realized that no one could help me. I would have to take care of this myself. How could I do it so that no one would get hurt? Finally, I thought I would begin the process by going to the leader whom I liked the most. He had been enthusiastic in the Technical Bereitshaft days, and I sensed that he was not entirely comfortable with the new Hitler Youth movement. He was less authoritarian than many of the other leaders. He seemed to genuinely like the boys, and he not only carefully explained things to us, but he listened to us and responded when we spoke. I had admired him for some time, even to the point of following him and copying the way he walked.

I had no idea how to broach the subject, but one day as we were talking I told him that I was having trouble in school (which was true) and that I thought perhaps I could not come to all the Hitler Youth meetings and outings in the future. To my immense surprise—in fact, shock—he responded strongly by saying that my school work took precedent over everything, and that perhaps I should drop out of all Hitler Youth activities for a while, in order to concentrate on school work. So on November 9, 1935, the anniversary of the Munich Nazi putsch (revolt), I left the Hitler Youth as quietly as I could. I just stopped attending meetings. It was very easy—too easy, I feared. No one came to interrogate me, and I heard nothing further from them. I never officially resigned, I just stopped going. A little later such a move would have been impossible. I have often wondered how this leader managed that, and how much he risked of his own position in order to give me a way out. How did he know how important it was for me to get out? It was a time, I was learning, that much was sensed but very little openly talked about. The next day I saw my first American movie with German subtitles, Ruggles of Redgap. I thought the movie was funny but superficial.

Public School

The previous year, Mother had decided to take me out of the Steiner school. (It was closed by Hitler in 1935 because the Anthroposophic movement was too far removed from Nazi ideals.) I began to go to the Wald (forest) school, a regular German high school, which was a 20-minute bike ride from our house. Coming from the Steiner school, I found myself one year behind academically. The new school was located in the woods and the classes were held in separate, one-story wooden buildings. All 500 students were there from 8:00 in the morning until 5:00 in the afternoon. We were given three meals: second breakfast at 10:30, dinner at 1:30, and coffee at about 3:30. We had supper at home at 7:30 p.m. We were certainly well fed, and in the summer we had classes under the trees and loved it. As the Nazi regime was established, we jumped to attention and yelled "Heil Hitler" when a teacher entered the classroom. Once a week we had assembly and had to sing both national anthems, "Deutschland, Deutschland über Alles" and the Nazi song, "Die Fahne Hoch" (Raise the Flag). We had to hold the right arm outstretched in the Hitler salute, sometimes for a long time. I always put myself in the second row or further back, so I could rest my arm on the shoulder of the boy ahead of me.

Every morning Admiral Dönitz (he took Hitler's place at the end of the war) and his son were chauffeured to the Mommsen High School gymnasium down the street, where the son attended.

There was one Jewish boy in our class, Silverstein, and sometimes some of the boys mocked him and even spat on him. I had never known such behavior before. He and I became good friends, and, sometimes, I could keep some of the other boys from hitting him. We continued to have both Catholic and Lutheran religious instruction but there was now no Jewish religion class, so he was excused from school at that time. We had a variety of subjects: German, of course, French, English, history, book-binding, gym, drawing, and many others. Coming from the Steiner school, I found these subjects very difficult. I also continued my recorder lessons with Cora Schröder, and studied the piano.

The comments on my report card now were different. I was a good "comrade" to the other students and I was reliable—a good German quality. I needed to show more self-discipline in order to achieve what I wanted, it said, and I needed to work harder.

My high school English teacher was Herr Kerl. He was tall and rotund, bald-headed and very cheerful. He made learning English fun. Herr Kerl had visited America and gone to a baseball game, which he described to us: "One person has a big club and another throws a ball at him. Sometimes the second person hits the ball with his stick so high it seems like it stays in the air forever, and if it lands in the bleachers the team gets a point." When he later learned that I was going to immigrate to the U.S., he gave me an A in English. He said he had met many Americans, had friends in the U.S., and thought his recommendation might help me if I was to meet some of them.

By this time our stealing days were over and we entered the age of Till Eulenspiegel-type pranks (practical jokes). I had a close friend, Andrew Blankenburg, who was the son of a high school teacher. He was a very gentle, fun-loving young man, and we roamed the neighborhood together.

Many of our tricks took place near the metro station at Eichkamp where there was a grove of trees through which passengers would have to walk after leaving the train. I often went there in the evenings to meet Al, who had given up his Auburn Cord for a small Opel, which he found very uncomfortable Most of the time he took the metro.

One evening Andrew and I put some marmalade glasses with burning candles in them all over a tree. It looked just like Christmas and people passing by admired the scene we had created.

Another night we stood on both sides of a path holding our hands at chest height as if we were stretching a rope across the path. Although there was no rope, quite a few passengers who had just gotten off the train stopped.

"Take that away," the first passenger shouted. We didn't budge. We looked at him innocently, as if to say, "Take what away?"

Another night I put on my mother's high-heeled shoes, her dress, and her hat. We went to the same grove of trees. When the passengers arrived, my friend Andrew attacked me (he was dressed in rags) and I started to scream, "Hilfe! Hilfe!" (Help! Help!). Two or three passengers ran after Andrew until he escaped. Finally, they came back to see how I was, but the "lady" was nowhere to be seen. Our friends and we thought these exploits were hilarious.

In January 1935 I started to write a diary. I began by mentioning that the weather was splendid. Church bells were ringing all over Germany because Hitler and the German troops had "co-opted" the Saarland, which was given to France at the end of WW I. Now the Germans had marched in and taken it by force. School was dismissed that day. Hitler had gotten away with it.

The real inspiration for the diary (later lost on the trip to America), however, was our neighbor's fourteen-year-old daughter, whose father was a doctor. My friend Andrew and I were both very shy and my greatest thrill revolved around seeing her from a distance of about 300 feet. When she looked at me or greeted me, I was in ecstasy. At night I had vivid fantasies imagining her coming into my room where I would give her candy. She had a very full figure and my whole body reacted to this scene. Sometimes, in my fantasy, she and I went for a walk into nature in our nightgowns. I was usually asleep, however, before I imagined us getting very far into the woods.

Across from her room, on the other side of the street, a community center was being built. When it was dark enough, Andrew and I climbed into the unfinished building, which had a balcony that overlooked her bedroom. We stood watching, always at night, of course, in rain, fog, and snow, sometimes for an hour at a time. We watched her reading, dancing with her sister, undressing, and going to bed. Sometimes she left the window open and we threw snowballs. Eventually we were discovered, and we paid a heavy price—from then on the curtains were drawn every evening.

Every Sunday as part of the divorce agreement, my brother and I met Father in Zehlendorf. We frequently rode our bikes to the suburbs, to Lake Wannsee, where we would picnic with our friend Hans Tremmel, and take small tours in his kayak. Father's maid, Hedwig, a full-figured woman who was living with him, accompanied us. Later, an opera singer moved in with Father, and the two of them made music together. These weekend meetings were uncomfortable, and I was always pleased to get back to Eichkamp, to Mother and Al.

Sometimes Father took us to the zoo, where his friend, Frau Dr. Heinroth, was the director. I loved that experience, and from it I developed a strong interest in wild animals, and their care and preservation. I learned many interesting tidbits: an elephant's penis weighs fifty pounds, for instance; and other "useful" bits of information. As we entered through the gate, the big elephants lumbered around behind a strong fence. One December day, Father gave us some peanuts to hand to the monkeys. I had my wool mittens on and one of the monkeys promptly took my mitten with the nuts. Father got very upset. He found the attendant and scolded him for letting something like that happen. I had never seen my father so angry. Finally the attendant climbed the fence and coaxed the monkey to return the mitten.

The zoo had a special exhibit one summer. As we entered the front gate we saw a huge crowd of people in front of us, watching an enclosure in which there were some tall, black Africans. Some were standing around a fire, spit-roasting an animal, and some were exhibiting crafts, and engaging in other activities. They were in their native costumes, which meant they were very scantily dressed, and they had big disks in their upper and lower lips. The scene had been set up to look like their home environment. Around the fence stood throngs of Germans, who had never seen black people before. After watching the Africans, the audience moved on to watch the other exhibits in the zoo.

When Father felt generous he took Chris and me to the Kurfürstendamm, which was (and still is) a major boulevard in Berlin. We sat at a table of a sidewalk cafe and had hot chocolate. When Father was in a very good mood, he also ordered a piece of cake for us while he had his beer and smoked a cigar.

One day I was to go skiing with Father and his current girlfriend from Hamburg to the mountain range called Riesengebirge. The highest mountain there was called Schneekoppe (snow capped) in the province of Silesia. Before leaving for the trip, I decided to fill my field flask with rum and lemon juice from Al's liquor shelf. My mother saw me, and when she asked what I was doing, I told her. She took the flask away from me, but I grabbed it back and poured it out on the lawn. Al stood by and watched as we had this fight in the yard. Later I wrote an angry, anxious letter—angry that she had defied me, and worried that she might throw me out of the house or do something terrible to punish me. I told her she could give away all my toys, all my books, and all my musical instruments, as long as she didn't toss me out or send me to live with my father.

Chris was also along on the ski trip to the Riesengebirge, and Father was drinking heavily. By the time we got there, he was hallucinating. I felt helpless as he lay there. His girlfriend, a dental assistant about 27 years old, and I went for a walk. I was able to talk with her about my misery and she listened. I was sure I was in love with her. Father finally sobered up, but I felt that helplessness whenever he had the D.T.'s; he had become dependent on alcohol, and he suffered tremors when he went without it. Later that same afternoon, the four of us had a good time in the snow. When we got back to Berlin, Mom and Al were glad to see us, and our altercation seemed forgiven and forgotten.

In the fall of 1935 I came down with a bad case of jaundice. I had eaten some spoiled fish and Al treated me. Because he was Jewish, he had lost his position in the city hospital, and he had established a private practice. He could take his patients to a Jewish children's hospital, where I stayed for four weeks. I turned yellow and so did all my bodily fluids, including my tears. I ate 56 bananas in one week to provide me with the needed potassium. Once when I was feeling quite ill, Mother came to visit me and she cried. I was totally surprised by her tears, and only learned later that I could have died. When I recovered, all that remained of this experience was that I was told I could never donate blood.

Confirmation Classes

After Easter 1936, Mother and Al arranged for me to go to the confirmation classes of Pastor Niemoeller. They wanted to expose me to a more democratic, religious philosophy. Mother had been brought up in the Protestant religion and many of her ancestors had been clergymen. Confirmation classes were an important way to learn about the Bible and theology, and they had left a great impression on her; it was probably her main experience with intellectual life. I had never been in a church except for my own baptism, and for marriages and funerals. God was depicted as a man with a white beard and I had never seen any evidence of Him (except at Christmas when Baby Jesus came to stand for Love and Harmony), nor was there much mention of anything approaching religion. I did not respond to the idea of drinking wine ("this is my blood") and breaking bread ("this is my body").

Pastor Niemoeller was a well-known Lutheran pastor, who preached and officiated at the modern Church of Jesus Christ in Dahlem. Since he spoke for the freedom of religion in a dictatorial government, his Sunday sermons and other meetings were well attended. Our confirmation class met as a group of about 20 young people, boys and girls, in one of the Church's small meeting rooms. I still have the notes from August 8, 1936:

> *"Confirmation means affirmation. We are to affirm the contract God made with us when we were baptized and accepted as one of His children. When we were babies our parents agreed to this contract for us, and now that we are older, we can agree to becoming confirmed Christians ourselves. And to make this contract with God we have to first know who God is and how he reveals Himself to us."*

Pastor Niemoeller was like a twentieth century Luther. "I stand here and I can do not otherwise," and he did not bow to Hitler as Luther in the sixteenth century did not bow to the Pope. Niemoeller demanded obedience to the will of God (Luke 6, verse 46). "We

must fear and love God," he told our confirmation classes, "We must be obedient and loving." (Ephesians 6,
verses 1-9) The themes of fearing and loving were also
woven into his Sunday sermons, and over the years, his
emphasis on love grew—unconditional love.

Niemoeller was unyielding to the point of rigidity,
and he was a deep feeling and thinking person who genuinely liked his students. His physical posture was military. He had been a U-boat commander in World War I,
and afterwards he studied theology (receiving a doctorate). He was never happy in the Weimar Republic,
which was an excellent democratic constitutional instrument, but one that could not be as effective as an auto-
cratic form of government, and Niemoeller like efficien-
cy and order. In 1932 he became the first pastor of the
Church of Jesus Christ in Dahlem. He had an assistant
(of Jewish background), Franz Hildebrand, who later
baptized my brother Chris in the village church nearby. I
came to love Niemoeller and my mother supported me
in this adulation. He was sensitive and spiritual and
stubborn at the same time. He looked me in the eyes,
and I felt accepted. His rebellion was a model for my
own rebellion. I felt my heart actually warmed by his
love for mankind, and he ignited my determination to
become a pastor. He lived in the midst of danger from
the Nazis, and he inspired me to take risks as well in my
own life. He appealed also to many Germans who
strengthened their own good intentions through his
inspiration and his model, and his church was always
filled to overflowing with those who were seeking respite
from the growing Nazi philosophy. Soon with the arrest
of some parishioners and many German pastors, this
aspect of the German Christian religion went under-

ground or disappeared altogether.

Niemoeller continued preaching and founded the Confessional Church, while the Nazis began a Nazi Christian Church. Arrests were made and edicts against Niemoeller's Confessional Church were issued.

The 1936 Olympic Games

Germany was chosen to host the 1936 Olympic Summer games. A big stadium had been built for the event near our house, and one afternoon, a friend and I decided to visit the site. We climbed through the tunnels, jumped from one row of seats to another, and inspected the big swimming pool. A sculptor friend of ours had designed the Olympic pin. Hitler spared no effort or expense to show his new Germany to the world. One week before the games started, food rationing was suddenly lifted and we could buy all the milk, meat, bread, and eggs we wanted. We could even buy coffee and bananas.

Having watched the construction of the stadium over several months, and being interested in track, I was hoping desperately that some miracle would occur and somehow I could attend. My wish was granted. Al came home with one ticket that a patient had given him—standing room only—up in the highest tier. Below were the VIP box and platform where Hitler was expected to appear. From my seat, I was able to see the javelin-throwing event, the shot put, and high jump, the disk throwing, and the hockey players from India who won the gold medal. To me the hockey players were magic; they used their hockey sticks with such great skill that the opposition often didn't have any idea where the puck was.

The most exciting events for me, however, were the 100- and 200-meter dashes, the 100-meter relays, and the broad jump. The hero in all four of these competitions was Jesse Owens, the American athlete. The crowd truly went wild, screaming and shouting when he exceeded the Olympic and world broad-jumping record by jumping beyond the small Olympic and world flags that had been stuck in the sand. He easily beat the other competitors in the 100- and 200-meter races. His movements were graceful and smooth. Finally, he helped the U.S. win the 400-meter relays. I was beside myself with joy and admiration.

Hitler was in his box below me watching the final broad jump. It was the custom, when the Führer was present, for the victor to run up to him and be personally congratulated. I saw Jesse Owens run like a gazelle up the stairs, when suddenly the Führer's flag was lowered and Hitler disappeared through a back door. When Jesse Owens reached Hitler's box, there was no one to greet him. Apparently Hitler did not want to shake hands with a black man. Below me was the camera crew who filmed the games. Leni Riefenstahl, the famous actress and personal friend of Hitler, was down there in the pit, directing the crew. Regarding the medal count, the U.S. had easily won in the track events; but, Hitler had added an art exhibit, which the Germans won hands down, and this gave them the highest total medal count. I had been rooting for the Americans. A week after the games we went back to food rationing.

That year, at age 15, I was at the height of my adolescence, and rebelled, especially against my mother. I became even more jealous of my brother Chris, who seemed always very sweet and compliant, and whom I thought my mother still preferred. Every night my mother would sit at the edge of his bed and read and talk to him. I lay in my bed hurting, but I could not say anything that would be admitting weakness, much less jealousy.

Often at night (and I thought it was partially because he felt sorry for me), Al would sit by me and talk to me about life. He loved to talk about his exploits in the Turkish campaign in World War I, which had been a high point in his life. As a surgeon, he had traveled throughout Turkey caring for German troops. As always, when Al was practicing his profession he was happy, and the appreciation and social contacts of that time meant much to him. I do not remember what it was he talked about, but there was an intensity with which he described his adventures. Often the subject would veer into his romantic exploits with the Turkish women, which he described as "very successful." He always considered himself a great lover and an expert on sex, so our discussions also often covered that topic, emphasizing the technical and anatomical aspects. In my advanced state of puberty I would often argue with him despite his obvious superior knowledge and experience. (He assured me, for instance, that from a medical perspective, withdrawal was the best way to prevent conception from occurring. Certainly, at that time, it was the most available preventative). I was also given Van der Velde, a popular book on sex that emphasized the novel idea that men should be "considerate" of women. My mother had told me that in regard to sexual matters, the important thing was to be "sincere." In spite of my parents' obvious sexual revolt from the restrictive views of the past, I also received strong verbal messages against sexual experiences before marriage.

In October of 1936 our entire high school class of about 16 boys and girls went on a trip into the country. Because of my interest in cooking (from Hitler Youth days and helping my mother in the kitchen), I was in charge of the food. I had three assistant cooks, all girls, and five additional girls who peeled the potatoes, scraped and washed the pots and pans, and did all the dirty work. I was in seventh heaven. Two boys broke the rules and took off for a long walk with two girls. As a silly sort of punishment for them, we put laxatives in their cereal the following morning. We were at that in-between age, between moral rigidity and a desire for excitement at any cost.

That same year I heard that two girls from our class, Helma and Christine, were planning a bicycle trip to Naumburg, an ancient city on the Saale River in Thuringia, and they were planning a first stop in Wittenberg, which was on the way. Naumburg Cathedral had a statue of Uta of Naumburg, which I had long admired in pictures. I thought it was the most beautiful object I had ever seen and I had always hoped I might be able to actually see it. I told a classmate, Pete, about the girls' plans for a trip. He was already in love with Helma and I with Christine. Both were beautiful, bright, and vivacious girls. We decided to follow them and eventually catch up, but we told the girls nothing of our plans. It was raining heavily when we started out October 12. The further we got, the faster we went. We could not understand why we weren't catching up with the girls. When we finally got to the city of Wittenburg some miles away, we were both soaked.

It was here that in 1517 Martin Luther posted his 95

Theses that got him in trouble with the Church. We were just entering the youth hostel where we planned to stay when we discovered that the two girls had already arrived. They had taken the train because of the bad weather, and they were very surprised to see us. We "decided" to continue traveling together. By this time it had stopped raining and we climbed the tower of the old church where Luther had posted his Theses. (The door had been replaced at least once.) I pulled out my C-soprano recorder, and Helma had brought her guitar. Peter played his harmonica and Chris, who had a lovely, clear soprano voice, sang. We sang and played German folksongs late into the night.

The following day we went on to Bitterfeld, and right in the middle of the highway, Chris's bicycle tire blew out. We pulled out our handkerchiefs and tried to wave down a truck. After about an hour of waving, a truck driver came along and took all four of us, as well as our bikes, to Leipzig, where people spoke in a Saxonian dialect that we began to imitate. We went to St. Thomas Church where Bach had played. I sat at the same organ and played a Bach chorale. The next morning we decided that the ride on the truck the day before had done us much good, and we found a truck driver who was willing to take us almost all the way to Naumburg. We then bicycled the rest of the way, and in Naumburg, we had our first warm meal—noodles. They were so poorly prepared, we called them Ersatznudeln (substitute noodles).

The next morning we visited the cathedral with the statue I loved. We entered the church and there upon a pedestal on the wall stood the small statue, Uta of Naumburg. She was very feminine with fine features and a flowing robe. I had imagined it far larger and more impressive. She was only about three-feet tall, but every bit as beautiful as I had assumed. She smiled benevolently down on us, and the gothic arches carried our view up to the heavens. Suddenly, the organist started to practice, and the music filled the whole church with eighteenth century harmony. I thought, If this is the Divine, I understand. This is something I want.

We left Naumburg and bicycled over to Merseburg and Halle (the town in which my father was born and raised) by the Saale River, and then to Bitterfeld. We took our time and saw many beautiful churches, castles, and cathedrals. When we arrived in Bitterfeld it was getting dark and the local youth hostel was already filled. Finally, we found an old barn on the outskirts of town. We knocked on the door of the main house and persuaded the farmer to let us sleep in the straw. We were all excited about the prospect of sleeping together; and at the same time, hearing the critical voices of our parents ... or someone. All barely 15 years old, we slept four in a row in the hay and the night passed without incident. The cold night gave all of us red noses. The next morning we headed back to Berlin, through rain showers and sunshine. We had been gone for about two weeks with our parents' blessings. We had come to the end of a wonderful trip.

My interest in girls and women continued to grow that year. Mom and Al had close friends named Kurt and Ilse Frank. Kurt was a patient of Al's, and deeply trusted him. Kurt had a bad case of asthma and, with the medical expertise of the time, Al recommended that Kurt move away from his wife and into a hotel. Ilse was a very attractive artist who dressed with great style. One afternoon, she offered to give me dancing lessons, and she showed me a few steps and asked me to put my arms around her. I had never held a woman that close and I was greatly embarrassed; I knew she must have been aware of my excitement. She was leading, and as I tried to move away from her, I came closer and closer to her bosom, and my face became redder and redder. She continued to teach me without mention of my embarrassment, and, eventually, I came to enjoy these lessons very much.

Emigrating to America

In Berlin the political-social reality continued to worsen. Although only Al was Jewish, we were considered a Jewish family. Germany was now saturated with anti-Semitism. There were anti-Semitic Stürmer newspaper boxes all over the city. I visited an ethnic exhibit near the Zoo railroad station, where they showed pictures of the genealogies of non-Aryan people. The Jews and the Slavs and the blacks were depicted as ugly and lecherous people. These displays were put up in the name of science, but they seemed to me obvious propaganda. Some of the exhibits were signed by a Professor Doctor. "Someone or other," giving them more credence in the eyes of the public. Many in the crowds stood around the boxes reading intently, and I felt they were accepting this as the truth.

I began to have more experiences with anti-Semitism. One day I was hiking near the beach of the Baltic Sea. The sun was shining, a few clouds drifted overhead, and a few flowers had blossomed on the dunes. I walked a long way, and just when I was growing tired, I noticed a bench in the distance. I eagerly walked toward it, but when I reached it, I saw stenciled on the back, "Juden sind hier unerwünscht"—Jews are not wanted here. I really wanted to sit down and rest, and I knew no one would see me. Though I was not a Jew, I would not allow myself to sit there; it would have felt disloyal to Al. Al had been so proud to fight for Germany in World War I and considered himself a good German. I found a soft spot on the ground nearby and sat, wondering about the unfairness of life.

Al and my mother had thought seriously of emigrating since the end of 1935 because the situation in Germany was clearly worsening for Jews. At the time I was unaware of any particular pressure to leave; it seemed to me that Al was simply looking for a place where he could work outside of Germany. He was offered a position as court physician with one of the Maharajas in India. Mother was concerned: "Will I be able to take my walks or is there a danger of being eaten by a tiger?" They decided against India.

We attended several meetings of the Zionist movement—an almost militant group that aggressively encouraged Jews to migrate to Palestine. Al took a trip to Tel Aviv, but came back with mixed feelings. He found the Palestinians were also anti-Semitic, and he was not eager to run from one anti-Semitic place to another. Meanwhile, we heard from Al's sister, Renate, known as Spatz (little sparrow) who was married to Ludwig Edelstein. These two

SPATZ, AL'S SISTER

had studied at Heidelberg and were known as experts on the history of ancient Greek medicine. When they had decided to emigrate in 1935, they had both quickly been offered positions to teach at Johns Hopkins University in Baltimore. I liked Spatz even though she often discounted my mother who in turn reacted strongly. Spatz saw my mother as flighty, unintellectual, and overly concerned with beauty and glamour.

Spatz had connections. She knew Senator Tydings of Maryland and Bettina Warburg from a banking family, a distant relative of Al's and her's. In order to emigrate to the U.S., we had to have two people from the U.S. who would vouch for us and make a deposit of $5000—a sum that would allow the family to live for one year. This was considered a generous sum, far more than the average wage earner made in a year. We were allowed to take from Germany only a small amount of cash (the equivalent of $10.00 per person) from Germany, and all of the belongings that we could ship. Many people found clever ways of getting their money out of Germany, smuggled in furniture or clothing, but we did not. We just took as much of what we owned as we could.

LUDWIG EDELSTEIN
SPATZ'S HUSBAND

Senator Tydings and Mrs. Warburg agreed to vouch for us, and Al, Mother, Chris, and I spent many days waiting at the U.S. Consulate in Berlin along with hundreds of Jews. Mother, Chris, and I were the only non-Jews there. We had to have a physical examination and a short interview answering easy questions. We passed that hurdle, and in January 1937, we got our exit visas.

Al and Mother tried to shield Chris and me from the worst of what was happening, and they did it very well. I was mostly unaware of their despair and their fears. My father had often been unemployed and looking for a job, so it seemed very familiar that Al should be looking for a job also.

A great deal of effort revolved around moving, gathering together jewelry and valuable furniture to take with us. My brother, who spent more time at home than I did, remembers my mother crying bitterly a great deal at that time, and others who knew her said she was as white as a ghost and growing thinner and thinner. It became a family legend that I had told Al and Mother not to worry; I would get a job and take care of the whole family.

I was excited about going to America, and it intensified the tensions of being in Germany for me. I could have stayed with my father, but I wanted to be with my mother and Al, and my brother; and, I already knew that I did not want to be involved with the Nazi philosophy or to live with those who were. I was very confused and frightened by much of what the Nazis were teaching me—about being killed, and about the Jews. It all seemed very evil, and there was no one I could talk to about it.

The Nazi laws against the Jews had become more restrictive. Jewish or anti-Nazi friends disappeared, and we were told they had committed suicide. One night there was a big commotion upstairs in our landlord's apartment. In the morning we discovered the Steins and their two children had suddenly disappeared. They had

heard through the grapevine that the Gestapo was coming for them, and they grabbed what they could and fled
by train to Switzerland, where Mr. Stein had citizenship.
In the afternoon of the next day three men knocked on
our door. They were from the Gestapo and they wanted
to know where the Steins were. We could not tell them.
They did not have a search warrant but went through
the upstairs apartment anyway. They did not find anything "subversive." We were afraid they might grab us
next, but they left us alone; for how long, we could not
surmise.

This was the point at which Al and Mom were
determined to leave. We knew many Jews who were certain that as good German citizens, they would not be
disturbed by these uncouth Nazis. Some did not escape,
or had much difficulty in doing so. When Al's former
wife and children later left in 1940, they disguised themselves as fisherfolk and sailed across the English
Channel from a beach in Dunkirk. When they arrived in
England, the adults were put in prison as enemy aliens,
and the children in orphanages. Eventually they were
able to get to America.

As we prepared to leave, we were referred by the
American Friends Service Committee to a Quaker family who offered to help prepare us for the U.S. I was surprised at their friendliness and generosity; they truly listened to us. They heard our questions, shared our enthusiasm, and were sensitive to our fears. I had never met
people so kind and respectful, and took this as an example of what America might be like. They invited us for
dinner. Since we could not take any money with us we
decided to spend quite a bit of it on clothes. We asked
what we should take in order to fit into the American

lifestyle. For me they suggested knickerbockers and leather jackets, popular when the Quakers had been in the U.S. several years before. They outfitted me in a sort of Great Gatsby fashion.

In March 1937 our timed departure to the U.S was nearing. We had been informed that we could take all of our furniture, and the movers wrapped everything very carefully: our custom-made Bauhaus furniture and the heavy antique chests that had been in my mother's family since the 1700s; mirrors and tables purportedly from the time of the Reformation in the sixteenth century; enormous boxes of special gold-plated china; and much silver, including flatware with nine pieces for each place setting. It seemed perfectly logical that we would ship such things; only later did I realize this was probably the only way Al and Mother could bring any disposable wealth with us. Fortunately, they did not have to sell much of it—shortly after our belongings arrived in the States, there was an accident on the boat in Tacoma, Washington (a stopover), and some of the crates were dropped 20 feet, breaking mirrors and chairs as well as an original painting by a student of Holbein's. The insurance for these items provided us with some immediate cash.

Al left the country first to prepare the ground. Chris and I stayed on in Berlin, he to finish the school year, and I to remain until my confirmation by Pastor Niemoeller. Mother, who was not very well, took a vacation trip to Yugoslavia. I also organized a farewell trip at our school. Four girls and six boys from our class made an excursion 50 miles outside of Berlin. Since I had a reputation as a cook, I was responsible for the meals. We slept in an open barn and engaged in much horseplay for several hours each day.

In April mother returned from Yugoslavia, and the next day she and Chris left for America to join Al. I was left all alone, remaining behind for my confirmation. I then moved in with Al and Lottie's friends, the Remisches. He was a sculptor who had a Jewish wife. They, and all my friends, were very nice to me as I awaited my departure for the U.S., although some expressed their worry that I would be attacked by wild Indians. Others feared that I would be robbed by gangsters as I went through Chicago, and there were those who had heard that in the West outlaws still held up trains.

On May 3, 1937 I bought my first suit with money Mother had left for this purpose, and prepared for the big date when one other young man and I would finally be confirmed by Niemoeller. When the evening arrived, the church was full. In the back, leaning against the wall, were four stocky men from the Gestapo wearing gray woolen overcoats, there to pick up any seditious pronouncements coming from Pastor Niemoeller. With his white Lutheran collar piece, the long black robe, and the Bible in his left hand, Niemoeller was an imposing figure.

After the sermon, the other young man and I walked down the aisle and approached the altar. The organist played a Bach chorale and we both knelt. Then, it became absolutely quiet and Niemoeller went through the ritual. The verse Niemoeller had chosen was suitable for my future in America. It came from 2 Chronicles 16:9 in the Old Testament: "The eyes of the Lord run to and fro throughout the whole earth, to show Himself strong in the behalf of them whose heart is perfect." We said a subdued "yes" as we dedicated our lives to God, and Niemoeller, in blessing, laid his hand on our heads. It was over. We were his last confirmants before he was sent to a concentration camp.

I was concentrating on the sacred ritual of confirmation and had no idea that the Gestapo would soon arrest Niemoeller, (nor did I realize that 60 years later, in my mind, I would still see those figures in heavy grey coats worn on a May evening in 1937.)

The following Friday, I visited Niemoeller for the last time. He looked sad and defeated. Half an hour before, the Gestapo had come and taken away his passport so he could not leave the country. We chatted a while. I thanked him for leading me to Christianity, and showing me the promise of religion. For the first time, I told him I had been thinking of becoming a pastor. We glanced at the map of Oregon, the state where I would rejoin my family. He told me that if I was retained at Ellis Island, I should tell the officials that Niemoeller was good friend of mine, and they would let me go because they knew him. He gave me his blessing and we said goodbye to each other. As I looked at him—such a good and wise person, aspiring to the best that man can be—the idea of becoming a minister became stronger and stronger.

On Sunday we celebrated my confirmation at the home of my piano and recorder teacher, Cora Schröder. It was also a farewell party and a birthday party since I had just turned 16. Father showed up, and he had been drinking heavily. Losing a wife, one son, and now his oldest son was more than he could bear. I was embarrassed because his breath reeked of liquor and cigars.

We had the traditional German Sunday afternoon

coffee and cake, and then Cora went to the piano, I picked up my F-alto recorder, and we played Händel's Sonata No.1 for cembalo and recorder. This was my swan song. I visited awhile with Father afterwards; then everyone went home.

Congratulation letters arrived, filled with advice and a little too much analysis of my personality. At first I became angry but later calmed down. "They mean well," I reminded myself. In that last week I said goodbye to a dear friend almost every day.

All was going well until a few days after my confirmation, when I got a message from the police that I could not emigrate because my papers were not in order. I had already packed my things and the boat and train tickets had been bought. I was called to Gestapo headquarters where I was so frightened my knees were actually shaking. I wondered, would or could Father protect me? I was interviewed by one of the officers who asked me whether I would remain faithful to the Fatherland. What could I say but "yes?" He stamped my passport and said the papers were now in order. I thanked him and got out of there as fast as I could. I was extremely relieved; some who were called to the Gestapo were not seen again.

The following Monday, the black day had come; it was time for me to leave Germany. May 17, 1937, two days after my sixteenth birthday, I met Father at the railroad station for the Hamburg trains. I would be with him only thirty minutes more after all our years together. We were both very self-conscious—all we talked about was the luggage and the tickets and passport. "Are you sure you have them all?" he kept asking again and again, and he made me produce them each time. We arrived at the platform and the train was ready to leave in ten minutes. He helped me into the train with the suitcases and then returned to the platform. I opened the window. Five more minutes! Father looked desperate with tears in his eyes, and I was crying. "I will see you again" he mumbled. Then came the sound of a long shrill whistle, (which I can still hear today.) The station master, wearing a red cap, was on the platform. He signaled for the engineer to start the train. Father shook hands through the window. His hand was limp and mine closed around his. I knew it would not be soon that I would shake his hand again. The last words I uttered were "Sei recht tapfer." (Be as brave as you can.) Suddenly there was a jerk. Father walked alongside the train. We looked at each other and said nothing. The train pulled ahead and Father remained behind. I felt like someone was pulling out one of my limbs. There was his familiar face, and here that big iron carriage tearing me away. Slowly the train rounded a curve. There was one more second I could still see his face. "Father!" something roared within me. And we were separated. It was all over. I cried like a small child.

The trip from Berlin to Hamburg was difficult. I stared out of the window lost in a world of pain and fear. I've taken many train rides in my life, but looking back, that seemed the longest, and I still remember every detail of the parting.

In Hamburg, I was met by Father's friend, Gretl, whom I knew from mountain skiing in 1936. She took me by bus to a Jewish family, friends of Al and Mother, who had arranged all this beforehand. They were to take me to the ship, but their religion forbade traveling by bus or streetcar or anything with wheels on the Sabbath.

They brought a small cart, we put my luggage in it, and what did not fit we carried. Since I was not Jewish I could pull the cart. We traveled over the cobblestones of Hamburg a long distance to the wharf. There was a huge passenger liner with U.S.S.Washington written on the bow and the American flag waving in the wind. I was entering a new world. I said goodbye to our friends, and walked up the gangplank. I was going across the ocean, then across the land, to a new home in America. I knew there were Indians who were admired and feared, there were gangsters, there was someone who knew my English teacher, and someone else who knew Niemoeller. Somehow there was a wonderful sense of opportunity and democracy, and I was certain it was all there for me.

Chapter 3

•

May 1937-February 1943

On May 17,1937, at twenty-six minutes past six in the evening, I left German soil for a trip alone across the Atlantic Ocean, for what seemed like halfway around the world. I was on the U.S.S. Washington, and a part of me could not believe this. I was still watching for the Gestapo to come running up the gangplank after me, but nothing happened.

I traveled tourist class (second class), sandwiched between third class and first, and the differences were noticeable. The third class passengers definitely had shabbier clothes, while those in first class wore fur coats and fancy jewelry. I felt very content where I was, and pleased with my roommates. The next morning the ship actually left the harbor. The farther we were from the German shore, the safer I felt. Yet, as long as we remained in German waters, I was still frightened that the Gestapo would pull up in a motor launch and call out for Ulrich Heinicke because something was wrong or missing in his papers, and they wanted to make sure he would remain a good German citizen.

Our first stop was Le Havre, where we had a few hours layover, and I went ashore for my first visit to

France. Almost everyone spoke French, and I practiced my French and found I was able to do quite well. My English was not so easily accomplished. The next stop was to be Southampton, but before we reached that harbor, we passed through an armada of warships from forty-six nations. We were moving very slowly, and it took us hours to get through this fleet. It was the coronation fleet in honor of England's new King George VI, the father of Queen Elizabeth. There were warships as far as the eye could see. I later learned this was the biggest fleet that had ever been assembled. Two years later these ships were in deadly combat with each other.

The food on the ship was a complete contrast to the German menus I had left behind. I had never seen such food and I gorged myself on it. There were twelve different desserts on the menu and I ate all twelve of them. When the ship left the channel for the open sea, there was a bit of a wind whipping up the waves. The boat rocked from left to right and up and down. I started feeling funny, and I soon knew I was in trouble. I barely made it to the railing before I lost all twelve desserts. The wind was blowing some of it back into my face. Soon there was a gentle tap on my shoulder. It was the third class steward: "Sir, would you mind moving toward the windward side?" (I didn't know what he meant, but he pointed to the other side of the ship.) "You are disturbing the third class passengers." For the next two days I was busy "feeding the fish" on the windward side of the ship.

In Southampton a young English woman came on board with her mother. She was about twenty-five years old with blonde hair, fine features, and a very personal and friendly style. She introduced herself and asked for my name. When I said "Ulrich," pronouncing it was beyond her, as it was to be for the many non-Germans I met later. My name had always been appreciated in Germany, but elsewhere it often brought a sort of gargling sound. She decided to call me Rikky, after Rikky Tikky Tavi from Rudyard Kipling's Jungle Book, and to shorten it. I became Rikky, a name I took for the next six years.

This woman was writing a novel and she said she would put my name into it, which further intrigued me. I was sure I was in love with her, and we played shuffleboard, took our meals together, and sat on deck chairs chatting (I wore out my dictionary), or we danced. As the ship dipped from left to right, I found I had gotten over my seasickness. Finally, on the last night at the captain's dinner, I ordered seven desserts with no untoward effects.

By May 25 we were nearing the coast of the United States, and expected to dock that day. Very early in the morning I went on deck in order to see the Statue of Liberty, which I had heard so much about and seen in photographs. The deck was crowded as the other passengers also had come up to see the statue. From a distance, she came into view, and very slowly we came upon her, a huge statue that demands attention and sends out her message of welcome. For me the experience was overwhelming. We all watched, as millions of others have watched, many who had to leave behind their homes and families and also their pains; I was part of those millions too. She is enormous and she seemed to welcome us to all the special things that America held. I had always been a German and I was leaving behind friends and father. Now I would be an American with all that that entailed, and I wasn't quite sure what that was. How did I suddenly become American and not remain German? What was I to do? I stared at the statue and felt all those hopes and prayers that had been laid upon her, and also the welcome that she was sending to us. Suddenly I became aware that there were tears streaming down my face.

We entered the harbor and docked. From the deck, I immediately recognized Al down on the wharf among hundreds of faces. My heart was beating fast as I set foot on U.S. soil. The dock was not as clean as the dock in Hamburg, but I felt the freedom there. I stayed four days with Al in New York in a daze. The heat was oppressive. New York was a bustling metropolis, noisy and dirty, full of people of varying backgrounds: Sephardic Jews, Blacks, and Italians; there were shopkeepers, hawkers selling fruit and vegetables out of pushcarts, the elevated train overhead, people standing on street corners. It seemed like a happy confusion to me, so different from Berlin. The heat finally got to me, and I was also eager to get to Mother and Chris who were already in Portland, Oregon, on the other side of this huge continent. People were friendly, but they were friendly in English, and I often could not understand what they said.

Al was looking around New York, hoping that he might find a position as a physician, but there were already hundreds of refugee doctors from Germany. Al knew that if he found nothing in New York, he could fall back on a good connection to a doctor, Ben Selling, in Portland. I set out by myself by train, knowing that I had to transfer in Chicago where I was very aware there were gangsters. I had pinned my passport and the few dollars I had to the inside of my shirt, confident that this would prevent the mob from getting at my riches. However, the transfer from one train station to the other in Chicago went smoothly (I looked, but was a bit disappointed to see no signs of gangsters), and I finally arrived in Portland after crossing the continent alone.

I was overjoyed to see my mother and Chris at the railway station. I knew Al would arrive from New York and we would all be together again. Mother had found an apartment (the Stelwyn Apartments) on Burnside and Twenty-third, our first lodging in the U.S. in Portland, Oregon—City of Roses. We stayed there for four weeks until we moved into a larger apartment.

Mother had decided to do all in her power to become American, and to bring us along with her plan. Her first effort was to pronounce an edict that we would not speak one word of German when we were together at the dinner table, so it was "Gif mee zee salt" or "Muzer, zee dinner was verry goot." And sometimes we sat silent rather than attempt to speak. It was painful, but we all did learn English quickly.

My Americanization

Since it was a hot June, we left the windows open, and it seemed like every apartment had a radio blaring loudly—either the latest popular songs or a baseball game. What a noisy country this was! I went shopping at the Piggly Wiggly supermarket across the street, where Mother had sent me for some Cream of Wheat and corn. I asked for gries (Cream of Wheat in German) and mais (corn). The clerk tried to help me and we ended up at the car lubrication shelf looking for grease, and then at the mouse traps (mais). We easily found the corn, but for the Cream of Wheat I had to return home to the dictionary.

Next to the supermarket was a drugstore, and for ten cents I could get the most delicious milk and ice cream concoction. I was hooked immediately, and to this day I love milkshakes with a passion, recalling that first marvelous experience America brought me that day. Vanilla, peppermint, and banana became my favorite flavors. This same experience also brought me a shock. A friend who had immigrated about three years earlier and was now in medical school invited me to feel beneath the counter. There I found all the gum that had been discarded, and with my good orderly German background I could not believe that Americans would do such a thing. I was upset for some time.

Soon after I arrived in Portland it was time for the Rose Festival Parade, which involved the whole city. The parade took place downtown on the main street, Broadway. Thousands of people lined the street on both sides. The atmosphere was one of relaxed anticipation. The occasional policemen were friendly, laughing and joking, and other than theirs, there were no uniforms. People were considerate of each other and stepped aside when a small child needed to see. Those with handicaps were given their viewing space without fuss or bother. I had never seen such kindness; the American cordiality was still strange to me. Sometimes I felt it was insincere and superficial as many Germans still suspect today.

As a child in Germany I had seen many, mostly military, parades. I was thrilled and half-scared to see the soldiers of the Wehrmacht goose-stepping down the avenue. There was a lot of "ta ra ra boom te aaa" or "umpa" music. The officer rode high on his steed, holding up an unsheathed sword. There were Nazi and military flags. The message was always precision, power, pride, and fear. The soldiers cast a spell on the onlookers, who gave up their individual power and pride to these columns of perfection. There was something about the beat of the band music, the enormous vehicles, and even the roar of the machines that (we know now) hypnotized and controlled the onlooker. At the time I could feel the physical effect. It was exciting for a people in hopeless poverty and defeat who love a good time and a good show.

Here in America it was different. I watched the parade—many beautiful and creative floats bedecked with roses, the result of people working together for weeks. But for me the high point came when I saw a real Indian in costume riding a magnificent horse. The Indian himself was decked out with great colorful feathers around his head and down his back. I could scarcely contain myself with excitement, for this was a thrill I never expected. In Germany they had warned me to "beware of the American Indians. They are still wild." The fellow on the horse seemed very friendly, as if he were enjoying himself immensely, waving and making his horse dance around. For a split second our eyes met, and I truly felt I was having an important experience. I wished my friends in Germany could have seen this. They would never believe it if I wrote and told them.

Slowly I began to imagine that the spirit of America was in this parade led by the Rose Festival queen, a tall, beautiful blonde sitting on the back of an open white convertible, waving and smiling to the people. She had been chosen from all the princesses—one from each high school—who followed her in their white cars. Rosarians in their white suits and white straw hats walked alongside the parade. It was not the stiff formality of royalty but the friendly greeting of a cheerful, young girl. Suddenly I flashed back to the time I had seen Hitler sitting in an open black car, stern-faced and grim, evoking fear and control. The Rose Festival queen evoked warm applause. I was overcome with the thoughts and comparisons going through my head constantly. Sometimes they were overpowering. I was having so many new experiences and so often they did not connect to—or could not build upon—what I had known in the past, so it was impossible to absorb or integrate what was happening to me.

A while later I saw another American parade. It must have been the Fourth of July. I was already working in Salem, Oregon at my first job in an American cannery. There was a military parade and the soldiers marched in rows of six. I was appalled at how sloppily they were dressed. Their pants were not pressed, their shirts slovenly, their shoes were unpolished, and they barely marched to the beat of the music. This seemed to be a holiday that was more the excuse for uproar and drinking than for patriotic expression. Some of the soldiers were drunk and had been placed in the middle so they could be steered, and even held up, by those on the outside. At this point I still had positive feelings for the orderliness and precision of the German military parade. Aside from the shock this parade in Salem produced in me, the experience also left a deep mark and I thought about it for some time afterward; there was something about the looseness I appreciated. I came to realize that my reaction to this haphazard parade was not altogether negative.

We soon became acquainted with many of the other refugees. They had all been relatively prosperous and middle-class in Germany—three or four doctors and some lawyers, but most were from the business world in the old country. They talked about the chauffeurs they had in Germany, the maids, and the big houses they lived in, and they were beginning to talk about the shortcomings of the U.S. Clearly, they did not have the recognition or the status in the U.S. that they had enjoyed in Germany, and it was clear that if they had not been Jewish, they would not have come to the U.S. Some of them had managed to bring considerable amounts of money with them. When we socialized with this group, we always had coffee and cake. After a few years the group fell apart. Some became busy in their occupations. One lawyer became a probation officer. One businessman founded a factory, another a winery. They made American friends.

My mother became friends with Ethel Sawyer and Elizabeth Hansen, two lovely ladies, one a principal of a private school, and her friend, a teacher. They introduced us to contemporary American literature and poetry, and they arranged for my brother to enter their excellent school.

In spite of my intense desire to be American, I did not catch on easily to the American ways of social interaction. It was easy to accept the role of "poor little refugee" that was assigned to me, although the attention it brought was not very satisfying. In addition, secretly I felt superior to the American young people, and this certainly did not make for an integrated or authentic personality, or one that was satisfying to know. Like many Germans coming to this country, I felt the Americans were superficial and childish. Young people seemed to know nothing of classical music, and they had no interest in the world's great literature. They seemed interested only in ball games and wearing the right clothes. I was vaguely aware that there was something very deep and free about the society, but I did not recognize it or admit it. What the Germans called deep feeling, the Americans called sentimental. What the Germans called childish, the Americans enjoyed and acted out freely. I also noticed that the Americans could laugh at themselves and still feel okay—a quality I never learned from my parents. Although both of my parents were known for their sense of humor in Germany, my father's was sarcastic and sometimes silly, and my mother laughed often, but did not understand American humor. I also felt my humor was not always appreciated. So, the American ways stood at my door, but I would not let them in. I had actually met very few people since my arrival—none of my age. Although I did not like Hitler, and the fact that many Germans were now following him with fervor, I began to get very homesick for my old friends with whom I had such good times. Also I missed the things I loved about Germany: the music and hikes. I knew I could not and would not go back. My Mother and Al were very good to me, but I was at the age when a young man begins to move away from his family, and I had no place to go and no friends with whom I could talk.

After four weeks in the U.S., my brother and I went to Spirit Lake Camp in the state of Washington at the foot of Mount St. Helen's. I was glad that my brother was with me. I could look after him and he was good company. The camp director was the executive officer of the Longview YMCA. His wife assisted, and their eight-year-old daughter was with them. The cook was a sturdy woman who cooked flapjacks and eggs. This was our first real American breakfast. Her husband was Mr. Fix-it around the camp. He had cancer of the lip, and his lip had been half eaten away because they were Christian Scientists and did not believe in doctoring, but rather prayed over such things. There was also Jerry, the camp counselor, a young Jewish student. What a difference there was between this group of young counselors and the leaders of the Hitler Youth! Jerry knew my name before we met. He asked me how I was, and he listened when I gave him a full reply. When we crossed a creek, he made sure we all got to the other side. He enjoyed our achievements. I was beginning to understand a little English.

One night the other boys and Jerry played a trick on me. They wanted me to experience the American custom of "snipe" hunting. It was already dark when we started, so I took my flashlight with me, and he gave me a stick with which to beat the bushes to stir up the snipes. I climbed up the hill with my flashlight, beating all the huckleberry bushes on my way. I noticed that the voices of the other kids got more and more distant. I grew suspicious, and decided to beat them back to camp headquarters and I got there first. They let me in on the secret—snipes don't exist—and we all had a good laugh together.

Another day we all climbed Mount St. Helen's, a 9,000-foot snowcapped mountain. We each had a big walking cane that resembled a broomstick. The timberline was definitely marked, and then came the snow and many crevasses, which we had to avoid. Falling into one of them would have meant certain death, but Jerry looked after each of us well. Finally we got to the top and had a tremendous view of snowcapped mountains: Mount Baker to the far north, Mount Rainier, Mount Adams, and Mount Hood. I felt so free and so important up there. The air was pure and we had luck with the weather. For a moment I thought of Germany, the hatred and tensions, and the yoke Hitler had put upon the people. There was nothing like that up here at 9000 feet. We each placed a pole behind us and, leaning on it, we slid over the snow, down 1,000 to 2,000 feet. Finally we reached the timberline and hiked back to camp. A week later we climbed the mountain again. This time I was chosen to be the leader.

There was a sort of hermit who lived on the other side of Spirit Lake who knew the ins and outs of the lake and the forest. His name was Harry Truman. There was no road around the lake and he had a motor launch, which he used to transport visitors and baggage. Sometimes the camp director invited him to come to our evening campfire and he spun many tales about the area.

We got letters from Germany regularly. One day I received a handwritten card from Niemoeller. The return address was Moabit Prison in Berlin, and he wrote some encouraging words to me. I was shocked, and for several days, very sad. What had the Nazis done to my hero? I felt very lonely. I climbed up the hill until I came to a fallen tree. I built a modest little altar with a cross and moss and branches. I had my Bible with me and read from the Forty-sixth Psalm: "God is our refuge and strength, our present help in trouble. Therefore will we not fear, though the earth be removed, and though the mountains be carried into the midst of the sea...There is a river, the streams whereof shall make glad the city of God. The holy place of the tabernacles of the most High." I went there every morning and evening, and I prayed for Niemoeller. Sometimes a squirrel and a few bluejays joined me.

Franklin Roosevelt had also become my hero. I had seen Hitler in person and had heard his disconnected, ranting speeches. Roosevelt seemed to me decent and considerate, without ego or mania. His silken voice came across on the radio, and I felt he was working for the individual, his rights, and his dignity and potency. He talked of encouragement and hope for all fellow Americans and initiated programs to give everybody help. I had never experienced anything like this in my life.

My mother was helping me open this door to democracy. Although in many ways she remained as demanding and controlling as she had been in Germany, she also immediately became a devout, enthusiastic, and informed democrat—with both the small and large D. Someone told her that if she read the New Yorker and Time every week, she would be au courant with all that was important here. This she did (until her very last days,) although in the beginning I am sure there was a great deal she did not understand. She always read these magazines faithfully and talked about what she had read. I was still clinging to my rigid German ways, but I was aware of a yearning within me to "hang loose" like the Americans, to let go of my ego. I was self-conscious in my dealing with the Americans, and aside from my own problems, my German frankness ("I simply want to tell you what I notice") did not go over very well with these kind and understanding people. My mother could say, "I want to be frank with you. That belt does not look right on that dress," and somehow she got away with it. People might laugh about her ways, but they still liked her and wanted to be with her.

In hopes of retaining her Protestant roots, my mother found a Lutheran Church. The dogmatic and authoritarian ways of this church, however, did not suit her, and she eventually joined the Unitarian Church where she found a community and friends who remained friends (for the rest of her life). She also found there an opportunity for singing and for social action, and an intellectual milieu that suited her, a place where she was appreciated. Al returned to the synagogue, even though he had never before attended faithfully. It was as if having paid for his Jewish roots, he now wanted to cultivate them. Often we would go to the synagogue on Friday night and to the Unitarian Church on Sunday morning. Later my mother joined the art museum, where she was a knowledgeable docent, and became more deeply involved in the social scene in Portland. She began to entertain, which Al also enjoyed, and where he was very successful with his continental, courtly manners. He was studying hard for his state medical boards with much hope. My mother and stepfather had lost a great deal socially and materially and had given up everything they knew to start over in a strange culture. They were living on borrowed resources, and yet they felt they were doing very well and that the future held great promise for them.

I was not doing so well. In fact it was a difficult and lonely time for me. I was inquisitive and intrusive. I tried to be funny and discounted others. And, I was sixteen years old with all the conflicts of separating from my mother and Al, yet needing them for support. This was a deep adolescent conflict, all the more painful because it took place in a land that was strange to me.

Eventually vacation was over, and it was time for my brother and me to go to school. (Summer vacation in Germany was six weeks and in America, three months.) My brother easily fit into his excellent private school. I presented my German credentials at Lincoln High School and found I had enough credits to graduate. My mother, Al, and I decided, however, that I should go to high school for at least one year before going on to college so that I could improve my English and learn American ways. So, one morning I set out for high school on my German bike in my knickerbockers, which fell just below my knees, a German sport shirt, and a beret. The kindly Quakers who had advised us about America prepared us well in all areas except fashion. My mother was always a bit original and eclectic in her fashion taste, but she always managed to look good, and Al was a bit more dapper than the average Portland physician, but my wardrobe could only be described as outlandish. It was a time when wide-wale, vanilla-colored corduroy pants and saddle shoes were the mark of a student who was "with it." I was totally unaware that clothes of a particular style should be so meaningful (and I have had trouble with that concept all my life). My wardrobe underscored my peculiar status and caused me great pain when I realized just how oddly I was dressed. Given our family's financial situation and the considerable investment that had been made in my Great Gatsby wardrobe, buying different clothes at that point was out of the question. No one actually laughed at me (that I

was aware of), and many people were very kind (or perhaps discreet); yet, for some time I suffered for the
advice I'd been given by the kindly Quakers about my
wardrobe.

The principal of Lincoln High School, Henry
Gunn, was very thoughtful and understanding in dealing
with me. He personally introduced me to the various
teachers and checked in on me quietly from time to
time. I was very impressed. He didn't expect adoration.
He was firm with me when he needed to be and always
encouraging—qualities that I had not experienced in a
teacher. Although I knew several languages to some
degree, English was the hardest subject for me. I was in
classes with others who had been speaking and reading
English all of their lives. I had been writing Sütterlin, a
gothic German script, and I had been told I had a very
fine handwriting. When I had to switch to the Latin letters for English, my handwriting became a combination
of the two scripts and has remained so, looking as if I am
writing in some kind of code so few people can read it.

My first assigned book was *The House of Seven
Gables*. I wrote the words that I didn't know in the margins, and on the first pages there was as much of my
writing as Hawthorne's. I just did not know there was
such a difference between knowing a language slightly,
and being able to speak and read it properly. Gradually
Hawthorne took over, and the margins became less and
less annotated. My speech and grammar took on a definite New England flavor for some time. Miss. A., the
English teacher, was a paragon of patience. Miss G., the
French teacher, who was a diminutive lady in her late
50s, developed a solid relationship with me. I had studied French in Germany and knew it better than English

at the time. She would call on me frequently, especially since I had a good French pronunciation. I advanced to French 5 and was grateful for this knowledge later, during the war.

Mr. W. was my civics teacher. He was in his middle fifties, with horn-rimmed glasses, wavy hair and a monotonous, slightly depressed voice. I learned a great deal about local, state, and national government from him, and I became excited by ideas of equality and opportunity for all and self-government. He was quite sarcastic in a humorous way, and very well informed. I am still grateful to him for the way he explained U.S. government to me and taught me to appreciate it. To this day I remember the foundation he gave me for an understanding of the American system.

Only the math teacher gave up on me. My ones looked like sevens and my sevens like Ys, and I did not understand what they were talking about in that class. It is probably a great deficiency, but I have lived my life since that time without an in-depth understanding of mathematics.

The other students were friendly, helpful, and kind to me, but I made no close friends like I had had in Germany. I rode to school alone, and I rode home alone. I didn't talk about the things the others were interested in, and sometimes I didn't even know what they were talking about. My English was a problem, and yet, I still thought I was superior to the others in certain ways, and this must have come across to them. Aside from my wardrobe, my behavior must have also seemed strange. Sometimes I went for walks alone late at night in the park and the hills, something that would have been common practice in Germany, but once caused a night watchman to jump out of the bushes and threaten to take me down to the police station in Portland. I talked him out of it in my thick German accent.

As Christmas approached, I had no place to go and no friends to visit. I felt particularly lonely, so one night, I sat down and poured out my heart into a Christmas story in my best new English.

A Christmas Fantasy

It was the twenty-fourth. The old town with its steeples, gables, and white roofs lay peacefully in the snowy valley of the now dark river. Snowflakes hurried quietly through the darkness. Now and then a star would appear in the vault of heaven, but soon it was lost in clouds of snow. One could hear the sleighs with their bells ringing, hurrying up and down the streets. Through the windows glittering trees proclaimed the joy of Christmas. The only quiet house was on Friedensgasse, opposite the church. Its dark windows stared gloomily into the gay street life, where busy parents did their last shopping before the stores closed.

Inside the house, Mrs. Schultz was lying in bed suffering with pneumonia. She was thinking of her twelve-year-old nephew, John. He had been with her since October. They came one day to arrest his Jewish father, but, Gott sei Dank, both parents had fled to a foreign country. She grieved that she could not help John celebrate the festival this year.

The door opened and John tip-toed into the room.

"Auntie," he said timidly, " Are we going to have a Christmas tree?" For John, Christmas was more important than any other day of the year. Auntie smiled bitterly.

"No, dear," she said, "I am sick and I cannot get up. But you go into the other room and there in the cupboard you

will find some presents for you in the third drawer from the bottom."

John was silent. A big tear ran down his cheek and he left the room as quietly as he had entered. He wanted to celebrate Christmas. He knew his former friends could not include him in their celebration this year because he was half-Jewish. His parents were gone—somewhere. He was all alone.

He decided he would celebrate Christmas after all, quite by himself. He took the Bible, and candy from his aunt, then went to the store and bought some candles with the few pfennige he had saved. He got some hay from the stable, filled a buggy, and soon was passing the last houses of the small town. Before long he had crossed the cornfields, which were covered with snow. There was not a breeze in the air. The snowflakes had settled on the ground. John listened to the forest, which spread its branches like a protective roof over his trail. It was like a medieval dome with all the columns. Now and then, the tracks of a deer would cross John's path.

Finally he reached a clearing. It was surrounded by big, tall trees. In the clearing, young trees lifted their green heads out of the thick blanket of snow. Over on the far side, close to the forest, was a real Christmas pine. It was almost as tall as John. Its green was covered with big white snow flakes. The nicest small cones one could imagine were hanging on its branches. John spread out a small blanket and put down his belongings. He fastened the candles to the twigs, then knelt down for prayer, as had been customary in his family. He took out the Bible, as his mother always had done, and read the story from the second chapter according to St. Luke.

Around him nature was quiet as never before. It seemed as though the trees, the snow, and the stars, wanted to hear *about the Child who was born in a manger. When John came to the place where the angel says, "For unto you a Child is born," he lit the candles—the Light of the World had appeared.*

After the boy had finished the story he took out his little flute and started to play all the songs his mother had taught him, "Stille Nacht," "Oh Tannenbaum," and many others. His songs caught the attention of a bird, ruffling its feathers, that had come to rest in the snow. It turned its head from left to right, and shook it up and down as if it liked the boy's songs.

Suddenly it said, "Cheep," and only a moment later, it sat on one of the branches of the Christmas tree, harmonizing its "Cheep, Cheep Cheep," to the songs of the boy.

The next visitor was a small squirrel. It had been stirred from its winter sleep and was now looking for some food. When it smelled the nuts the boy had brought along, it rushed to the bags in a bold squirrel manner, and started eating.

Soon a little mouse looked curiously out of its hole in a tree, and rushed over to the place where the squirrel was busy.

The next one to join the party was a gray rabbit that had slept in the neighborhood and was awakened by the noise.

Soon they all came: the deer and a buck, the fox and the hare, the birds, and all the animals that lived in the forest. They came to John and he fed them. When they were satisfied, he took his flute again and played. All the animals sat around him listening to his sweet melodies.

Suddenly the sky became very bright. Each star looked like an angel, and they all seemed to come closer and closer. They were the Messengers of Peace, and were seen by no one but John and his companions. The flute sounded clearly into the night "Glory be to God in the Highest," and the angels joined in "Peace on earth; goodwill to men."

Three days later, a regiment of stormtroopers was playing war games in the big forest. At the clearing they found John, frozen in the snow. His hands were clenched around his flute, and on his face was a soft smile, for now he was in happier fields than they.

• • •

My social life just did not blossom. I decided to try an American church since my mother had been so satisfied with hers. I chose a very high Episcopal church that was close to where we lived. The congregation was largely quite well-to-do and politically conservative. In their youth fellowship, many of the young people had known each other most of their lives, and knew what seemed a special code of behavior. (My future wife attended these meetings, but neither of us remembers the other from that time.) I attended church faithfully every Sunday morning and the youth fellowship every Sunday night. No friendships developed out of this, however, partly because I just did not fit in anywhere, and this group of young people was already tightly knit. I thought they were just unfriendly.

As my English became better, I was often invited to talk about Germany. One of my first talks was at an African Methodist church where I talked of my love for philosophy and religion and about my relationship with Pastor Niemoeller. They seemed enthralled, but I was confused when they continually interrupted me by shouting "Amen."

Once I was asked to speak at a large high school, Grant, on the east side of town. There was an assembly of about two hundred students. I told stories that I thought would be humorous to them and they listened. I told how confused I was when I saw the girls in the U.S. chewing what looked like jelly in sticks. Eventually I found out that this was lipstick, which girls in Germany would not have been allowed to wear. I talked about how at the beginning and end of each class, German students had to stand and shout "Heil Hitler," and I told them about how the one Jewish boy in the class was treated. I explained that we had individual religion classes. I told them that the German teachers were much stricter and more distant, and that there was more rigidity in the whole school system. Again and again in different ways, I talked about the respect that the teachers had for the students in the U.S., and that there was a gentler atmosphere here. In spite of explaining often that it was impossible for me to return to Germany and live under Hitler, and that the American system was far easier and more pleasant, they asked the same question again and again: "Which do you like better?" And so I explained again and again, in a heavy German accent, that I was happier here, and privately I hoped that I would soon fully believe this.

Making Our Way

In the meantime, our family life continued to develop. We often rented a cottage near Cannon Beach in Oregon. In spite of the very real struggles we were all going through, my mother managed to have many of the experiences that she wanted, and a vacation at the beach was one of her life's necessities. There was a small cluster of vacation houses there. The whole family swam in the cold ocean, picked blackberries, went on hikes, and on Sunday afternoons had my mother's coffee and cake. More often than not the weather turned nasty, but I remember it as a happy time. My brother and I became good friends despite our five-and-a-half-year age dif-

BROTHER CHRIS NEAR
CHAPMAN SCHOOL.

ference. Mother determined our social activities, and Al continued to study for his Oregon medical boards which included chemistry, physiology, and many other basic courses that he had taken in Germany.

After a year in Oregon, Al passed the state board exam. He was the only one of the refugee doctors who succeeded, and he opened a practice in the Medical Arts Building. Many of his patients were those whom he and my mother had met socially, and, for some reason, a large part of his patient load also came from the black population on the east side. He was loved devotedly by many of them, and this con-

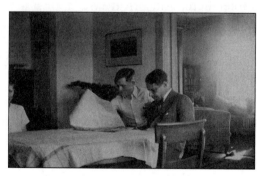

AL AND RIKKY IN 1949 IN NORTHRUP.

RIKKY: HANDSTAND NEAR
CHAPMAN SCHOOL

tinued throughout his life. Al seemed to love his work, and as long as he was busy with his patients he was happy. He and my mother joined the Urban League. We were often the only white people there and met many interesting people, such as the poet Langston Hughes. My mother often invited the members of this group to her dinners in an era when it was unusual for the races to mix socially.

There were also special friends like Dr. Selling who continued to give Al much support. The Selling family lived up on the hill in an exclusive part of town and often invited us to dinner. My most memorable experience there was learning to eat artichokes. They also invited us to their seaside resort on the Washington coast. They had a large Buick, which we drove to the beach over the coast range. Dr. Selling often repeated as we drove up a steep hill, "First class passengers remain seated, second class passengers get out and walk, and third class passengers get out and push." I thought this was true humor. Mrs. Selling and my mother became close friends and remained so all their lives.

We also came to know a Dr. S. from Astoria who convinced Al about the virtues of vitamin A long before it was popular to consider that vitamins could radically effect health. Al (and my mother) remained devoted to this belief. They took massive doses of many vitamins,

AL

LOTTIE

which I am sure no doctor treating them knew about, and, (which we now know,) were probably toxic doses. They did remain looking very well, however, until they were quite elderly.

Then, in the midst of Al and my mother's growing adjustment to America, there was a startling blow. Al was denied permission to operate in any of the Portland hospitals, even though he was a thoracic surgeon, and had studied and worked with the world-famous Ferdinand Sauerbruch. Our suspicion, which was later confirmed, was that he was refused because he was Jewish. This was a blow not only to Al's career, which meant so much to him, but to all our great hopes and idealistic beliefs in America.

Reed College

By the fall of 1938 Hitler had taken over Austria. Chamberlain had returned to England after a visit with

Hitler, saying, "There will be peace in our time." It was a few months before Kristallnacht, the time when Jewish businesses were destroyed and open attacks upon the Jews began. There were still some refugees leaving Germany and managing to get to America, the Von Trapp family among them. They were not Jews but were political refugees simply because they opposed Hitler.

It was at this time that I entered Reed College. Friends told us that this was a remarkable school with very high academic standards, claiming to be the fourth highest in the nation. After my experience with Niemoeller, I was clearly planning to be a minister, but a Unitarian minister. Reed seemed to us the fitting place for me to begin my professional preparation, and it was very conveniently located in Portland. Although Reed was a non-denominational school, we knew it had some informal ties to the Unitarian Church. An early minister of this church, Thomas Lamb Eliot (a name to which I was to become personally deeply attached) suggested to Simeon and Amanda Reed that they "use their riches to found a Reed Institute of Lecture and Arts," and this they did in 1911. The first graduating class was in 1915. Eliot strongly influenced the philosophy, educational methods, and selection of the faculty, and he became the first chairman of the board of trustees.

In Portland, Reed had a peculiar reputation as a Communist school that espoused free love, did not participate in national sports, and was anti-religious. The streetcar conductor would announce the stop for Reed as "Red College." It is true Reed took a certain pride in being unlike other colleges. Sloppy clothes were a fad there at a time when they were not acceptable at other universities and colleges. Some girls could even be seen to be wearing jeans on the grounds, although not to class. I knew of some students whose parents were probably connected to the Communist party, and one of my favorite professors had leftist leanings. However, love was scarcely free in those days before effective birth control when abortion was illegal and might mean severe injury or even death. And the football team actually celebrated their losses, when they lost to any of the local industries who fielded a team. When Reed won, they lowered the flag to half-mast. As for being anti-religious, I spent four years there preparing to become a Unitarian minister and heading the religion club, and I never was aware of any disapproval of my religious interests.

I entered Reed one year after arriving in the States, with limited knowledge of English, the American culture, and the social scene. Reed enrolled me without the usual stiff entrance examination, which I probably would not have passed because of my limited English. The college provided an excellent hands-on learning experience, with regular lectures in the chapel, and, above all, small group discussions of the weekly topic with ten to twelve students and the top professors in the field. I was scarcely able to keep up with the deeply intellectual discussions. In fact, I could barely keep up with the English, but this did not inhibit me. I managed to enter most conversations, and I thought the others seemed to understand me. This is where I learned about the small group discussions and the democratic give-and-take.

In the lectures we all faithfully took notes. Barry Cerf, chairman of the literature department, stood on the stage behind a podium. He was a short man, and we could see just his head from behind the lectern. He looked like a Jewish Zeus, his white hair standing up and lit by the light beam from behind. He had brought his notes, yellow and old, and he carefully unfolded them. Sometimes they were turned around or upside down, but he would quickly straighten them out, and read to us about and from the Greek tragedies.

Rex Arragon taught beginning history (History 11) and was the brilliant head of the history department. He brought the Budapest String Quartet to Reed many times. He was my faculty advisor and I was in awe of him. Having come from Harvard, he carried his books in a green cloth bag over his shoulder. Dr. Arragon impressed me as an excellent teacher and discussion leader. In his lectures he used slides of Egyptian sculptures and of Greek temples. Literature 11 and History 11 were parallel courses, so when we read Greek plays, we also read Herodotus, considered the father of history, translated from the original. Reed emphasized learning from the original text or from direct translations. To this day I am grateful for having taken these two courses, which influenced me in many ways. (When my wife and I traveled to Greece fifty-six years later, all our knowledge from Reed about the ancient world came back to us. We even recognized the landscape.) At Reed, however, when I was having a difficult time with English, translations of the originals of Thucydides and Homer were a considerable strain.

My stay at Reed was not an easy one. I lived off campus at first and I was not very much into the social scene, nor was I an academically brilliant student. Most of the courses were very difficult for me, and I often had to work as much as 40 hours a week as the night watchman, a job that gave me startling views of the extracurricular activities at the college. I watched the students coming home to campus at night drunk and getting sick all over the dormitory. I watched them hang their whiskey bottles out of their dorm windows into the ivy. Liquor on campus was against the rules, but very much a part of expected behavior. As I came upon couples in their cars or in the canyon behind Eliot Hall, I was embarrassed.

Later I worked for two years as a janitor and morale-raiser for the patients in the Glenn Chesney Quiett Infirmary under Catherine Holden, a nurse. It was while listening to the radio in this building on Sunday, December 7, 1941, that I heard about the Japanese attack on Pearl Harbor. I later heard President Roosevelt talk about the "day of infamy." I stood next to the radio and cried quietly, wondering what would happen to my new country. Will this mean we go to war with Germany? It was too much for me to comprehend.

Since I was considered an alien, I only received 35

REED PROFESSORS: CHITTICK AND REYNOLDS

cents per hour, not the usual wage of 40 cents per hour paid by the National Youth Administration. One of the jobs every winter was to prune and clean Reed's raspberry fields. I still remember the cold and rainy weather and the pricks of the raspberries. Bill Barratt, another student, worked with me, and we became good friends and remained so, even into graduate school after the war. I painted the inside of the dormitory under Scottie, the contractor, who was a hard taskmaster and had a deep Scottish brogue. I also cleaned Reed's football uniforms after each game. The work I was involved in was an important part of my experience at Reed; I hoped the academic aspect would leave as lasting an impression.

For fun I joined the Glee Club. At Christmas we marched into the Commons (the dining hall) carrying a pig's head at the front of the procession while singing, "Boar's head I bear, bedecked with bay and rosemary."

One day in Eliot Hall I met Professor Chittick, whose course in American literature I had taken. He was over six feet tall and had a hoarse voice. He had a big smile on his face. "Rikky, when are you going to teach me the recorder?" he asked. "What are you doing tonight?" I replied. He said he was free, and that night I gave him his first lesson on his F-alto recorder, which he had bought the week before. He and I became very good friends. It was a strange combination, but we remained close for many years. His wife, Edna, whom we visited in Seattle until she was 101 years old, was a pianist, and she gave me piano lessons in exchange for Dr. Chittick's recorder lessons. Although I never excelled academically, Chittick accepted and supported me totally. He and his wife never had children, and from time to time they became close to certain students, and I was one of them.

Soon we started a recorder-madrigal group with two other students, three professors, and the head of the culinary department. We played before a packed house in one of the weekly student assemblies, and we played in each other's homes, in the woods, and on the Reed front lawn.

GROUP OF LIBRARY 'RECORDER' PLAYERS WITH INSTRUCTOR

From left—Miss Mildred Cline, Miss Minnie Elmer, Miss Rosella Knox and Miss Bess Allen of Central library staff, members of the Library recorder group, and Ulrich Heinicke, their instructor. Members not in photograph are Miss Nell A. Unger, librarian; Miss Jane Gilbert, Miss Claire Bryson, Miss Harriet Akin and Miss Doris Wildman.
—Les Ordeman, The Journal.

RECORDER GROUP IN THE
PORTLAND CITY LIBRARY

There was even a picture of us in the Portland paper, The Oregonian. The Portland Public Library heard about the group, so the head of the music library, as well as the head of the entire library and two of the other librarians, formed a recorder group also. Thus, the recorder was introduced in Portland, and for me, it was the beginning of a social life and of some very happy experiences.

At Reed I met Sir Thomas Beecham, the great Mozart conductor, the diminutive Béla Bartók, the Budapest String Quartet, and many others in the living room of the college president, Dexter Keezer.

One of my most memorable courses was one on architecture where, among other things, we studied cathedrals. I learned about the styles, the aesthetics, and some of the engineering. All the talks with my father about cathedrals fell into place. I loved that course, and wished once again that one day I could visit some of the

REED PROFESSORS: CERF AND ARRAGON

great cathedrals, but I could not imagine how it would ever be possible.

In the psychology department, psychoanalysis had not yet arrived at the academic setting, and we were taught Pavlov and the behavioral theories. The psychology professor kept us amused with his many jokes on the level of "Marriage is an institution and who wants to live in an institution?" I continued to struggle with many of the courses. Economics was the most difficult, and I frequently came home deeply depressed, even though all the teachers were very kind and supportive. I often felt closer to some of the faculty than to the students generally, even though there was much kindness and acceptance among the students, and I always felt heard and understood. With a student body of less than 400, we all knew most of our fellow students.

Because I was planning to be a minister, I majored in history and philosophy, although there was nothing spiritual, and certainly nothing religious, in these courses. I decided to cover this lack by founding the Religion Club, which I am quite sure had never been done before, in spite of the college's link to the Unitarian Church. We were a group of about six to eight and met regularly. We were even assigned a meeting room. Although we were a very small group, and our interests were unlike those of the other students, we felt easily accepted, and we tried to address some of the transpersonal aspects of life, in which Reed did not offer courses.

I stayed in touch with Reverend Dick Steiner of the Unitarian Church in Portland, where my mother had become deeply involved. Steiner was of Jewish descent, and had been raised in a family that knew Tolstoy. He was not only a close friend of Lottie and Al, he also took a fatherly interest in me. He became a guide and counselor for me, and informally groomed me for becoming a Unitarian minister. Thus, my family was assured that my education would be of some practical use.

Al and Lottie had hoped I would go into business where they thought my persuasiveness and determination would be rewarded, but the commercial world did not appeal to me. Dick Steiner represented a liberal approach to religion, and there was no dogmatic approach to God. I was already at Reed College during the week, but I "religiously" attended his Sunday services. The music they played and sang appealed to me. Steiner and I had many personal conferences and he thought he could help me get into the Unitarian seminary in Boston. He was not so powerful as Niemoeller, but he was democratic to the core, and I enjoyed hearing from him about the history of the Portland Unitarian congregation, which had been founded by caring and community-minded people. He spoke also about the

Unitarian Church in England, and others in the United States. Later, during the war, Dick Steiner read my letters from the war to the congregation. Everything—politics, the war, the human community—was a part of religion in his eyes.

The biggest blow of my college career came at the end of my junior year when I did not pass the junior qualifying examination, and consequently could not write a senior thesis. I went to my room and cried. My whole body ached; I can still remember the feeling of that experience physically. Yet Reed let me stay on because it was permissible to take the examination a second time. My parents consoled me as best they could, but I knew it was really my responsibility. I tried to convince myself that I had done everything that I could, that I had worked hard, and that, as a person, I was okay. I loved humor and music, and I had acquired some very close friends. I wondered if perhaps Reed was not the right college for me, yet I was proud to be a Reed student and desperately wanted to remain there. I did not blame my 40-hour work week for my problems. It was the Depression era, and there were many students who had to work a great deal in order to earn their room, board, and tuition.

Finally, Al's medical practice was making enough money to enable him to partially support me, so I moved onto campus into Doyle House. In the spring of 1942 I took the junior qualifying exam again, and this time, I passed it. Dorothy Johanson, a history professor and member of the recorder group, helped me a great deal. I had now done all the course work to graduate except for the thesis, and I finished that during the summer of 1942. The title was "The Struggle Between Church and

State in the First Part of the Fourteenth Century." I was
greatly interested in the political maneuvering between
Church and State, and I thought at the time the topic
was very important. I read original sources with fascination, in French, Latin, Italian, German and English,
about Boniface the VIII and Marsilio of Padua.

Enemy Alien Status

Because of my German citizenship, I had to register
as an enemy alien, abide by a curfew, and stay within a
radius of five miles from home. These were the only
restrictions placed on the Germans even though some of
them retained strong attachments to the fatherland. The
Japanese, on the other hand, who may have been in this
country for several generations and were American citizens, were forcibly removed to distant "relocation" camps
in the U.S., losing much of their assets. The grocer on
Twenty-third Street and Hattie their daughter, a friend
from Reed College, had to leave. I was upset that the
United States would do something so unfair.

Since I also had a home on the Reed Campus in
addition to my home with Al and Lottie, I was allowed
to travel within a distance of 10 miles. At one point, the
apple farmers in Hood River on the Columbia River
were in dire need of workers for their harvest. This was
more than ten miles from my two homes, so I went to
the U.S. district attorney in the federal courthouse, and
he gave me a special permit to pick apples at Hood River
during the school vacation. The Secret Service did come
to our home once during this time to make sure our
radio had no short wave. While I was restricted in these
ways, I nevertheless received a "personal" letter from

President Roosevelt with "Greetings," inviting me to register for the military draft.

In looking for source material for my thesis I discovered that many books were in the University of Washington library in Seattle, far beyond my permitted radius of travel. I took my plight to Dr. Chittick, who suggested a thesis conference on Whidbey Island in the Puget Sound where he had a summer home. (He was not my thesis advisor.) He suggested I spend some time in the university library, and then visit him on the island. So again I went to the U.S. district attorney with an additional travel request, and he approved a written travel document. Another Reed student who played the recorder and was also a good friend of Chittick's decided she would join me. We went off by bus, first to the University of Washington library, where I found many excellent sources for my thesis, then to the island, where I had my thesis conference. We had a wonderful time hiking, playing our recorders, talking and laughing, and eating Mrs. Chittick's wonderful cooking.

After I submitted my thesis, I had to defend it before the chairman of the history department, his assistant, and one other faculty member. I was scared but did an adequate display of the main points. They sent me out of the room, and as I stood in front of the door, I could hear them talk about me, my work at Reed, and my character. Finally they called me in and congratulated me. After such a struggle at Reed I had finally made it. I am still grateful to Professor Dorothy Johanson, who believed in me and supported me, and also to Dr. Chittick and many other professors who worked hard to help me.

Being Drafted

Now the draft stood before me. I had only been deferred long enough to write my thesis and get a bachelor's degree. In college I had joined the Fellowship of Reconciliation (FOR), a pacifist organization that was headed locally by a man who worked at the YMCA. Under this group's influence, and feeling in principle opposed to any kind of violence and war, I planned to register as a conscientious objector. As a ministerial student, the draft board probably would have deferred me. My experience in Germany, where I watched the growing hatred and militarism, was still deeply disturbing to me, and I wanted no part of anything like that. Mom and Al supported my decision not to register for full combat, and yet I surmised that they were not really comfortable with it. I was in a country that had welcomed us and saved us from the Nazis. If I fought in a war against Germany, I would be fighting against my friends whom I had loved and with whom I had grown up. I wondered what was happening to them now. My feelings for them were mostly those of sorrow that they were compelled to follow such a path, which, I believed strongly, was wrong and had to be stopped. I knew that if I had remained in Germany, I, too, would have been forced to fight against the Americans. It was only because I had decided to follow Al and my mother that I was now an American. Who was my enemy now? I was strongly anti-Nazi but not anti-German. I wrestled with these questions painfully for some time until I was totally confused. Finally, I decided to register as 1-A-0, which limited me to medical service, and the army accepted my decision without question. Again my family supported me, or rather, they did nothing to dissuade me.

Was I a coward? How many boys would die in this war? I had been faced years earlier in the Hitler Youth with the demand that I must be prepared to give my life for Hitler's ideal. Thus, at a young age, I had wrestled with the question of when and for what I would be willing to give up my life. At that time the ideal in question was Hitler's, and I was clear I did not want to give up my life for him. Now I wondered if I was more concerned about my personal welfare than about saving democracy or stopping the evil that I knew was coming out of Germany. Again I struggled within myself and finally decided to register 1-A as a "good American," even though I was an enemy alien. I had more reason than most to know the danger imposed on the world by Hitler, and to recognize the values we had in America and how important it was to save them. Once I made the decision to go, I was prepared to do whatever necessary, to give up whatever I must, in order to carry out the mission of the United States in World War II.

While waiting for induction I worked for three months in a cabinet shop making crash doors for the Liberty ships, laminating and gluing them. My boss was a German immigrant who had strong German leanings and who was often visited by the FBI for his pro-Nazi views. There was no suggestion that he should move to a relocation camp. It only added to my confusion and strengthened my decision to join the army as a "good American."

Chapter 4

•

February 1943-June 1944

inally, my orders came to report to Fort Lewis, Washington for induction into the army. I had the usual physical examination in Portland, which included seeing a psychiatrist who asked me if I had any friends. I said "yes," and passed. I said goodbye to Mom, Al, and Chris and went by train to Fort Lewis, Washington. There we were issued GI clothing and saw innumerable training films, including one on sex where a soldier with an obvious sexual disease says, "Doc, I thought she was clean" in a hoarse voice. We saw this film five or six times, and by the second time the whole audience repeated with a hoarse voice at the proper moment, "Doc, I thought she was clean."

Entering the US Army

After one more visit to Portland I was assigned to basic training in Fort Warren, Wyoming. The army had deferred me so that I could finish my thesis and get a degree. Apparently they felt my knowledge about the struggle between church and state in the first half of the fourteenth century would best prepare me for a truck driving regiment. At Fort Warren, where the climate was arctic and miserable, I learned to take a GMC (Chevy) two-and-a-half-ton truck and engine completely apart and put it together again so that it would run. At the end of the training, I was the first to be recommended for officer's training school until it was discovered that I was an enemy alien and the order was withdrawn.

At Fort Warren I wrote home still concerned with heavy philosophical thoughts about the war.

March 1943

Dear Mamm [my mother],

I enjoyed Dick's [the Unitarian minister] sermon, "Faith in Crisis, Faith in the Future" very much. How far away all that seems here in the Army. How few people in Fort Warren move these problems in their minds. And again I must say that I am not in the least worried about the outcome of this war. The big question is, will the common man—civilian or soldier—realize what the bloodshed and

YOUNG RECRUIT

destruction, the hatred and uncertainty were about? Few people realize that a revolution is going on, and fewer people know that the tide can turn for the better. And I think that we can count on our fingers those who sincerely believe that acting with faith in the Christian principles or ideals is the best solution. And I don't mean "put a nickel in the drum and Jesus he will come, put a nickel in the drum and you'll be saved!"

I've been waiting to get the Tao te Ching. I'd like to translate it from the German for the fun of it, even though it won't be very good. It's been very long since I had a chance to do something along creative lines.

I enjoy my new room very much. I go to bed one hour later, get up one half hour later. Simple arithmetic will show you that does not make life any easier, but it makes it

THE LIBRARIAN AT FORT WARREN, WYOMING

more exciting because after I come home from the library job I can stay up until 10 or 11 p.m. and read. Thus I manage to keep busy, which is a good thing. I sort books and magazines for the librarian, Miss Goodrich, and in the morning I help the baker. The boys in the barracks think I am crazy to take on all these jobs and responsibilities. But I like it far better than sitting around and reading funnies and listening to them talk about sex.

Is there anything you'd like to have while you're 43 or older? During war time, birthdays have to be planned weeks ahead. I still haven't quite got it in my head that I actually own such a beautiful watch [sent for my birthday]. Is there anything I should know about the case? Is it waterproof, shockproof, etc.? Well, be good and have an envelope full of thoughts and more of love.

P.S. Please give my best regards to Amy G. I wish she'd quit being sick. Get me Johnny's address.

And to my brother, I wrote:

Dear Chris,

I hope you won't feel that this is the first letter I wrote you since my induction. I was certainly amazed at your taste in choosing the right present. I do love halva even though some of my buddies made faces when they tasted a piece. I hope that the enemy alien curfew, over which I was very surprised, won't bother you too much. Remember that the most beautiful things in life often take place in the daytime.

Good luck.

As ever,
Your brother Rikky

And another to Al and Lottie:

Dear Mamm and Al,

Friday we had California sunshine. Saturday Oregon rain prattled on our raincoats, and today an ice cold snow storm beats around our ears. Such is life in Wyoming, or simply, such is life, period. In answer to your gardenia-bread-and- butter letter I only say this: After you and Al have done so much for me I don't worry about spoiling you. For the idea cannot spoil you, and a gardenia without an idea is empty. Concerning your faults and mine, I shall keep still. I don't feel that any words have to be lost on that subject right now.

Now, to come to my birthday: You all certainly did an excellent job making it a cheerful day. It was not until noon Saturday that I realized that I was twenty-two and that is the truth. I could not figure out what in the world that insured package contained. It was to look like something from Woolworth, yet very expensive. I still wonder at that terrific machine [watch] which somehow got onto my wrist. I thought about chipping in. I only wished I could turn the two hands to Western daylight saving time (not just in fantasy). It might look better. Concerning the cake and cookies, being modest or not modest, I enjoyed both of them tremendously and so did some of the boys. Although the hairbrush was a sort of anti-climax to the tremendous watch, it was still gladly received for the cause of cleanliness.

All of your letters meant much as birthday presents. Ever since I have been in the army I have come to know that a sincere letter is irreplaceable. Of course we love to eat. Saturday evening I worked in the library. We had a nice little snack: cake, halva, and Coca-colas. The librarian who is under army regulation is extremely nice to all the soldiers. This, my first birthday away from home, passed, and I should say that the material and other presents made it worthwhile to become twenty-two. Adelaide S. surprised me with a $5.00 check and a very nice letter. I will write to her soon.

Now, to answer some of your questions.: I will return all the tin boxes that the cakes were sent in as soon as they are empty. Don't be surprised if you find a bunch of socks to be mended in there. There is no hurry for them, however, and I can wait weeks. It's just the fact that I have some torn socks strewn over my locker.

Concerning my health: it is very good. My tummy goes haywire only rarely and my nose ... well, my nose ... it's still there.

I'll be very glad and interested in translating some Tao te Ching (or whatever the name is). I fear, however, since you have done so much in that line, I might not be of great help, but send it anyway. We have English-German dictionaries in the library.

Soon after, I was sent to Camp Philips in Kansas and was attached to the 513th Quartermaster Regiment. I had the feeling that, with my college degree and erudite knowledge of church and state, the army didn't really know what to do with me, especially since I must remain an enlisted man, and not become an officer. Therefore, they made me chaplain's assistant to a Southern Baptist minister. Being a chaplain's assistant in a quartermaster truck driving regiment was not a heavy assignment. The chaplain himself had very little to do except occasionally when he had a message to deliver from a soldier's family. There was very little demand for spiritual guidance or religious advice in this unit, and I think he actually spent much of his time sleeping. It was my duty to awaken him a few minutes before noon every day so that he could appear on time at the officer's mess hall. I would find him with his head on the desk fast asleep and sometimes snoring. As the rays of the sun came through the window they hit his head and made his lieutenant bars shine. There I stood, Private Heinicke: "Lieutenant, Sir, it's time for lunch." He jumped up, grabbed his glasses, and headed out the door, while I went to the enlisted men's mess.

I recognized that this experience was to be my first opportunity to practice in my chosen profession, even though there seemed little chance of much practical learning. During the week I spent a good deal of time practicing the organ for the Sunday services. I used my knowledge of the keyboard to learn the unfamiliar hymns by ear, and I made up a system of working with the pedals. By the end of my time at Camp Phillips, I thoroughly enjoyed my self-taught method of organ playing, and it has given me much joy throughout my life. My lack of technique has never inhibited my enthusiasm for the organ.

The services were unlike anything I had ever experienced. The chapel was always filled by boys who accepted Sunday services as a necessary life ritual. Whether this particular form of worship suited them all, I do not know. Ringing in my ears still is the melodic intonation of the chaplain as he admonished everyone to "Come to Jeeeezus to be saaaaved and healed." It was never entirely clear to me what that entailed. There were many warnings of what not to do and commandments to be followed. Again I was asked to give my life—this time to Jesus—without specific instructions about the process. The chaplain also always spoke about sin and venereal diseases and dying for one's country, with an unspoken promise that if life were lived according to specific rules, somehow one would be protected from dying in battle.

I also had the job of preparing the Sunday services—finding flowers in Kansas and laying out the hymnals. During the service I sat in the balcony playing the organ. Since there was no mirror in which I could see the congregation and since the organ made up in loudness for what it lacked in tone, I often could not hear the weak, late-adolescent voices singing with unaccustomed softness. Often I would have to stop playing in order to turn around and see where they were in the hymn. Otherwise I kept going at my speed and hoped it matched their tempo. I tried sincerely to catch the spiritual nature of this whole experience, but truthfully, it was the beginning of my doubts about the relevance of becoming a pastor.

The first group of Afrika Corps German prisoners was held at Camp Phillips. They were a proud, haughty bunch, and we were not allowed to talk to them. One day as they were weeding the ditches by the road in front of the church, I opened the chapel windows as wide as I could and put the organ register on full volume as I played "Deutschland, Deutschland über Alles," the German national anthem. There were about thirty German prisoners and they all snapped to attention and stood there until the end of the hymn. The Americans had no idea what was going on.

In this camp I also had my first experience of how the army treated homosexuals. I was seated at regiment's headquarters when in walked two MPs with a tall, blond soldier in tow on the way to a court martial for engaging in homosexual acts. I didn't know much about homosexuality then. The boy was nice looking, and headquarters staff sneered at him yet seemed embarrassed at the same time. I felt very sad about their ruthlessness and disregard for the soldier's dignity. I don't know what happened to him. He may have been sent to jail; I was not around long enough to know the outcome.

While still in Wyoming, I became eligible to take my citizenship test and become naturalized. I had been in the United States for five years. I easily passed the historical and constitutional material. Then, in my naturalization interview I was asked, "Did you ever belong to the Communist party? Are you favorable toward Russia? (Russia was, of course, fighting on our side at the time.) Do you follow leftist politics?" I said no to all these questions. At the end, the interviewer added, almost as an afterthought: "Of course you've given up all allegiance to Hitler?" I nodded yes. I was very proud to officially be a part of my new country. It was too late to become an officer, but I did not particularly care.

A few days later there was a commotion throughout the regiment. Ulrich Heinicke had received some top secret orders from the War Department to report to Camp Ritchie, Maryland. I was no longer just the chaplain's assistant, but suddenly I was handled with great respect. I was headed for the army's top secret intelligence camp because apparently someone in Washington D.C. had discovered that I knew German and French, as well as English, and that I had a college degree. So, I packed my bags in a hurry and went off to Camp Ritchie in the Maryland mountains near Hagerstown. All I knew about Hagerstown was that it had the highest veneral disease rate in the States, and I didn't know what that said about U.S. Intelligence.

The student body at Ritchie was a motley crew, refugees from all nations, soldiers who had majored in foreign languages in college or whose fathers had come from the old country. It was not the typical American scene. There were soldiers with heavy foreign accents, older men, and many Jewish refugees, all in American uniform. Once someone who had recently come from Romania became the center of interest as people gathered around him to get the latest news from Europe. They asked him how many languages he spoke, and he replied, "I speaken zee Rumania, Francais, Cherman, Italiano, a little Schpanish, and Russic, and English." Someone in the group asked, "Of all those seven languages, which one do you speak the best?" And he replied quickly in a barely decipherable accent, "Uf awl zee zeven lanwitches, I speken zee Enklish zee best." This became a code phrase at Ritchie for some time. Many of us were not far removed from his situation, and we understood why he did not appreciate our laughter.

Ritchie had a definite and rigorous program, which was a challenge to me after the vagueness of my previous assignment. We knew we were being trained for something very special, very dangerous and super-secret, but we had no idea what it was. We had to learn all the ranks, weapons, uniforms, and planes of the Germans and Italians. We shot many German guns and learned to use various kinds of foreign weapons. We had to find our way in the dark forest with just a compass and no map. In an effort to teach us to listen carefully to the meanings in the inflections in speech (in the event we were interrogating prisoners of war), we were given a phrase such as "Noch ein Stück Gänsebraten?" (Still another piece of goose?) We had to spend hours saying this with the emphasis on different words to understand how the emphasis changed the meaning. For instance, with the emphasis on "noch ein" (still another) it meant we already had one, and on "ein Stück" (one piece) meant you could have one more, not two. We practiced faithfully even though we often ended up howling with laughter at the whole procedure. At least it took up some training time.

At the graduation ceremony, Colonel Banfield announced that we had been the worst class of all the thirteen classes they had had thus far. Considering the danger they constantly assured us we were going into, and the skill that we would need, this was hardly encouraging.

Name Change

The night before we were to be shipped overseas, we were asked to volunteer for certain assignments. We had been trained for interviewing prisoners of war, and one assignment for which we could volunteer was working behind the German lines to rescue Allied personnel who were caught there. I thought this would indeed be important and useful, and when I eagerly volunteered for the assignment, I was accepted at once. I was thrilled at the prospect until I suddenly realized that with my German name, Ulrich Heinicke, if I were caught, I would be considered a traitor, and I would be tortured or killed at once rather than taken prisoner as an ordinary American soldier would. I rushed to the Adjutant General's office, and the captain, who was a lawyer by training and well-versed in the legalities of war, heard my story and told me to change my name at once. "What will your new name be?" he asked. I had never thought about it, and begged him for some time for such a major task. He granted me a half an hour!

With no idea of how to go about choosing a name, I rushed out of his office and came upon a rack of phone books for the entire United States. I grabbed the thickest book, which contained all the Brooklyn phone numbers, and opened it to about where I thought the Hs would be, as if that would be the best place to start. From experience I knew that H had always seemed a good place to be in the alphabet. It was early enough in the alphabet so that I wouldn't miss out on the goodies if they were given out alphabetically, but neither would I be chosen first for guard duty or to pull KP (kitchen police). Based on such thinking, I began my search for a new name. I moved my finger a bit to the left of the Hs and came upon the Gs. In Brooklyn this was Greenbaum, Greenberg, Greenthal, etc. Somehow that did not seem fitting, so I moved a bit to the left and found a whole column of

Fraziers. Frazier was one of the founders of the Unitarian Church in Portland, and I thought that would be a great name to carry on. The name Thomas just came to me as a first name. I had always liked that name. It was a good, clear name that sounded right in all the languages that I knew. Everyone could pronounce it and understand it. Thomas Lamb Elliot was one of the founders of the Portland Unitarian Church as well as the first board member of Reed College. I became Thomas Lamb Frazier, and have remained so.

When I came back to the Adjutant General he said, "That's a fine name, and if you behave yourself in the army you can take back your old name when you are discharged." He rushed the name change to the local superior court to make it official. The following morning, when they did a final muster at 5:00a.m. as we were shipping out, I did a double-take when they called out "Frazier!" I yelled back, "Here!" Ulrich Heinicke had served me well in Germany. It was a good, understandable German name, but in America it was often pronounced with a sort of gargle and cough. I loved my new name. It was a good American name taken from two admirable men. I couldn't imagine I would ever want my old name back.

I already had dog tags with my new name, but I kept my old number—39326590—etched in my brain. We were taken by truck to a huge luxury liner, which was a British ship, with a British captain and crew, and British chow. The ship was much bigger than the one on which I had come to America in 1937, but the liner had been converted into a troop ship, and the accommodations can only be described as terrible. We slept crowded in hammocks and narrow bunks. Many of the men lit up cigarettes and gathered in circles around a deck of cards. Some had to leave to go to the open deck with a reverse peristalsis from the rocking and weaving of the liner. I got sick, too, and puked into my helmet. This was the way most of us began our experience of war. After three days I ventured on deck. My abdomen was at peace by then and the fresh air helped me recover my normal senses, but it was cold! We were heading due north to avoid a pack of German U-boats. Our ship was faster than the U-boats, but they could still have sunk us with a torpedo. We learned later that the same week we were in the area, a troop ship with 700 U.S. soldiers aboard had been sunk by German submarines, and all men had been lost. My family had heard this news and knew that I was expected to travel the same route at the same time. For two weeks they were anxious and worried until they received my V-mail from England.

England—Ireland

We landed in Liverpool safely and immediately boarded a British train for Scotland. At night in England all the lights were out because the Germans continued their air raids. We stopped at Stranrear in Western Scotland, took the ferry to Belfast, and then to our new billets in Bangor, east of Belfast. To house their military personnel, the English had built thousands of Quonset huts that were made out of sheet metal and looked like jelly rolls cut in half. Again we were cold. By this time I realized that being cold and trying to get warm would become a major effort for me throughout the war. We got some of His Majesty's blankets with the War Department insignia on them, but they scarcely

Stranraer

Belfast

IRELAND

Liverpool

WALES

ENGLAND

Oxford

London

Beaconsfield

Bristol

Plymouth

Utah Beach

Isigny

St. Lo

Caen

BEL

Brussels

Paris

Rembouillet

Chartres

Melun

Auxere

Autun

Châlon

FRANCE

- Grenoble–Bourg St. Maurice–Val d'Isère about 110 miles
- Val d'Isère– Val Savaranche (Degioz) about 30 miles
- Cogne–Aosta about 16 miles
  map not according to exact scale

helped, and since it was February we shivered all night. There were long lines to the bathroom, and our bladders were really hurting.

I was struck by the poverty in Northern Ireland. People were very friendly and clean, and yet wore gray, threadbare clothes. Even the local railroads looked poor, with narrow gauge tracks and small cars. One day I developed a high fever and was rushed to the nearest British hospital in Belfast. I was so sick I was afraid they might ship me back to the U.S. and thus end my war effort. I recovered, however, and soon they sent us to Beaconsfield near London, which had been the Hollywood of England. Now it was a top secret intelligence training camp for the British and a prison for high-ranking German generals. We could see them strutting behind barbed wire fences in the yard with golden braids and bright red collars on their uniforms.

One of the first things we had to do was to sign a little black book promising that we would never divulge throughout our whole lives what we saw, heard, or did in this camp. Actually all I saw were the British soldiers in formation, stomping around with their knees raised high and their feet coming down on the pavement with a clack. We also saw British Intelligence movies in which every now and then the picture of a completely naked woman would appear behind a fishnet just to keep us awake.

We got British rations. I'll never forget my first breakfast: liver, cabbage and mashed potatoes, a cup of tea, and an over-sweetened dessert. I also had my first motorcycle lesson. The brakes were on the handles and I had difficulty catching on to that. When I thought I gave it gas, I braked, and when I thought I braked, I gave it gas. After an hour or so of this I decided I could ride on my own. I took off and promptly mixed up the gas and brakes. There were two English soldiers parked with the two front wheels of their motorcycles touching, so I steered between the two wheels hoping to pry them apart. I did, and I crashed, cut my lip, and bled. A first-aid man put a Band-Aid on the cut and I went on with my lesson, but afterward I was always leery of riding a motor bike, especially on cobblestones after a rain.

April 9, 1944

Dear Folks,

It's still kind of difficult to realize that today was Easter Sunday. I had wished to go to a nice old English church with all its ritual and tradition. Instead I was put on KP at the last minute. Thus Easter turned out to be an ordinary day. I might quote T.S. Elliot and say, "This is the way the war's won, this is the way the war's won, this is the way the war's won, not with a bang, but a dish rag." Anyway, my thoughts have been with you, even though we are far removed from each other in space and time by 6,000 miles or eight hours. Right now it is ten minutes to 11 Pacific Standard Time. You are probably waiting on Al who went to see a patient. In ten minutes you are going to be sitting in church, dressed in your best. The English landscape continues to be more pleasant every day. It is very difficult to meet any decent Englishmen—should I say gentlemen—they are quite reserved. Even Anni [Al's sister] found it extremely difficult to break into Oxford society, although she had been teaching at the university. I have been fooling with the idea of studying over here. For instance I might spend half a year in Cambridge or London. The English are in many aspects more cerebral or even progressive than we are. They do have their highly stratified society (and I don't like it), and they have a fellow like Lasski, the Red Dean, and the government does sponsor papers with all sorts of opinions. Practically speaking, I believe that the average Englishman is more adult and more interested in his government than the average American. In the economic field their problems are more difficult than ours.

I should like to repeat my request for the New Republic. Send the New Yorker. The mail service is very slow, and I expect it will get worse as the war progresses. Mamm, please read your letters before sending them. The last letter contained two sentences which made no sense. On a V-mail form, that is a big loss to the recipient.
I hope that you are all well.
Best wishes and love,
Tom

P.S. Regards to Steiner

While in London I visited Al's mother (Maemmschen), his sister Anni, and Hugo, who was retarded from having had scarlet fever as a child. Because of Hugo they had been unable to immigrate to America, but it was fortunate they had been able to get to England. Anni, who had taught me English in Berlin, was in bed with terminal breast cancer.

April 3, 1944

Dear Mamm,
This letter might not turn out to be quite as cheerful as you expected it. But before I report on Anni, I should like to

tell about two places I have visited recently. The first was the grave of William Penn, with whom I think you're well acquainted. Well, he is buried somewhere in England. The whole thing is very simple, in Quaker fashion, and yet very impressive. It's a quiet little country graveyard right by an old Quaker meeting house, in a small dale, surrounded by big trees. The grave itself consists of a modest stone slab with the name of William Penn written on it. There are no flowers, no fences, no distinction from the other graves. I was very much reminded of Grey's "Elegy to a Country Churchyard." I also saw Milton's cottage, which has withstood weather, visitors, and time for 400 years. Unfortunately I didn't have a chance to go inside.

Well, I finally visited Oxford, a charming, small town, dominated by the famous university with its many colleges. I went to see Anni and Maemmschen right away. My first impression of Anni was one of horror; I hadn't expected quite such a change. The constant pains have worn down her whole physical being. Since she hasn't eaten very much in the past week or so, one can almost see the outline of her skull. Her hair has changed to a gray color interrupted by stands of white. Naturally her hands and arms have become quite thin.

But all this suffering has given her face a beautiful expression. She was very cheerful and seemed to be happy that I visited her. I was very much struck by her attitude: she is not at all self-conscious, and she refuses to talk about her ailments. As Maemmschen told me, Anni had hoped for an earlier ending of this suffering; and yet she has made up her mind to stick it out.

Fortunately she feels a little better quite often (or occasionally) and that's when I was allowed to visit her. The bottom of her bed is raised about one foot. Of course, she can-

HUGO AND MAEMMSCHEN. AL'S
BROTHER AND MOTHER.

not move about very much. Her sight is getting worse and she is dictating most of her letters. Recently she has had a little difficulty hearing.

Now, let me turn to something more pleasant; and that is Maemmschen. She stays with Anni from morning until 8:00 p.m. She does all of the cooking for Hugo and most of Anni's. She does all the shopping and some washing. The trips from Rawlings Road to Leavensden Nursing Home are no cinch, especially when she has to wait for those buses as much as 45 minutes.

Despite all of this, she looks very well, better than she did in Berlin. Her disposition has changed: She is not so cranky any more, is very alert and observing, and does not argue half as much as she used to. Anni concurs with this opinion. It is amazing to see the old lady hustle about busily doing her many tasks. She'll get up from the dinner table at least five times and she'll stoop under the buffet "with the greatest of ease." As we said in Germany before 1933, "I'd prefer a Jewish grandmother any day."

Hugo does not seem to have changed much. He is happy when he is working. He makes 1 shilling (20 cents) per hour cutting grass, raking leaves, pulling weeds, and sweeping sidewalks. He does some of the housework now that Maemmschen is so busy with Anni. The house is inhabited by three or four other people, all Germans. This has only one advantage: Hugo can talk with someone, since he knows no

English, and Maemmschen prefers to talk German. The owners of the house are honest-to-goodness German gossip women. They'll go so far as to stand behind the door and listen to Maemmschen's conversation. It is extremely easy to step on those ladies' toes. One of them has a lot do in the local German congregation. She gave me Hildebrandt's [Niemoeller's assistant] address in Cambridge. Some day I shall try to look him up. He has married an English girl recently and supervises all German church work in this country.

Anyway, Maemmschen pays about $50.00 for the two rooms. It includes use of all furniture and dishes and kitchen and supply of bedding and sheets. This brings me to a financial point. If you send a few dollars in the near future I am sure M. would appreciate it. As Anni's condition gets worse, expenses seem to increase. I have given her my last two pounds, and I hope to give her a pound or two once a month. But as you know, a private, even in Uncle Sam's army, has his financial limits. I hope to visit them again soon, only this time I shall stay at the Red Cross. Also you can cheer up Anni by writing more often. Maemmschen has one wish: send her, either directly or through me, some Nestle's coffee.

While I was on pass in Oxford I saw Christ's Church and attended a service there; typical English Gothic style—long and low, compared with French cathedrals, which necessitates a small flying buttress construction. Instead of the simple French cross vault, there is a sort of mushroom arch. Embarrassing enough, the congregation sits on both sides of the aisle, both halves facing each other. To a stranger, which I still am, this is a deviation from the Englishman's love for privacy; for one can give everyone a frontal inspection from top to bottom. This also means that man no longer faces God, or the Holy of Holies, at the altar, but faces man.

However, I am not criticizing. This way one must learn to concentrate. The choir was excellent, and consisted of boys and men. They sang a Palestrina, and it made my heart jump. The whole atmosphere is very "high-churchy": a lot of prayers and psalms are being rattled off. It is a pity that, in such a beautiful cathedral, with a nice organ and an excellent choir, one must find such a sterile atmosphere. I must cease now for the censor's sake. So far I have had no letter in reply to one of mine from England. Be good all of you and write.

Meanwhile Annie had died.

May 15, 1944

Dear Mamm,

I suppose you too had mixed feelings about Anni's passing away. I had half-heartedly expected it, and yet I refused to accept such a dreadful thought. Now the suffering is over, and Annie will live in our minds as a great person. Her good deeds and thoughts will live on forever. Perhaps such concepts of infinity are difficult to grasp, but I am sure that it does good to have faith in such goodness. With this faith one need not ponder about the machinery that will get us into heaven or hell. I have come across a very nice epitaph by Grey—his elegy. I will put down the send it to you. It might suit the occasion:

Here rests his head upon the lap of Earth
A youth, to fortune and to fame unknown,
Fair science frowns not on his humble birth,
And Melancholy mark'd him for her own.
Large was his bounty, and his soul sincere,

Heav'n did a recompense as largely send:
He gave to misery all he had: a tear.
He gain'd from Heaven ('twas all he wish'd) a friend.
No farther seek his merits to disclose,
Or draw his frailties from their dread abode,
(There they alike in trembling hope repose)
The bosom of his Father and his God.

Maemmschen wrote me a letter appreciating all my efforts. I hope that we can get her to the States as soon as possible.

It looks as though times are quite exciting for Chris. I had somewhat hoped that he'd stay out of the army. I hope my last letter to him did not disillusion him too much, but that's the way some of us feel, if not worse. I hope he won't be quite as disappointed in the army. I am very glad that Larry, a former Reed roommate, passed by recently. I only hope that our friendship won't be interrupted by this war. Received a nice, very enthusiastic letter from Dick Steiner. Please be sure and show him as many of my letters as possible. If you don't mind, they're addressed to him as well. That in answer to your twin V-mail letters, which took two weeks.

Now returning to my miserable self. Yes, this cog of the big machine reached another zenith in the annual revolution. Twenty-three—an ugly number with neither rhyme nor reason, nor of great importance in the past of mankind. From now on, you are getting younger, and I may start counting my gray hair; for no longer am I able to say that I am half as young as my mother. Wait until I beat Al to that status. Of all my birthdays, this was certainly the most miserable one. Taking Easter Sunday as a precedent, the army decided to assign me to a rag, some water, and too many pots and pans—KP. Furthermore, there was no mail to make this day, at least mentally, a happy one. No package has as yet shown up. Concerning your birthday, I shall send off a modest package within the next few days. It contains a picture and two or three books. More of that later. Eagerly awaiting The New Republic.

In England I visited all the cathedrals I could. St. Albans was typical. Like many English cathedrals, it is located in the country, unlike the Continental churches, which are in the middle of town, surrounded by houses. St. Albans had low naves and the English tower with no spire. I went there often and listened in awe to the organ music. Sometimes I sat in front of the church on the green grass overlooking a pond with swans on it, and thought, what a wonderful world this could be if people would not wage war. I also thought about how lucky I was to be alive. I loved England. The people were so delightfully different from any I had known. I sometimes had difficulty with their class distinctions and standoffishness; yet, they had respect for each other, especially in the lower classes. I met many English girls. We danced, laughed, walked, and held hands. These were quiet relationships, and I was very happy. London was a mess, and yet there was little confusion. Thousands of beds were put up in the underground (subway) and people slept there, sometimes whole families, but mostly mothers, their children, and the grandparents. One night I was sleeping in a hotel when a bomb, probably a V2, went off next door, destroying the whole building. I was so tired I slept right through the explosion. This seems unbelievable to me, but my memory is that in the morning, when I woke, I was surprised to see the building next door completely gone.

I also saw Midsummer Night's Dream in Regents Park and heard many symphonies. I went to the Tate Galleries where I saw a fine collection of Gainsboroughs. England was in many ways so much the opposite of the culture in which I grew up. I was impressed by the Englishman's respect for the other person, the freedom to express oneself (as demonstrated in Hyde Park), the calm of the people, the landscape, and the political system, which reflects the feeling of the people more immediately than even the U.S. system. My whole visit was an idyllic time for me, and I probably have since viewed England through the distorted glass of my affection for it then.

One day I went to a restaurant downtown and I was very hungry. The waitress put down a tray of sweets, so I decided to eat them all. When she came back her jaw dropped. Since there was rationing, I was supposed to take only one. I apologized wholeheartedly.

All in all, I had a good time in England. The weather was nasty, the food lousy, but the people were tremendously friendly to me, and this small country had stood up for democracy with great sacrifices, and we were there to help. One day I went out with a young woman who had lost five members of her family in a recent bombing. I was so ashamed of being German-born that I never told anyone and no one guessed. My accent was enough the result of learning British English, coupled with a Portland accent, that many people guessed I was Canadian or that I was from some other more exotic part of the Commonwealth.

An exchange of letters among my brother, an army buddy of mine, and me follows:

From Chris, who was 16 at the time:

Dear Rikky,

Often I have speculated about the idea that you might not come back, and so I thought I might tell you how I feel about it. Although all the men engaged in this battle have often had tough times, I still think it is a great privilege to fight and perhaps die for these great ideals, and I know whether or not I carry a gun, which I now think is necessary, I shall always fight for these great truths. I hope to join some branch of the service where they let you stay in college for six months so I can first finish a complete year of college.
Chris

My dear Chris,

I want to thank you for your birthday greetings and tell you that I surely appreciate your thoughts. I was a bit disturbed, however, by your outlook on the army and on war. Although I have been in the army for a while and have been very observing, I don't feel to be an authority on war itself. I showed your letter to a good friend of mine. He immediately wanted to write, and I've enclosed it. He's a young chap who has faced death, and I mean death (not à la Tom Sawyer attending his own funeral) many times. Please don't take all this to heart. It's just another person's point of view. I surely hope to hear from you soon.
Faithfully,
Your brother Tom

The following letter is from a remarkable young man, a commando who had climbed the cliffs of Norway from the sea when that country was held by the Germans.

My dear Chris,

Your brother, who is a great friend of mine, showed me a letter you wrote to him a short time ago and said that I might reply. Please forgive the liberty I take in doing this.

I am a British soldier and have served in the army since 1939. I took part in the Norwegian campaign, was in the Commandos for four years, and have recently returned from North Africa. It is this service that I use for writing as I do.

You write that a man should be proud to die for great ideals, but may I suggest that there is a difference between being proud and being ready. You lose sight of the simple fundamental: that we are fighting for a new way of life not a new way of death. To reiterate, we are fighting to live, not fighting to die. While no one should regret having to give his life, he can and does expect that those who remain shall make a decent world of the chaos that now exists.

You also forget that while men will fight for great truths, they will also fight for great lies.

There is no privilege, no glory, no happiness in dying for one's country; only heartbreak to those we love and to those who love us. There is little idealism in war. There is no credit in shooting a fellow man. It is a job that must be done. A man believing he is right shoots no better than a homicidal maniac. The only difference lies in a man's own conscience.

Personally, I want to live. A muddy piece of ground and a blanket is an anticlimax to the castles I have built in the air for after the war.

We have a saying in Britain that it takes only nine months to be born but seventy years to die. I wish to enjoy my three score years and ten before I cry, "Enough, I am coming back!"

Yours sincerely,

Ron

My brother replied:

Dear Rikky and friend,
I want to thank you both first of all for taking such interest in me. I appreciate it very much. Most people would probably just have said, "Poor little kid, he'll learn." I have thought a great deal about what I wrote, and I talked also to other people and soldiers. I still feel the same as I did before, and I think our misunderstanding lies more in the fact that either I failed to transform my thoughts into the proper words, or perhaps you misinterpreted them. You say there is a difference between being ready and proud. If you have read Browning's "Incident of the Trench Camp" you will perhaps see what I mean when I say "It is a privilege to die for ..." etc. As for being ready, I think that I am as ready as any boy in the United States. You know yourself that my courage was never low, nor was my spirit. You write of the paradoxes that I must be going through. In the same breath, I fight and go to college. Being ready is being equipped, mentally, morally and intellectually. Your friend also writes that he expects those staying at home to make a decent world out of this chaos. I can think of no better way of improving society or being properly equipped than a good education. Besides, I have given up my summer vacation and I am going to Reed till I am eighteen, when I will be drafted like the rest. The army college could have given me no more. I agree there is little idealism in war, but I believe that right now it is a part of the eternal task of achieving our ideals. This war is a job, and a hard and cruel one, but don't forget that men have been fighting in one way or the other for centuries, and they will go on doing so. Fighting, I hope, not with guns but with the forces of truth. I know the clouds look black over there, and it is a hard life, but you must not lose sight of the

thing we are fighting for. Too many people think it is just a job, and when it is done we can come home to our girlfriends, Cokes, and hamburgers. You and I and all of us young men are the ones that will determine, to a large extent, whether we will have another war. You must tell all about the horrors, but you must also help to build a structure that can resist and prevent war. I know you wonder how I can say these idealistic things when I have never faced the real thing. I have seen, heard, and read a lot about battles, and some of the minor inconveniences I have experienced myself. All these things I add together and multiply by three, and it is a horrible picture, but still I believe in my idealism. I know I will be scared stiff, but not afraid. I want to live too, that is only human nature, but before I die I shall have tried my best, and if God wills it, I shall die, whether I am reading a book or helping the poor or firing a gun. Shooting men I like no better. I know that the Germans are basically like me—human people. When I shall shoot to kill, I will not only be shooting to preserve myself, but also shooting to kill the great lie for which the Nazis have been led to fight. It is our duty as good citizens of our respective nations to see to it that we know how to tell the good from the bad, and then try to help other people. These are my thoughts. I may be wrong and I would appreciate very much if you would write again. This letter may also be unfriendly, but these things lie very close to my heart, and they burst forth sometimes quite uncontrolled.

Lots of love and good luck,
Chris

I was touched that my brother had written so openly to me, and was thinking so deeply about the war and about me.

Rescue Team Forms

EDDY AND JOHNNY

Finally, the rescue team we had come to England to form was ready. There were seven of us. The leader was a captain who was often away taking care of important administrative matters, I supposed. The lieutenant was a graduate of an Ivy League college and a former ski instructor there. He was from a well-known family and spoke a fair amount of French. He was fun to be with and I looked upon him as tremendously sophisticated and glamorous, comfortable with the rich and famous, and quite able to accomplish whatever needed to be done. We were an odd couple, but we were together much of the time, and he helped me overcome many of my socially awkward ways. We went through much of the war together, and in some ways we were buddies, but the army distance between officer and enlisted man always remained.

There were two other enlisted men besides me. Junior was the youngest, and we treated him like a kid, which he was. He was from Texas, the ideal go-fer, very sweet and always eager to be helpful. We all liked him. There was a common story told about American ingenuity. It was said that the Americans won the war because they could fix an engine with a safety pin and they were great at using string or paper clips, whereas

OUR TEAM: LT. PHELLAN, SGT. WADA, TOM,
LT. OFFARD, LT. WOODS, JOHNNY AND JUNIOR

the Germans had to have rigid instructions to follow.
Junior was the original "make do" GI. He managed to
stick anything together or find simple solutions to complex, mechanical problems. He also had a restricted
repertoire of Texas songs about Mexican ladies, which he
would sing over and over. (To this day, those songs with
their catchy tunes will sometimes come back to me and
will not leave my head, and I find myself smiling as I
remember Junior.) The sergeant, Eddy was a tall, red-
headed fellow with a slow Southern drawl who was a
master mechanic as well as a master of anything else that
needed to be fixed. He also found and got to know
many women in a manner that was a great shock to me
with my chaste ways. Even without speaking German,
he and Junior always managed to be helpful. Then there
was Dodig, the Italian opera singer from New York, who
had an immense repertoire of bawdy stories. There was
another private from Texas, and Lieutenant Moraud,

who bragged that if we followed him we would not be killed. The seven of us were a motley crew who were given the task of somehow figuring out how to get behind the lines held by the Germans and search out the Allied soldiers who were caught in enemy territory. I thought our team members were all "real Americans," and I was immensely proud to be part of this group.

My mother kept writing letters faithfully and these messages were so very important. We were stationed in Bristol, where the Germans had destroyed 30 churches in one night's bombardment. I was billeted with a lovely English couple who treated me like their son in a quiet, accepting way. The fact that they had a daughter in her late teens helped as well.

Before we were to begin the trip across the channel, I wrote a last letter to my mother and Al, explaining my reasons for fighting:

May 1944

Dear Mamm and Al,

These are great moments in the history of mankind. Whether all these events are glorious and promising for the future remains to be seen. It won't be long that many of us will be over there on the Continent doing our share, minute and unimportant as it may be. I want you to do me a favor. When you think of me, don't worry about my physical well-being, but pray for those other things which may be found on the higher levels of our lives.

Concerning the war, I have to confess that I have joined the majority of soldiers in this army who long fought hard just to get home. The author of The Battle is the Payoff *(his name has slipped me just now) realized that long ago. One is beginning to feel that one is powerless; the things that are interesting, beautiful, and revolutionary simply don't belong in the army. I am leading a double life these days. That is why I am hoping, perhaps more than you in America are, that the war be over soon, that the time will come where one can make bigger sacrifices for greater ends than a physical victory. It seems to me that we are fighting not so much for freedom, equality, etc., but for the right, the possibility to strive for those truths after the armistice. Of course, this concerns me and perhaps millions of other soldiers.*

As I have mentioned before, I have seen some interesting things, and met some very charming people in this town. The other day I saw a play by J.B.Priestley, They Came to a City. You may remember from his book Midnight on the Desert that his plays did not go over very well in the States. I can now see why. In the first place, we have really no equivalent playwright in the States who takes off as strongly on the social scene, keeps down to earth, stresses the spiritual, the emotional, and yet makes hardly any practical suggestion. I'd say that E. O'Neill goes too far to the extreme on the social side in The Hairy Ape. Will Saroyan touches more on the psychological, picturing the big-hearted, good-old American Jim Dandy. Thornton Wilder would probably come closest. But compared with Priestly, he is too much up in the air, perhaps too old-fashioned. He is one of the few American writers who gets away from the more materialist philosophy.

Priestley's play has nine people in it, all so-called typical Englishmen. They are the aristocracy, the laboring class, the middle class, and include a banker, and an old woman who is somehow detached from all this. Well, they all go to see the city of the future, where everybody is happy and works hard. And as they come back on the stage they give their impres-

sion of this new place. Two of them flee to the new city, and four return to the status quo. A husband who is married unhappily is dragged back by his wife. The two people from the working class decide to go back to the old place, so they can fight for the new city and show the people where it is. Thus the play has a slightly Marxian touch. Anyway, I enjoyed it tremendously. Paid only a shilling for each of the seats (20 cents to you). So you see, even the proletariat can invade the theaters of the upper class.

I had no mail from you this week. May God bless all of you.
A big invasion kiss from "Tom"

Preparation for Invasion

The invasion started on June 6—D-Day—and the news spread like wildfire. Surely we would leave in a few days ... if only we knew when. Sooner or later this life of comfort had to come to an end. No more private billets, no more girlfriends, no more concert halls or theaters— just K-rations, a foxhole, and the enemy a few hundred yards away. But why jump the gun?

Before long we were alerted, and that same night we left Bristol for Plymouth, driving 15 MPH with only the black-out lights on. It was a GI trip if I ever saw one. As a private, I was a driver, alone in my jeep. The only thing I could see was the glimmering light of the jeep ahead. How many times I went off the road I do not remember; but I am sure that some good angel, who was more awake than I, kept me from breaking my own trail off the curve or down a cliff. The staging area was just a conglomeration of wet tents, waterproofed vehicles, and an atmosphere of expectancy. I tried to forget the big

question that loomed overhead: "When will we leave?" I
worried about the little things—the new French money,
the delivery of mail, the card game, the last phase of
waterproofing. D-Day had been so recent that no
rumors had as yet reached the staging area about what
had happened on the beachhead. But they said that the
winds were playing havoc with the English Channel,
making a crossing, much less a landing, very difficult.
After three days of anxious waiting we were finally herd-
ed to the point of embarkation. It was fascinating to see
the dock workers pick up one of those seven ton "jobs"
of heavy equipment and heist them into the hold of the
ship as though it weighed only a couple of pounds. It
seemed as if they were going to stow away all of
Plymouth in that one Liberty ship.

We knew that since it was not essential that we be in
the frontlines, as it was for the infantry, we had been
held behind for a few days. Finally we were told to get
our gear together, throw out all souvenirs, and take only
what we could carry on our backs in rough terrain. We
also had to get our jeeps ready to drive through shallow
water up to the hood in order to reach land. Near the
staging area we were directed to a distribution center for
waterproofing materials where a sergeant instructed us
how to attach a piece of hose to the exhaust pipe and tie
it to the jeep so it would protrude two feet above the
windshield. We were then given a big glob of kosmolene
(a pliable sort of silly putty) to plug up the drain holes in
the jeep floorboard and other water-sensitive spots. We
had to protect the battery terminals and the spark plugs,
and soon it seemed that everything under the hood and
around the engine block was full of kosmolene. As the
driver of one jeep, I was to get it on land somehow and

then meet up with the officers and other enlisted men in our team later when we were in France. Up and down the staging area were dozens of other soldiers who would be driving jeeps or vehicles that carried weapons or heavy equipment. Now they were struggling with kosmolene, eager finally to go into action, and putting all their energy into preparing their machines, knowing that the condition of their jeeps and the strength of the kosmolene would determine their very survival. Finally we drove onto the ship and spent the night in five-decker bunks until the ship took off in the morning.

Chapter 5

•

June 1944

This time the embarkation really meant business. There was no WAC (Women's Army Corps) band, no Red Cross workers handing out doughnuts, no England waiting for us. We were no longer unassigned replacements, we had a job to do. Slowly the English coast faded away, and it hurt to leave England.

The trip across the Channel took about five to six hours. There were soldiers of all sorts standing on deck: combat troops, officers and men, truck drivers, and special soldiers like us. We filled the hours by asking the ship's crew endless questions about conditions on the beachhead and about the landing in Normandy, which had occurred a few days before. There was a strange combination of feelings abroad—eagerness and determination to get into the war, and an almost overpowering fear of what was in store for us.

The Invasion

Finally we saw the shores of the Continent in a blue haze. We passed the Cherbourg Peninsula which was

still held by the Germans, and which the Allies wanted
to use as a harbor. As we approached the shore of Utah
Beach in Normandy, where we were to land, we could
see hundreds of war and cargo ships scattered all over
the coastal waters. After our anchor had been dropped,
we put all our earthly belongings on an LST (Landing
Ship Tank) and I drove my jeep onto it. We were hell-
bent for action, or thought we were. It was really quite a
lively scene off the French beach. Black troops (the military was not yet integrated) were cruising nonchalantly
through the water in ducks (amphibious trucks). All
around us, LSTs were being loaded and dispatched
toward the beach. Most of the cement wharves had been
shattered by the storm. Many of the underwater mines
had not been removed, and warning signs were everywhere. Once in a while, the body of a dead GI floated
by. I shuddered. For most soldiers this was the first taste
of the reality of war and each dealt with it in his own
way. We had been taught to leave the concern for the
bodies to the medics and to avoid them. I did my best
not to think about them.

My attention was suddenly drawn to a Liberty ship
that looked as though it had been hit by a mine. As we
went on we saw another one directly behind it in the
same condition, and another one behind that one,
dozens of them, all neatly lined up parallel to the beach,
serving as breakers. It was painful to see those ships resting on the bottom of the sea, split in the middle, or with
big cracks in their hulls. To begin to figure out the working hours, the money, and the materials that were resting
on the bottom of the ocean leads to an awareness of the
terrible waste in modern warfare. It was too much to
think about the human suffering, and we had not been

advised to avoid thinking about the tremendous material waste, so I poured my feeling into these broken pieces of equipment.

When we were about fifty yards off shore, we passed a very curious sight. Amid all these hustling Ducks and LSTs, standing out against the dead hulls of the sunken Liberty ships, was a pile of junk in the water. It consisted of equipment that had been shot up on D-Day, and the waves had piled it up until it extended at least ten feet above the water's surface. On the top of this odd-looking pinnacle was balanced a most comfortable, leather-cushioned and fairly new armchair. Sitting in it, looking very much at ease, was a GI taking down the numbers of the incoming ships.

All of a sudden our LST hit a sandbank just offshore of Utah Beach. This was down the coast from the famed original D-Day landings on Omaha Beach with its high cliffs, which would have been impossible for vehicles such as my jeep to land. The tide had not yet fully receded, and there was still water between us and land. Some other jeep drivers were busy putting the last globs of kosmolene over their spark plugs and distributor caps in hopes that the jeeps could make the short distance to the shore. Finally the gate of the LST was lowered and we left the ship. After the last jeep was off, the LST pulled out, leaving me stranded in my jeep on a sandbank between England and France. There I was, all dressed up and ready to do my part in the war, and no way to get to it. What a picnic this would have been for a German fighter plane! And we could tell by the tracer bullets, which were chasing something behind the clouds, that there were planes around. (Every fourth or fifth tracer bullet lights up, so that the GI can see where he is shooting, particularly at night.) Suddenly a German reconnaissance plane flew directly over me and no one shot it down. Now I knew I was in the war. I sat alone in my jeep, caught on the sandbar, water up to my chest, with a German plane flying overhead. There was absolutely nothing I could do. The engine of the jeep, protected by the kosmoline, was still running, but it would not be able to run much longer, and I could not move because the water was so deep. Was this to be the end of my life—caught on a sandbar trying to get to a war to do something that would count? Was this to be my last and only moment in the war? After anxious waiting and many reviews of my life, the tide went down enough so that I could drive my jeep ashore. I put it in four-wheel drive and the jeep moved slowly toward the beach. Now I was on the Continent, headed for Berlin by way of Paris.

Our team (Lieutenant Woods, the sergeant, Junior, and I) had remained together, and before long we were assigned to a field surrounded by hedgerows on all four sides. After all this excitement we were exhausted and our first thought was to find a good place to sleep. Stretched over us was a dome of tracer bullets, all out after a German plane. A beautiful sight but very noisy! Now and then I could hear the peristaltic humming of a German plane. Everything up in the air after dark was to be fired at by the AAA (anti-aircraft crews). We were too tired to worry about such "trifles," so I slipped into my sleeping bag and crawled under the floorboard. I left the infantry to worry about the enemy. Around midnight I was awakened by a steady stream of water running down my neck and into my sleeping bag. In my sleepy state I sat up, only to hit my head on the floorboard. After I had gathered my wits I realized, too late, that I had left open the drain holes in the floorboard of the jeep.

The following nights we pitched tents, made ditches around them to hold the rain, and camouflaged them, like good soldiers. Perhaps the Soldier's Handbook 21-100 was right about immediately pitching a tent in combat. We stayed in our wet pup tents with the infantry for several days and nights, and I learned well how to live with my jeep in mud and rain, which was to become a major challenge for the next year.

Like the infantry, we slept in wet tents, we slogged through the mud, and we waited anxiously to start our work. Waiting around with little to do was to become another of the great challenges in the army for me. So after landing on Utah beach, we were on our own. The infantry had moved on although we could hear the guns and the fighting. Lieutenant Woods immediately talked to the partisans, establishing a grapevine, or a communication line, to several partisan groups who might know where Allied soldiers were in hiding behind the German lines. This was an essential task. Meanwhile, I got my jeep in order, taking off the rest of the kosmoline, checking the spark plugs, and changing the oil. To me it seemed that my contribution to the war effort would revolve around the mechanism of my jeep. We inspected our weapons and scrounged for food (mostly K- or C-rations). We spent time getting acquainted with the French population and took part in village life, and I practiced my French. Getting to know the local people was a big part of our assignment.

On the third day we had our first French conversation with "Simone" who was herding her cows past our tents. Before long we had her whole family with us. Everybody was gesticulating wildly, condemning the boches (pigs, referring to the Germans), who had taken everything with them—everything except a dozen fresh eggs and four bottles of cider, which they gave us in exchange for the little odds and ends of our ten-in-one rations. (We later traded our eggs and cider for some bon-bons.) Meanwhile, when the German planes flew over, everybody dove into a ditch, under a tree, or wherever they could find shelter.

After "soldiering" (the term used for waiting) for two or three days in tents near the town of Crocqueville, a few miles from the beach, our team finally moved into a chateau six kilometers north of Isigny. This chateau looked more like one of the better farmhouses than an ancient castle. The Germans had just moved out, and it took a whole day to clean up the mess and eliminate the stench. We found our first German uniforms and the first recent Nazi propaganda in this house. The two ladies who lived in the house treated us as special guests, with an excellent introduction to the French cuisine. The Isigny cream and butter are well known throughout France, and it didn't take much tasting to discover their excellent quality. We were still near the frontline troops who found housing as they could or slept in their tents.

Eventually our officers received their orders. Although we were in the American Army, we were attached to British Intelligence. The head of this organization was a one-armed British colonel who carried a swagger stick under his shortened arm. Our main mission in IS 9 (Intelligence Section 9) was to gather Allied personnel who had escaped from German prison camps or had been shot down and were hiding with the protection of the partisans.

It was our job to learn where the men to be rescued might be by getting in touch with the French partisans or groups in the Underground Railway. The partisans were French soldiers, citizens, peasants—men as well as women and even children—who formed a paramilitary group and worked with tremendous energy against the occupying Germans. They took great risks and when caught by the Germans they were often brutally tortured, but few of them talked or gave out names. They were called the FFI (Forces Francaise Interieure) or the macqui (named after an underbrush weed in Corsica) or just "partisans." They were often our main protection.

Lieutenant Woods was the chief organizer of all our activity. We constantly had a partisan representative with us who was the link to these captured Allied soldiers. He also protected us with information about which areas were rigidly held by the Germans, and where the lines were loose and we could travel with the least chance of being caught.

All through our European experience, (France, Belgium, and Italy) we would always find a spot where we could go through and behind enemy lines, gather up the soldiers, and bring them back to Allied positions. To get to them, we drove our jeeps and quarter-ton trucks, or we walked through fields or cross-country when the roads were held by the Germans. Sometimes we retrieved just one man, but often many. We used our vehicles to bring them back, walked with them, or hired buses. We had several close calls from the Germans but our partisan colleagues always managed to protect us. The liberated soldiers were, of course, elated to see us.

Some had been in captivity for long periods of time and others had just been shot down and they were hiding.

The First Rescues

We reached Normandy intending to rescue Allied soldiers who were caught between the lines, and sometimes behind the lines, as the Germans were retreating before the Americans. It was not easy to pass through the German lines. There was the constant fear of being caught, the roads and the paths (if there were any) were difficult, and we were challenged by physical hardships—rain, mud, lack of food; and again, always the fear that an armed German troop could come around the corner. I carried a .38 caliber revolver and a carbine and the lieutenant had a .45 caliber pistol. Some of the partisans brought British Sten guns (automatic). When we used our vehicles we had to make sure our tanks were full and that we carried at least one five-gallon GI can full of gas. Since we were from SHAEF (Supreme Headquarters of the Allied Expeditionary Force), we could scrounge our supplies from any regimental or division headquarters. But what saved our lives were the many loyal partisans who gave us the strategic information we needed and who went with us on our trips behind the German lines to give us protection.

At first, most of those we rescued were British flyers who had been shot down, taken prisoner, and escaped; or they had been rescued and hidden by the French partisans. The widely believed story we heard was that when Americans were captured, they made the best of their prison situation, adjusted to it, and somehow managed; but when the British soldier was taken prisoner, he spent every bit of energy to escape and very often he did. Certainly they were taught escape as part of their training. Most American soldiers were not. Our special wire-cutting knives, silk maps to be sewn into our uniforms, buttons that could be put on a needle to be used as compasses, and various other escape tools, were all supplied by the British.

Normandy had been suffering under the German occupation for about four years and during that time some of the French, especially the Partisans, had developed a strong system of opposition, the Resistance. Part of the Allied planning for the landing at Normandy was dependent on the French for the destruction of rail lines, roads, and radar communications.

In Normandy many of the lost Allied personnel were downed parachutists. In preparation for the landing, Britain had been sending in parachutists, and because the planes and the men's equipment were often old, many of them were lost. These parachutists were a special breed. All were volunteers, men who wanted extra adventure, saw the challenges of their job as excitement, and were confident of their ability to accomplish their extraordinary feats. They looked on it as a sort of wild sport, and they were indeed considered tremendous national heroes.

The French partisans gave us the location of Allied soldiers hiding with them. We poured over maps to find the best routes. As the U.S. forces moved forward, we also began to pick up American GIs who had become lost. The danger of being caught by the Germans was great, and although we carried some weapons, our job was to locate and liberate Allied personnel, not to conquer German territory or soldiers. Our mission kept us very busy not only with the rescue attempts, but also with preparations for the expeditions. We had to find soldiers to go with us, get equipment and gear ready for the trip, and meet with partisans who could help.

While we were waiting to undertake our assignments, we continued to make friends with the local people who were particularly excited to find anyone who spoke French. They poured their gratitude and exuberance for the American liberation forces on us, and we accepted it in the name of the United States. But we also knew it really belonged to the thousands of GIs who had climbed the cliffs of Omaha Beach and been wounded or killed.

We had much freedom and often I would have wild and determined ideas, which Lieutenant Woods would restrict with reason. He himself, however, was very talented in making the most unlikely things happen. Jr. and the sergeant added their common sense and savvy in special areas such as scrounging gas and food, fixing cars, and generally encouraging us. Lieutenant Woods and I often went alone or with partisans while the others took charge of preparations and remained behind. They did not speak French, and they were not eager to risk their lives when there was no purpose in them doing so. I was always ready to go anywhere. We all had become friends even though we came from totally different backgrounds. We worked together smoothly as a team, we all loved joking together, and we each supported one another.

One particular trip in those first few weeks stands out. It probably represents more of our youthful enthusiasm and daring than well-thought out planning. Clearly it was not conceived by experienced military men. We heard through the partisan grapevine that 150 RAF (Royal Air Force) boys who had been shot down during the previous few months had been captured by the Germans, but had escaped and were hiding about 35-40 miles from the Allied lines in land held by the Germans. We decided to ram our way through German-held territory to get them to the safety of our lines. We were able to assemble a crew of over 100 wildly exuberant French, Belgian, and Canadian soldiers, and British paratroopers, who were eager to accompany us on the rescue mission. All of us were armed to the teeth with knives, grenades, Schmeissers, Thompson sub-machine guns, Stens, pistols and revolvers of many different makes, English and American machine guns, carbines, and a "hell of a fighting spirit" that was somehow combined with absolute deathly fear. We acted as if we were prepared to take on the whole German army. (We knew we might have to deal with some of it.)

We went in a motor convoy consisting of three jeeps (one of them mine) and six dilapidated civilian cars, which had the doors removed. (This provided for a speedier exit of the occupants and for a larger space from which to fire.) Bringing up the rear, were five old French buses, each of which had a big charcoal burner mounted on the back as part of their means of propulsion. Every twenty kilometers or so we had to stop to stoke these burners and to replenish them with wood. Huge flames were spouting out of the rear of these strange buses and it often looked as though every one of them was on fire. When we got to the edge of Isigny, one of the buses broke down from old age. Fortunately, the other four were destined to survive the whole trip. As decoration and for the purpose of recognition, almost every car or bus had a French or British flag fastened on it. Paratroopers that had joined the task force were sitting everywhere—on top of the buses, on fenders, on the hoods, on the bumpers, and some even inside of the vehicles! The local French people looked at us with their eyes and mouths wide open. Even the Allied tank people we passed as we neared the frontlines could not figure out to whom this circus belonged.

Fortunately, we met no enemy opposition on the trip. After passing through two villages, my jeep looked like a flower shop, for the French were throwing huge bouquets at us. Whenever we stopped for more than two minutes people would come running out of their houses waving a bottle of wine in the left hand and a glass in the other. Every now and then civilians would tell us of some German patrols who had passed through on their motor bikes about an hour before. Occasionally an FFI soldier would jump out of the bushes, hanging on to his captured weapon with one hand and waving us on with the other. After all the wine and champagne, we started to feel really good. The Germans were reported to be in a forest we had to pass through, but they never bothered to call on us.

We found the British fliers camped in a deserted school, where they had been brought together and were being fed by the local people. Most of them had been captured and held as prisoners of war until they some-how had escaped, found partisan help, and made their way to the schoolhouse where they were waiting for us.

The elation of the British at being rescued can scarcely be described. Like so many other rescued sol-diers, their greatest interest at that point was for ciga-rettes, and we did our best to provide them. We loaded the men into our rickety old buses and lit out as fast as possible, without incident, back to our own lines, continually passing on roads well within German territory. We had to stop frequently, of course, to stoke the rear furnaces of the old French buses. If we had been a strange sight coming, we were an even more peculiar sight returning, with an additional exuberant 150 rescued British airmen hanging on to the vehicles. Just as we arrived safely in Allied territory, to our surprise, we met two columns of American tanks and a regiment of infantry that were just setting out to attack and occupy the exact German area through which we had just cruised without incident. That evening we went to a rather exclusive nightclub in Le Mans where we paid $2.50 for two cups of marché noir (black market) coffee. It was all in a day's work.

As these flyers were rescued, very often the first thing they asked us was, "Got any cigarettes?" We came to find this was a major issue throughout Europe. Often, when we reached the soldiers who had been hiding, along with their exuberance at being rescued, came the cry for cigarettes. We soon learned to carry some with us. The cigarette shortage all over the Continent was acute, and everyone, rich and poor alike, craved American tobacco. Two to three times a day, a Frenchman entered our lobby and nonchalantly emptied all the ashtrays into his coat pocket. The manager of the hotel was more subtle in his manners: he only picked up a butt here and there, when he thought no one was looking. Some of the Frenchmen sent their exotic-looking and highly perfumed wives to our hotel, and these ladies accosted us right in front of the hotel and rattled off the question we had heard so many times since landing on Normandy:

"Have you got unee cigarette for mee, non?"

Later on, in Germany, it was the same story; well-dressed and well-fed Germans stood in front of many a GI movie theater relieving the soldiers of their half-smoked cigarettes. It did not take the Germans long to learn that smoking was forbidden in the U.S. Army theaters and that the soldiers waiting outside would throw away half smoked cigarettes before entering. Whenever and wherever a crowd of American soldiers gathered, there would be little German children who had been sent by their fathers to search for cigarette butts. As soon as a GI had thrown down the butt of his cigarette, ten to fifteen of these little ones scrambled furiously to the ground. One day, in Munich, I was stopped by a fellow who had placed his bicycle in the middle of the road so that I simply could not proceed with my jeep. Before I had a chance to say something, he flung back the flap of his jacket, displaying a big yellow star. With his thick, guttural German accent he said, "I am a Tschew (Jew), pardon me, and I have papers from an American soldier to show that I was in the concentration camp. Have you got a cigarette for me?"

Meeting the People

Often between assignments we became involved with what was going on in the villages. One day I had a unique experience as a milker, a job that turned out to be a fiasco. I approached the cow very gently, overflowing with all kinds of bovine mental telepathy. I lowered the three-legged milking stool (it only had two legs) carefully to the ground. I pressed my helmet gradually into the thighs of the beast, and I reached for the "faucet" when the animal became distrustful and moved a few yards away from me. So, with a bucket in my left hand, the milking stool in the other, I went from one spot to the next. Every time I reached her, she would budge a few yards. She came from a good family and was not going to have any monkey business with a helmeted stranger. Once I got two "sqoits out of de woiks," as someone said, but that was not sufficient even to identify the substance. In America we say, "it was only a drop in the bucket." Naturally I felt rather silly following this feminine creature around to no avail. I had to retreat with milk all around me and not a drop to drink.

After my experience with the cow, I put down some thoughts on philosophy for my mother. I was not free to write of any experience connected with the war, so I began a conversation with her about struggling with my calling as a minister.

June 25, 1944

Again there is little I can say. Sometimes this censorship is getting to be quite a nuisance. Naturally one can write little about the war, and I hate to get personal because our immediate superiors are reading this "stuff." So you see, we are fighting for freedom of the press.

The main book [the book I was reading] is John McMurray's Reason and Emotion, an excellent book. I wish you'd give it to Dick Steiner before you read it yourself. I have seldom been as fond of a book. I have recently (within the past four months) changed many of my ideas and this book might give you an idea along what lines this has happened. I have often hinted at it in my letters. There is a passage in one of R.L. Nettleship's letters (MacMillan 1897) which could very well have been written by McMurray: "The only strength for me is to be found in a sense of a personal presence everywhere. It scarcely matters whether it be called human or divine; a presence which only makes itself felt at first in this and that particular form and feature. Into this presence we come, not by leaving behind what are usually called earthly things, or by loving them less, but by living more intensely in them, and loving more what is really lovable in them; for it is literally true that this world is everything to us, if only we choose to make it so, if only we 'live' in the present because it is eternity."

The soldier bill [GI bill] sounds almost too good to be true. I am still hoping that Uncle Sam will make an arrangement for some of us to stay over here for one half to one year and study. The international situation looks somewhat better ever since D-Day. Churchill seems to be quite optimistic. It would be wonderful if the war were over by Christmas. But then one musn't be counting on that.

That's about all I have to say right now. Be good, all of you.

Best wishes and a kiss from Tom

Before leaving Isigny, we were involved with another major incident in the town. It revolved around Pilou, a fine horse, only two years old, and having his full share of joie de vivre. One morning his happiness came to an end with an accident. We found him right after breakfast, with his hind end stuck in the bottom of a deep, wedge-like German air raid trench. Soon the whole village population had come together and in a typical French manner, all of the farmers were talking at the same time about each one's individual salvage plan. Many of the soldiers and infantry nearby were also

deeply involved in the rescue. Poor Pilou was groaning
and puffing and twisting himself in agony, straining his
innards to the utmost. Our whole team was working in
shifts trying to liberate the horse's rear end, but to no
avail. Every time Pilou moved, he only forced himself
deeper into the trench. Finally, as a last resort, we called
over the GI medics who were beyond the nearest
hedgerow and they came with their half-track vehicle (a
vehicle with round rubber tires up front and caterpillar
tracks in back). By slinging the winch cable over a strong
branch, we half-hoisted, half-slid poor Pilou out of his
tight spot.

Meanwhile, everybody was invited for a glass of
cider, even though our worries were not over by a long
shot. Pilou was much too exhausted to move even his
head, much less walk. Our next challenge was to get him
upright. Again the medics came in handy, not only with
their half-track, but also with a couple of men who had
been handling horses all their lives. We put Pilou on a
tarpaulin and pulled him by half-track to the next big
tree. Then we put some straps around his belly, slung the
winch cable over a branch, and hoisted him up, hoping
that his blood would start circulating again. We mas-
saged his legs, talked to him, and fed him all the equine
delicacies we could find. That evening in the home of
Madame de la maison, all the conversation revolved
around poor Pilou.

The next morning the French veterinarian showed
up—an important-looking, bespectacled, pot-bellied,
well-dressed bourgeois who spent more time evaluating
our opinions than the actual condition of the horse. The
farmers looked up to him with awe as the Big Medicine
Man. Finally he took off his kid gloves and with great

professional gestures he examined the beast from front to rear. Suddenly he stood up straight. He folded his hands behind his back, thus making his belly protrude all the further; and as he rocked back and forth from heel to toe, he came to an important decision: Pilou needed an injection. So, an injection he got, while Monsieur le Docteur took a shot of something else. We faithfully continued pampering, massaging, and even feeding Pilou. The little daughter of Mmes. Elizabette even included Pilou in her evening prayers, and yet, next morning, whether by divine predestination or by sheer force of nature, Pilou was dead.

It was Sunday and the GIs (who attended our first church service on the Continent) put on overalls and tended to the burial. We searched extensively all over the countryside, and finally found a hole made by an abandoned anti-aircraft gun position, where we dragged Pilou. A corporal on our team who had been a butcher in civilian life severed Pilou's four legs so that he could fit into the hole. When the horse was finally in his proper place, we threw the good earth over him and covered him up for eternity. That evening at the funeral party we had a merry old time with two young ladies over some honest-to-goodness steaks, crepe suzettes, and a drink or two, or three or more. We were definitely "getting to know the local people."

Finally, after more land was taken by the Allies so that the soldiers in hiding were freed, we moved to our next stop, the town of Carentan, which was still being shelled by the Germans. Every evening a German plane came over strafing the town to let us know that the war was still on. It was easy to forget that the frontline was only twenty minutes away from our hotel. Our team slept in feather beds with white sheets (or rather I should just say sheets—they were hardly white) and we thoroughly enjoyed our ten-in-one's or C-rations, thanks to the ingenuity of the hotel cook. We had our first real lessons in the exchange of food articles. We took the rations that we did not like to a Frenchman and exchanged them for cognac, butter, eggs, Calvados, or whatever we wanted. We soon found that if a Frenchman has something, you can usually talk him out of it, even though it is necessary to talk fast, literally as well as figuratively.

On the evening of July 10, 1944 I again wrote to my mother about the French and expressed further thoughts on religion and philosophy:

Dear Mamm & Chris,

France continues to be very interesting. I have by now talked to many civilians. They are excellent hosts. They have little food that they can offer but what they have they share gladly. And believe me, it's well prepared. So far I still like the English [people] better. They are not quite so overbearing in their speech—not just because I can't get my two cents worth in edgewise—they are more easy going. Of course, the French have excellent wines and champagnes. Yes, I've been drinking champagne twice the past few days. I have also come to appreciate a good French kitchen.

Here is a thought from Stevenson's Pulois et Unbera: "It is not strange if we are tempted to despair of good. Our religions and moralities have been trimmed to flatter us, till they are all emasculated and sentimentalized, and only please and weaken. Truth is of a rougher strain. In the harsh face of life, faith can read a bracing gospel."

This letter may look a bit confused; perhaps it reflects something. I am quite well.
Love and two kisses.

It was at the same hotel in Carentan that I also had my first and most shocking experience with the French urinoir. I went into the courtyard and found a blue sign with white letters: URINOIR. A white arrow under the sign was pointing left, so I looked to the left, but saw only three filthy, almost featherless, bad-smelling ducks that were wasting their lives on a cement floor. There was a small drain hole in the middle of the courtyard, but that was too exposed to be a urinoir. I decided to go to my room and look out of the window, and wait for someone to set a precedent for me. Before long the hotel owner came out of the house, and to my surprise and embarrassment, he headed straight for that small hole. Meanwhile, people in the windows of the surrounding four-story houses were looking down from all four sides. One woman was hanging up her laundry, the hotel cook was getting food out of the cooler, the maid was scrubbing the cement floor, and to top things off, the old man, while relieving himself, called over his shoulder to another maid, Marie, and told her to fetch two buckets of water from the pump. All this was done in a very matter-of-fact fashion. Any embarrassment was all mine, but many American soldiers who considered themselves very broad-minded also had considerable problems with this kind of French openness.

In Carentan I saw my first French Gothic church. It had been started in the twelfth century, when approximately five hundred churches and cathedrals were built in France. Some of them were finished in the eighteenth. The exterior was unique. It had a tower similar to the older of the two towers at Chartres. The flèche (spire) was perforated with small rosettes. There were other unplanned holes, slightly larger and not as beautiful, made by artillery shells. The Germans had the nerve to place a sniper up there, and our troops were forced to fire in return. The gargoyles and other monsters protruding from the oddest places were weather-beaten. There were a few other sculptures that had also been worn down by wind, rain, and time.

Inside, a service was going on. Women dressed in black were kneeling on the prayer chairs and the priest was speeding through the prayer book. Every now and then his sing-song voice was interrupted by the women who injected an "Amen" or "Gloria," or other similar words or phrases. They sang beautiful old chants written in the modal scale, and everything went smoothly, as it had for centuries. The odor of incense permeated the air. The place definitely had an atmosphere all its own: the colored windows in the background, the beautiful sacramental wares and receptacles, the embroidered gowns of the priest, the curé, the altar boys, and the sacristaire (a glorified janitor, known as the Keeper of the Sacraments), the dark and sorrowful colors of the women, the nuns, and the little girl sent to church by her mother. In the midst of war, it all still went on—the singing, the prayer, the Amens, the changing of the priest's garments, the hollow faces. I thought of T.S. Eliot: "We are the hollow men, we are the stuffed men..."

Suddenly it was over. Most of the women left. Some lingered on in prayer, but even they soon departed. Now I could approach the sacristaire who was busy putting back all the garments, the containers, the tablets, etc.

into their proper places. He looked interesting, about twenty-four years old. His hair, with the help of a strong dose of grease, was combed back, giving the impression that he was soft and gentle. A black formal suit hung about him loosely and sloppily. He must have inherited this formerly fashionable suit from a much larger predecessor. After dishing out two scanty bits of information concerning the church, he immediately got down to business. "We once had an American soldier here who promised me a lot of cigarettes, but he never returned. Being tied down to this church all day, I never have a chance to pick up what's thrown overboard from the passing American trucks."

Fortunately, I had by this time found it always paid to carry along some cigarettes even though I did not smoke, so I was able to give a pack to the sacristaire and immediately I belonged. However, he still volunteered very little information, so I decided to take a tour by myself. I was getting tired of talking to him about snipers, bombardment, trucks, candy, cigarettes, and all the usual topics of war life.

Finally, I had the whole church to myself, and was able to recognize the conflicting architectural features in the interior: the simplicity, power, and quiet striving of the pure Gothic style, the drama and affectation of the stage setting, and the lightness of the Baroque and eighteenth century influence.

In the Gothic style, the columns, the pointed arch, and the crossed vault were harmonious and beautiful, and they fulfilled the function of uplifting the onlooker. Unfortunately most of the colored windows had been shattered by the war, but several remained in the apse and, with their deep blues and reds, those were particularly beautiful. On the north end of the nave's west side was an old picture of Peter receiving the keys to the kingdom from Jesus. It was more beautiful than all the other pictures in the church. It was a wooden panel from an old altar and must have dated back at least to the thirteenth or fourteenth century, for there was hardly any third dimension or perspective, and the human figures lacked a certain amount of proportion. The faces very bravely gave away the characters of the Apostles: one spying Peter with envy, another regarding Jesus, one lowering his eyes in embarrassment, and another looking quite businesslike about it all. The subtlety of the picture lay in its simplicity. Along the side were several chapels dedicated to various saints. Each had a money box within easy reach of the worshipper.

In the baroque aspects of the church, the chancel, the high altar, and some of the saints statues had been added later, especially during the eighteenth century. To me, of course, they were out of place stylistically. The high altar in the middle of the central nave particularly spoiled the atmosphere. The fluted columns were twisting their way upward like four corkscrews. Only a twisted mind could produce such a twisted column, I said to myself. Unlike the clustered columns, these stopped suddenly, halfway up, supporting nothing but an involved ornament or a fancy spiral.

Finally I sat down at the organ. The first notes I played were much too loud and startled me. Slowly, as I gained more confidence, the notes became more intimate, more harmonious, not just self-conscious individual noises. As I played an old Bach chorale, I forgot the wickedness of man. The past was forgiven, the present seemed real, and the future looked bright. A spiritual experience? A religious experience? It was something special. I left the church through a small side door where the village beggar was waiting for me with: "Got any fags?" "No." "Are you sure?" "Yes, I don't smoke." "Will you bring me some tomorrow?" Unlike the sacristaire, the secular beggar could approach me directly.

One morning a Frenchman came up to our head-quarters and offered us his civilian car, which he said was stored in a garage just outside of town. He was unable to get gas for it. His idea of "just out of town" turned out to be a fifteen kilometer drive past enemy heavy artillery positions, through shell holes, past machine gun positions, and over a hill that exposed us to enemy observation. We did not know about all that, of course. When we got to the village, which was very badly damaged, we found that the man's car, which he was offering us, had been intentionally wrecked by the Germans, and his house had been destroyed by artillery fire.

On our return from the village to our base, we were suddenly challenged by American soldiers. They jumped out of the ditches, planted their bayonets, and told us to raise our hands. They marched us to the command post, where we were informed that we had just returned from a village where intense fighting was still going on. They could not figure out how we had driven through the frontlines with two civilians, no passes, and no password. Later we found out that the Americans must have been changing guards when we passed by unnoticed on the way to the village.

Our next move was to St. Jean de Daye, where we stayed seven days. While staying there, we were able to drive all over Normandy, from Cherbourg to Bayeux, from Isigny to St. Lo, searching out Allied soldiers who were lost. The roads were dusty and neglected; many of the shell holes had not yet been filled. All vegetation had the same color, the color of dust. The civilians were glad to see us, and yet they could not quite forget that the Americans had done their share of the destruction. St. Lo was hit worst. We saw it just after it had been taken. Once a beautiful small town, it was now a pile of rubble. As we approached St. Lo, we encountered the most horrible stench rising from dead horses and cows, which were lying on both sides of the road. Their legs were sticking up into the air, their bodies bloated, and their innards hanging out. Next to them lay dead German soldiers covered with either a shelter half (small tent) or an overcoat. Every now and then we saw a large German gun pointing our way, but fortunately they were all deserted.

St. Lo lay in an agony of twisted, silent ruins. Not a single house had been left untouched. In most cases only a wall was standing. If it was made from dust, to dust it had been ground again, not by God, but by man. From the smallest rubble down by the river to the church high on the rock, we could see the devastating effects of the whip of war. Here man once created; and here much was destroyed: he, his children, his cattle, and his hearth. That's why there was nobody to ask for "cigarettes pour papa." People had fled from the battle into caves, under houses, into shelters, or down the road. And many were crushed under the big wave of war—two thousand of them in this town alone! Out of the stench of dead flesh, the column of vehicles, and the clouds of dust, rose the ruins, as if there were a sha-dow over all. Walls were without windows. Everything was hollow. Bits of chairs, curtains, mirrors, and stairways were strewn about.

High up on the rock, man had built a beautiful temple. We could not imagine that the terrible wave of war would reach the summit of that rock. However, one splash had been enough to deface the beauty, break the graceful lines, damage the spire, shatter the windows once full of color, cave in the roof, and stain the altar. And that was "the rock upon which..." Perhaps it was necessary, perhaps a coincidence. Down in the valley the war passed on: trucks with men and equipment going in one direction, refugees with their bare possessions in the other. Nobody seemed to talk about his plight, everybody was intently going somewhere. And yet, I wondered whether all these refugees were not going to be disappointed once they got wherever they were going. News of St. Lo soon disappeared from the headlines.

Our next move was to Villedieu des Poêles, a charming small town which had not been ravaged by the war. Since we were the first Americans there, we got quite an enthusiastic welcome—our first big one in France. Again this was the welcome that belonged to the infantry that had climbed the beaches of Normandy. The owner of the hotel dragged out an ancient gramophone and played the "Marseillaise", the French national anthem, while people were shouting, "Vive l' Amerique! Vive l' Amerique!" In Villedieu we were besieged by the deprived French. "Avez vous du chewing gum?" "Vous n'avez pas une cigarette?" We had not yet reached that part of France where the Resistance movement could enlist the support of the population as a whole. This section was very Catholic and much too conservative politically for extensive underground activities to be found. People were openly for Pétain, the French president who had been a hero in WWI, but was now the head of the

Vichy regime (the puppet government of the Nazis) because he was a good Catholic and because they felt politically he could not have done other than he did. One of the girls even gave me a pin with the Vichy insignia on it as a souvenir.

In Villedieu I had my first date with a French girl. She worked for the French Red Cross and was studying to be a nurse. She was very intelligent and courageous and a charming person with great ideals for service, and yet, in a secret corner of her heart, she hated people who did not have any physical handicaps. As a child she had had infantile paralysis, which made her right leg twice as big as the other. Of course, she limped, and she was often sneered at, usually behind her back, by the other girls of her age. In fact, people turned around when they saw us walk through the streets together. That is why she wanted to be a nurse, and why she told me that, "if I do not get married by the time I am thirty years old, I will take care of lepers on an isolated French Island." This was almost an ultimatum, as if there were no other choice. And she added with bitterness that, "In this profession one usually dies of leprosy." She spoke of wanting to serve the world and suggested there were other ways of doing so besides becoming a part of the church. In spite of her bitterness, she was a lovely person, and I truly enjoyed being with her until she decided that she wanted to marry me. (There had been no romance.) Her sad letters followed me for some time, and I did feel sorry to add to her disappointments in life.

She was like many very intelligent girls in France who, for some reason, had been frustrated physically, financially, or socially because they were women. They felt that in order to be themselves, they had to go to

Africa and teach birth control to Arab women, to a lone island and care for the lepers, or to French Indochina and better the living conditions of the natives. The women that I met in France did not see much hope for an emancipated life.

One night at 11:30, a few German planes came over and dropped seventeen flares. In the distance we could hear the weak sputtering of our anti-aircraft guns. The flares floated down gently through a veil of mist. They were giving a clear outline of the gables, roofs, and towers of the dormant medieval town. The irregular humming of the planes soon died out. No explosions followed, and everything was quiet except for the bell on the church tower, which rang out the midnight hour.

I took a trip back to Carentan when it had become the rear echelon as most of the Americans had moved on. As so often happened later on in our drive through France, the enthusiasm of the French for the liberating army died down in a short time. The first day we arrived, we were given a royal reception by cheering crowds with music, flowers, and wine. A few days later, the wine would still flow, but the civilians expected something in exchange for it. Still later, little children would approach us and ask for things directly, and the girls would wave and smile with the hope of getting a fruit bar or K-ration cigarettes. After that, people would turn away disappointed if the GI did not feel like giving away anything at all. I never saw the final stage in which, according to rumor, girls who had dated German soldiers would have their hair completely shorn by the French after the Allies arrived.

When I arrived in Carentan, I went to our former

hotel and found, to my surprise, thirty very pretty American Red Cross girls. I had not seen an American girl for such a long time that I thought them a somewhat slaphappy, carefree, and noisy bunch. Seeing thirty American girls in one room all talking at the same time, many of them with broad and noisy Southern accents, is quite an experience after being in war-torn France.

Soon we hit the road again. On the way to Paris, the enthusiasm of the French for their liberators mounted steadily. The first people we had met in Normandy had suffered under the American bombardment and were more cautious with us. And, they are known to be more reserved than the French in other provinces. From this time on we met many partisan groups. We heard for the first time about people who had fallen into Gestapo hands, or about the Nazi torture chambers. The advance of the U.S. Army was so rapid that on our next stop in Laval we stayed only two days. There was no reason for us to stay in territory that had been liberated. Off we went to LeMans. The highway was littered with huge amounts of abandoned German equipment: guns, tanks, trucks, stolen civilian cars, horse wagons, and even some pushcarts.

Before entering LeMans I wrote my mother:

Dear Mom,

Almost two weeks have passed, and I have not written one word. It would be silly of you to worry over much newsless times. But you may believe me—I simply have not had the time. Today I had a lot of mail: one French military dictionary from Maemmschen [Al's mother in Oxford], nice stationery from a girlfriend in England, several letters and last, but not least, two letters from you. Also got Dick's ser-

mon with a newsletter. Congratulations to the D.D. The new church program for the kiddies sounds good. The church has always needed a good youth director. I was interested to hear that Chris is changing from medicine to something else. I finally received your ballot. (Could you send me the Republican and the Demo booklets?) Also you might let me know as to what you think in general, or whom the rest of our crowd favors (ask Dick and Warry). You know yourself that I'm leaning more and more to one side (the left).

You won't believe it, but the other day I went kayaking for the first time in eight years. What fun. A charming little river that winds itself through pastures, ancient villages, over sluices, etc. Naturally I couldn't help diving into the cool waters. And it's been two years since I have taken a swim.

My French is at times fairly good. It's fun to burst out in machine gun fashion in a language that has as yet not reflected my natural emotions. Yet I've been taken for a Frenchman many times. I even dream in French (after only six weeks on the Continent).

Well, that's all the little gossip for today. Be good and take a big kiss.
Tom

The reception in LeMans was really quite cheerful. We arrived there with the first troops, who always get the full blast of exuberance and gratitude. People were eagerly inviting us to have a drink of wine with them. Big welcome signs, which had been hidden from the Germans, were stretched across the streets. The French, English and American flags could be seen everywhere. A few people had even dared to put out the Russian flag. The rumor was that even the whorehouses allowed the

GIs free entry. It was not until Le Mans that I took my first bath on the Continent. I think they are still trying to clean that tub!

In LeMans I had my first opportunity to see the famous French Gothic. I spent several hours looking at the inside of the cathedral. How detailed the work, and yet how simple the construction; how huge the edifice, and yet how intimate the feeling it aroused. The three naves dated back to the twelfth century; the transept and the apse were of a more recent date. Most of the colored windows had been stored away for safekeeping. One of the priests told me that the colors in the fenestration on the three sides of the cathedral (two naves and one apse) varied in shade and intensity according to the three times of day (morning, noon, and afternoon). It was the simplicity in construction of this cathedral that struck me most. The interior was not as richly decorated with pictures, stone carvings, flags, side chapels, etc. as, for instance, the cathedral of Chartres or the Notre Dame de Paris.

Next day, a British paratroops captain and I visited a chateau near St. Calais. The conflict between the Catholic and Protestant churches of France once centered here. Alfred Musset lived and wrote in that castle. As we approached the front entrance we saw the owner, his family, and some relatives having their five o'clock tea on the front porch. What a picture! One old man was in a wheel chair, another had so many nervous twitches that he could hardly hold on to his cup of tea. The ladies were holding their cups (it looked like some eighteenth century set) in the most graceful manner; their small fingers were gingerly suspended in mid-air so they could display a precious ring or two. Their dresses were made out of what looked like very expensive material, bordered by very fine lace, yet the styles of the dresses were about one generation out of date. Suddenly a big door leading out to the porch was opened in grand style, and a servant paraded down the steps. On a silver platter he carried some green apples, which he formally offered to each one of the obviously worthy people present. There were many servants who were surprised and quite flattered when I walked over and talked with them. This put me into a lower category of people in the eyes of the noble creatures who were sipping their tea. The only thing I could think of at the moment was, "Workers of the world unite, you have nothing to lose but your chains," the cry of the Communist movement. The inside of the mansion, which we could see through the open door, was a conglomeration of junk dating from the seventeenth century to the Victorian age. There was something very tragic in seeing these people desperately trying to hold on to their former prestige ... to their past.

Our next stop was Chartres. We found that the town had not yet been taken by the Allies. The shutters of every house were closed tightly. Every now and then the civilians would open their doors a fraction of an inch to see whether the Germans had left yet. Mortar shells were falling all over the place. Every corner we turned, we got a German reception with a nine mm gun shooting from a distance or some unseen place. Since we were not combat troops and without decent weapons, we had no way of protecting ourselves, and we felt the boys in the tanks and half-tracks could do a much better job without our help. So, we decided to return to Chartres the next day. And what a change there was then. The population of Chartres seemed to have gathered in full

strength in the mar-
ket place. They were
out with flags and in
their Sunday dress-
es. They crowded
around our jeeps
and made us drink
one glass of wine
after the other.
When I had just
finished my eighth
glass, we got orders
to move on. So on

JEAN & RENE

we went until we got to Jouye, a small village seven kilometers outside of Chartres.

In Jouye we got about the most sincere reception we
could have expected anywhere in France. Again, as we
were the first Americans there, we received the full
intensity of the gratitude meant for American liberators.
People came running out of their houses with flowers,
cakes, and all kinds of wines and liqueurs. Women and
children wanted to be hugged and kissed by an
American. Again we had to drink the ever-present glass
of wine. I did not dare to move out of my jeep. I was
afraid of not ending up where I wanted to go. That
evening we had a big reception dinner given in our
honor at the schoolhouse. Again more wine. Yet I managed to navigate. That night we were told that the
Germans were still in strength in the woods a few hundred yards away from the village. Some "brass" thought
we should pull guard all night, so two of us guarded the
bridge with boxes of plastic anti-tank grenades and
Tommy guns. The family that lived next to the bridge

CHARTRES CATHEDRAL

supplied us with drinks and all kinds of delicacies. They were refugees from Paris—Jean, René, and the two babies—and we became good friends for many years. There were no other U.S. troops in the vicinity and we were sure that the Germans would never show up, and they never did. For three days I stayed with Jean and René. We went riding in a folding boat, we took pictures, we laughed, and we swam. We even went fishing with our bare hands. Apparently some GI had thrown a few hand grenades into the river; the fish were just floating there.

One afternoon we took a bicycle ride to Chartres to see the famous cathedral. If I had gone on a pilgrimage in Europe, this would have been the goal, for I had read Henry Adams's books, *Mont Saint Michel and Chartres*, had seen many photographs, and had heard much about this most perfect example of Gothic architecture. But I had hoped for too much. Mars had cast his shadow over Chartres. All the portals of the cathedral had been covered up with sandbags. The precious colored windows had been stored in a safer place. The inside was neglected. Huge, ugly scaffolds destroyed the graceful upward movement of the Gothic arch. The high altar was entirely removed, and a piece of baroque interior decoration cluttered up by wooden angels, flowers, and twisted columns produced a theatrical effect. Yet in spite of these drawbacks, there were many features that were certainly outstanding in their architectural beauty. The first thing that struck me were the perfect proportions of the right tower. I was thinking of what my professor at Reed once said about the Greek Doric column, namely, that this particular form cannot be improved. The more recently built tower on the left, although its stone carving and ornamentation were much more elaborate, did not give me the same feeling of simplicity, peace, and perfection. The flying buttresses looked graceful and full of life, and one could hardly believe that they were counterbalancing the tremendous thrust that was exerted on them from the pointed-arch vault. The inside was a big disappointment, particularly since all the colored windows, including the frontal rose window, had been removed. The windows were intricate and interesting as designs, but they looked dead, cold, and impersonal without any colors. In one of the side naves was a large counter where one could have one's sins forgiven for a certain amount of money. I thought Jesus would have driven these moneychangers out of the temple. As I was looking at the history of Jesus' life done very delicately in stone relief along the passage in the apse, which surrounds the high altar, two GI nurses and their officer boyfriends came whizzing by, mentioning casually the beautiful stone carving, while a minute later they were talking about the French woman collaborator who was getting a haircut in the middle of the market place. On another day I visited the cathedral's basement, consisting of several chapels dedicated to various saints and a statue of the Miraculous Virgin—a mysterious place if I ever saw one. This underground cathedral was the oldest part of the church at Chartres. The age, the darkness, the flickering candles, and the mysterious and rich colors made us walk on tiptoes and talk in subdued voices.

Again we hit the road, this time for Rambouillet, which had just been entered by the first reconnaissance troops. We looked for the local partisan chief, and finally found him in the most unexpected locale. He lived on the far end of town in a beautiful area in a house that resembled a luxurious palace. There was a big swimming pool, stables, garages, greenhouses, buildings for the servants, beautiful flower beds, and all the things about which an ordinary mortal only dreams. It would take too long to describe the meals we had there. The owner and host was a big, husky chap. He wore brown riding boots and a brown riding uniform. His face looked as though it had been stolen from a Dick Tracy character. He had two pitch black eyes, one of which appeared bigger than the other and set further back (perhaps it was a birthmark). When he smiled or laughed, he shifted his mouth entirely to the right cheek, directly under that big black eye, producing a very weird image. He had married a 20-year-old who was much too beautiful, too fragile, and too romantic to be described, and who obviously was not very happy with her husband. Later on we heard more about this "nouveau riche." Ever since the beginning of the Nazi occupation, he had been very friendly with the Gestapo, and he had operated a huge black market, one of the biggest around Paris. He was said to have gotten most of his money through this illegal profession. About eight months before the invasion, he realized the German cause was lost, and he started using his Gestapo acquaintances for very extensive partisan activities. This was highly unusual. Of all the hundreds of FFI I met during the war, I never met any others who had played both sides as he had.

In Rambouillet I saw many newspaper reporters (including Ernest Hemingway), who were all waiting to get into Paris. The town of Rambouillet was taken, but we were told that the area around it might still be infested with Germans, so again

Yvette

we had to pull guard. This time the shift lasted all night, and the post was on one of the big roads leading into town. We were three British and two American soldiers, with a British captain in charge. At midnight it began to drizzle, and by two-thirty it was pouring cats and dogs. We were neither mentally nor physically prepared for such a wet stunt. We tried to crawl under the jeep, all five of us, but there was always at least one who got the wet end of the deal. Finally we decided to walk back toward town and seek shelter in the first open barn or garage. However, our search was to no avail. At three a.m. we decided to wake up a civilian, so we picked a house with an American flag in the garden. We knocked on the door, and when someone peeked out of an upstairs window, we told them that we were Americans (the poor people thought the Germans had returned) and that we wanted to sleep on their garage floor. A few minutes later, the front door opened and a very beautiful young girl in her negligee said with a thick French accent: "Pleese coam een." Her features were extremely fine. She had those famous French dark eyes, and her black hair was flowing down to her shoulders. For a minute we were all flabbergasted and tongue-tied. Soon her parents came down. That morning between three and four o'clock we were celebrating the fall of Rambouillet over some champagne, cookies, and peaches. As far as I know, the Germans never did come down that road. I returned several times to this house, paying a visit to Yvette, who was really quite a girl for her nineteen years. Besides being very beautiful, she was an accomplished painter and we spent quite some time talking about the French impressionists. She played Chopin for me on the piano. Her French was clear and concise; there was hardly a sentence where I did not have to interrupt her and ask the meaning of some two hundred franc words.

Chapter 6

•

June–October 1944

Our team tried to sneak into Paris from Rambouillet, but every time we thought we were getting somewhere, we were turned back, once by a German patrol armed to the teeth, and another time by forty-eight German tanks. Everybody was waiting to know, who was to have the honor of driving into Paris and thus be the official liberator. Finally, the biggest all-French Allied Division turned up–all 19,000 of them. They were all over the countryside. They moved a few kilometers and then stopped for hours. It seemed as though every time a French soldier came through his hometown, the whole division stopped for un coup (a glass of wine). In Rambouillet we saw one of their columns of half-tracks, tanks, and jeeps go by our hotel window five times within one hour. Perhaps they had fallen asleep during map reading courses, or they wanted to be sure they had taken advantage of all the wine available. One day we went to the French division command post and asked G-2 (intelligence) why the French were so slow and did not move on to Paris. The G-2 looked out the window and gave us this classic answer: "What god-awful weather in which to take Paris!"

Foul weather or not, we all had a great itch to get into Paris. According to the latest information, the Germans were still ruling the city with an iron hand. The curfew there lasted nearly twenty-four hours a day. It was suicide to walk in certain sectors of the town at any time. We left Rambouillet to spend the night at Gif, planning to sneak into Paris the next day. We arrived in Gif still unopposed by the Germans. The temptation to move on was too great, and so on we moved, disappointing a hotel owner who had hoped to have some customers at least for one night.

Liberating Paris

On to Paris—through the woods, over dirt roads, through the fields, and past truck gardens (small plots of land that had been planted with vegetables and flowers). Slowly the atmosphere began to change. Farmers were standing by the roadside passing out all kinds of fruit and vegetables to the dust-covered troops. Naturally we could never quite come to a halt, and I remember many a tomato exploding on my windshield, splashing over our uniforms, or apples hitting our faces at twenty miles per hour. Our jeep was soon covered with all kinds of flowers, and tomatoes, apples, and carrots were scattered over the floorboard. Suddenly, as we reached the top of a hill, we saw the Eiffel tower. Our hearts began to beat faster. There was the Mecca of our journey through France. We had forgotten about the rumor that the tower had been scrapped by the Germans for its steel. Soon we reached a big boulevard. The three traffic lanes were fully occupied. I have seldom seen such an assortment of vehicles, all speeding madly toward the city's heart, which was still held by the Germans. Jubilant crowds lined the road on both sides. After we had passed the city limits, there was just one narrow lane where one could speed through; the rest of the street was completely filled with overjoyed Parisians who cheered, applauded, and tried to shake hands with us. If we had stopped for a moment, we probably would not have been able to proceed another inch. Finally the crowd thinned out. We had reached the frontlines. FFI cars were racing through the streets at a terrific speed with all kinds of ancient and modern weapons sticking out of the windows. Every now and then we could hear the piercing sound of sniper fire or the sputtering of an automatic weapon. Someone was trying to climb up into the copula of the Dome des Invalides to get at a sniper. The French soldiers were constantly saluting their officers, while their officers commanded their men with great and dramatic gestures. Across the street a band played the "Marseillaise" in honor of DeGaulle's arrival in Paris.

Our destination was the far side of the river, where Lieutenant Woods had managed to reserve a fancy hotel. So we crossed the Seine River, passed burning buildings, saw wrecked vehicles that had been used as barricades by the FFI, went up the Champs-Elysées, and finally landed at the Hotel Reynolds near the Arc de Triomphe. This was a magnificent luxury hotel. Since we were with SHAEF (Supreme Headquarters of the Allied Expeditionary Force), directly under Eisenhower, we had certain prerogatives, even though we were not in a high echelon. I had a beautiful suite with a special entree, private bathroom, oodles of cupboard space, all sorts of direct and indirect lighting, private phone, and room service. That evening I was introduced to Genevieve, a

GENEVIEVE

Parisian blonde who was wearing a nurse's dress that had blood splattered all over it. She was sporting a Red Cross armband, and on her fancy hairdo she had balanced and anchored down an FFI cap. Of course, she was "all excuses" about her ferocious makeup. She told me that she had just come down from one of the roofs in the neighborhood where an FFI soldier had been shot in the arm by a Milice (member of the French fascist militia). With those words, she pulled a tiny .25 caliber pistol out of her pocket and said, "Thomas je crois que je viens de tuer un homme." (Thomas, I believe I just killed a man.) Apparently she had fired at a Milice soldier. All this sounded much too dramatic to be true. Anyway, we ordered some champagne, and celebrated the liberation of Paris, le coeur de la France. I never saw Genevieve again.

The following day the shooting was still going on. The FFI were armed to the teeth. People carried weapons, and the hot-blooded Parisians fired aimlessly at the slightest provocation. We were more afraid of the many stray bullets from our Parisian friends than we were of the few well-aimed bullets of the milice. That morning I had to go to St. Denis alone. Whenever and wherever I stopped to ask my way a big crowd gathered around me tout de suite. The girls wanted to be kissed by the first American they saw. The men asked me to step inside and have a drink with them. When finally I was able to ask the location of a certain street, four or five Frenchmen got into a heated discussion about the shortest way to get there, each trying to be more helpful than the last.

On one of those stops, I had an interesting experience. My face was already covered with lipstick and powder. People were thanking me personally for the liberation of Paris. They asked where I was from, and then they were very interested in Oregon, though most had never heard of it. Suddenly I noticed a commotion about 100 yards down the street. One of the women next to me said, "Look Mr. American, we've got something to show you; we brought this especially for you." She had hardly finished her sentence when the crowd opened up, and a narrow lane about thirty yards long was leading directly to my jeep. At the far end of this lane were three armed, ultra-patriotic FFI men with their typical berets, extinguished cigarettes butts dangling from their mouths, shoddy and sloppy suits, and worn-out shoes. If they had not been sporting the FFI armband, they could have been mistaken for robbers. In front of them they were kicking and pushing a rugged-looking individual whose sex I could not make out until she was within five feet of me. This lady had really been worked over by the French. She was about thirty-five years old, fairly heavy, and of medium stature. Her black eyes were full of fury and "the devil," according to the crowd. Her whole body was quivering with rage. Her head was completely shorn, and on her forehead someone had painted an inverted swastika with iodine. Apparently this woman had slept with Germans. I was expected to make an amusing remark, but I simply could not. In fact, I lowered my head in embarrassment and blushed. When they had taken away the "treacherous" woman, I decided I had to make some comment to let my position be known. So I asked them, "Will a French girl who sleeps with an American soldier receive a similar treatment?"

"Mais c'est tout à fait différent," they quickly retorted. (That's a horse of a different color.) I continued in flawless French that amazed even me, "What can you do now to help France and her people?"

On the way back I ran into trouble. As I was driving through the busy streets, I suddenly heard the ringing shot of a rifle. The crowds all dispersed within a few seconds, all seeking refuge in some entrance. A minute later the shooting really began. I was walled in on both sides and could go no place with my jeep. There wasn't a tree, ditch, or driveway that could give me protection. Police were running through the streets waving their pistols. The Parisians were far too trigger-happy for me. Two of the shots came dangerously close to my jeep, and a woman stuck her head out of doorway yelling, "Save yourself, Yankee!" I began to feel very uneasy. Though I managed to get my jeep moving, whatever street I turned on to, the shooting seemed to be worse. I found myself driving around in circles. In my despair I finally ordered a Frenchman to climb into the jeep and asked him to direct me to the Arc de Triomphe. Rifles and pistols were still popping off all over the place. To make myself as difficult a target as possible, I forcefully stepped on the accelerator, and in three minutes we arrived at the hotel where my team was waiting with Tommy guns, pistols, and carbines.

Before long, due partially to an acute food shortage, the enthusiasm of the recently liberated town calmed down. The American soldiers gave away their own supplies or traded them for French souvenirs, but this was not enough to feed or clothe the Parisians or to keep their automobiles going. Soon after liberation, prices soared again, and the black market flourished as never

before. The first bottle of
champagne I bought in
Paris cost me 165 F
($3.10); the last one 750 F
($15.00). Yet, if one spoke
French, one could manage
to have a reasonably good
time without laying out
large sums of money.

I was invited to many
parties, went sightseeing,
and some of my new well-
to-do friends invited me

COLETTE

to nightclubs and black market restaurants. These parties
consisted mostly of young people who thoroughly
enjoyed their new freedom. Some of them were Jewish
and had been hiding from the Nazis for four years. One
young Jewish girl, Colette, had been hiding from the
Nazis all during the war. Some had not wanted to do
forced labor in Germany, and some had been in the
Maquis (the French underground). Others had returned
to their beloved city with the French forces from Africa,
or they had just been liberated from a Nazi prison or
concentration camp.

One evening we were on the seventh floor of a modern apartment house, dancing, drinking, singing, laughing, and having a hilarious time, when suddenly, around
one o'clock, a French policeman showed up at the door.
The neighbors had been complaining about the noise,
and now he was going to take down our names. We
invited him to have a drink, which he accepted gladly.
And when an American soldier offered him a cigarette,
he said, "Oh, you are an American! I didn't know there

were any Yanks up here." He quickly gave up his original plan to administer some kind of punishment, and we gently ushered him out the door after promising that we would be good children.

In September 1944, I wrote to my mother:

I haven't written for a long time. And I hope you won't ever worry. There simply isn't any time. One can see now that the war is coming to a close in Europe. Before long, we'll be on German soil. I don't quite understand why the Germans are holding on as they do. They must have a terrific fear drilled into them.

Physically I am well and busy. Mentally I've become lazy like any other soldier, and that is a terrible feeling. I hope I will recuperate from that after the war. I took a lot of pictures recently. As soon as I have a chance to have them developed, I shall send you some snapshots.

I hope you are not angry with me for writing such a poor note. C'est la guerre. Please say hello for me to the rest of the family and take a kiss.
Tom

We often stood on a corner of Champs-Elysées and watched the girls pass by on their bicycles. But the sightseeing in Paris included more than just reviews of the opposite sex. Of the many buildings and monuments, I especially remember visiting one: the Notre Dame de Paris. It was a beautiful Sunday morning. A few white clouds were drifting casually across the deep blue sky. The Parisians had put on their Sunday's best, and most people seemed to be in a happy mood. I went with Simone, a frail, medium-sized girl, who had recently spent two years in a German concentration camp, which had left a deep mark on her. She was nervous, tense, and disillusioned, but that was only because, in her words, she "had not gained the moral strength to set herself a new goal." She despised all institutionalized religion, and she had never tried to find spirituality outside of the church. This morning we were going to try to get as much as possible out of our visit to Notre Dame.

My first impression was: What a beautiful church! The delicate spire rose out of a maze of flying buttresses of numerous, monstrous gargoyles. There were five portals and thus five naves. Each portal was richly ornamented with a relief sculpture of biblical history: apostles, saints, angels, kings, patrons, etc. Inside, nuns were selling trinkets, tourists were moving through the aisles, worshippers were saying their prayers, and the constant humming of hushed voices could be heard everywhere. We tried to ignore all this commotion. I was amazed to see how a physical structure could uplift my spirit. One architectural feature was pointing to another, higher one. It was wrong to look all the way up to the keystone of the arched vault, for then the height appeared purely a physical one. So my eyes stopped about three-quarters of the way up in order to attain the right feeling. I was reminded of Goethe's "constant striving," or of Wordsworth: "How sweet it is with uplifted eyes to pace the ground, if path there be or none, while a fair region around the traveler lies which he forbears to look upon; pleased rather with some soft ideal scene, the work of fancy or some happy tone of meditation, slipping in between the beauty coming and the beauty gone...."

This upward sweep was being accentuated, if not realized, by the various tiers. At first there was a heavy, simple, restful, and yet upward-pointing Gothic arch, and then the eye came to rest on the galleries. The arch in this tier was of a later Gothic than the first. It was lighter, more ornamental, with a slight Byzantine touch. Then I noticed a rose window with a delicate and intricate stone design. Clustered columns with tender and pure lines were rising through these tiers. Finally I saw the fenestration, with deep and pure colors, which were being struck by the rays of the sun. Passing clouds now and then hid the sun. As the light struck the windows with differing intensity, the colors came alive; they changed, they moved. And it seemed as though the saints, the patrons, the animals, and the plants pictured on these panes were coming to life. By this time I felt the upward striving of the pure Gothic arch had been transferred directly into my heart. And as I closed my eyes, a trumpet began to sound—a real trumpet. It seemed as though the angels were announcing the coming of a king. As the last note died in its echo, the organ began to play gently, first with one voice, a flute, then another, sounding more dramatic. Soon there were five or six voices, and finally, the big bass of the foot pedals joined in. By now the music had become very powerful. I could not hear the distinct harmony anymore. The sound reached every corner of the huge cathedral; certainly it filled all of me, and at last this earthly music became almost "*too much, too terrible, too strong for our weaker existence ...*" (— R.M. Rilke)

Then came the downfall! As I was experiencing all this, and was nearly transported into another state of consciousness, Simone suddenly pulled my sleeve. I opened my eyes and noticed a nun holding a money bag in front of my nose. I took out my purse and had my soul saved for ten francs...and lost whatever spiritual awareness I had almost attained. And I lost much more permanently. I was deeply shaken by the schism between the beauty and hopefulness of the church and the reality of the material world.

Paris night life was restricted to a large extent because of the material shortages. Yet even at first, a few nightclubs were open, and they were packed. The Boef sur le Toit featured a good orchestra, an overcrowded dance floor, champagne at fifteen dollars per bottle, and the French za aou, which corresponds roughly to the American zoot-suiter. The girl wears a dress with a low-cut bodice, the hem of the skirt reaching down almost to her knees, her hair hangs down to her shoulders in wild disorder, and she can be seen passionately accentuating the syncopation of a modern dance rhythm in the middle of the dance floor. We also had some excellent black market meals in Montmartre (the Greenwich Village of Paris) at twenty dollars a plate. When we entered a harmless-looking bar there, my friend winked at the barkeeper, who nodded knowingly. He then led us through a small door into a back room where everything was prepared for a possible police raid because of the club's heavy black market activity.

A few days after the liberation of Paris, a WAC major and her detachment decided they needed our hotel. It was far too rich for our status or our needs anyway. Many big units connected with headquarters were arriving, and it was time for us to move out. Our next stop was to be in the British sector. Brussels had not yet been liberated, so there would be many allied soldiers waiting to be brought out.

Liberating Brussels

Our team moved on to Brussels, Belgium, but we were stopped at Mons a few hours before we got there because the Germans were blocking all the main highways leading into the city. The next morning we decided to go on anyway—do or die. This was land between the lines, which were constantly ever changing. Officially it was British-held territory, but the Germans were still on the roads, and we drove with our hands on our guns fearful at any moment that we would be ambushed. Just before arriving in Hal, on the outskirts of Brussels, we passed three huge mounds of dead German soldiers piled ten feet high. It looked as though they had been thrown there by a dump truck, with stiff legs and arms showing up against the sky, and bluish-white faces, dismembered bodies, and bloody and torn pieces of uniform. The stench was so horrible that I could scarcely bear it. German prisoners of war were burying their comrades. For some time I was overcome by the enormity of all this, the insanity and the horror. This was the enemy, and it was our job as soldiers to destroy them, but all I could see before me were their wives, children, parents, brothers and sisters, aunts and uncles, and friends who were going to be crying for and mourning these dead. I paused a while and pondered, Could I have been among them? If it had not been for the meeting of my mother and stepfather, would I be in a German uniform in just such a pile?

We happened to arrive in the center of Brussels, at the Place de Broukère, just as it was being liberated by the British. Therefore, inadvertently, we became part of the tremendous excitement in the city, and received the reception meant for the Allied liberators. This time, instead of being kissed by young girls, we were surrounded by a huge crowd of autograph hunters who were waving their papers and pencils right in front of our faces. I felt like a famous movie actor or a crooner who was being accosted by bobby-soxers. Since we Americans were only a very small minority among all the British soldiers, we received special attention. The crowds had converged on the Place de Broukère, the center of town. All day long people danced around the big monument, and sang "Tipperary" in English, and they asked for our shoulder patches. When I asked a policeman for directions to a certain street, he not only offered to take me there himself, but also invited me to his home for lunch. I was somewhat surprised, and for a minute I did not know whether or not I should accept. Finally, after hesitating for a few moments, I told him that I would be delighted to come if his wife would not berate him for bringing a luncheon guest on such short notice. We climbed onto a streetcar which took us into the very heart of the working class district. We entered a dead-end street and climbed up a few stairs in an old apartment house. Lunch was ready to be served, but when the Madame heard there was going to be a Yankee guest, she got out her meat ration for that week, dug into her reserves, and gave me half a cake that had been baked for the coming Sunday dinner. To finish off in grand style, she served me a cup of real coffee, which was a rarity anywhere on the Continent. After lunch, I had to accept all sorts of trinkets and souvenirs. By now this warm enthusiasm and generosity had reached a point of embarrassment for me. I had seldom had a more sincere and touching reception anywhere. (Some 20 years later I visited Brussels at the Place de Broukère and looked around. Remembering my welcome of long ago, it seemed strange that nobody recognized me, or knew of the reception we had received that first day of the liberation!)

The Belgians had borne a big share of the Nazi oppression. Yet, their underground movement, the Armée Blanche, had been very effective and was better organized than the FFI (the French), and they were operating under much more adverse conditions than the French Maquis. We saw towns and villages that had been partially or wholly rebuilt after the destruction in World War I. This time the Germans had set fire to these buildings only two days before our arrival, and they were still burning. This was the second time in twenty-five years.

In Brussels, I saw my first American movie in five months. After leading such a serious and tense life, I was shocked to see the lightheartedness, the informality, and the casual treatment of sex. I had not seen anything as jovial and relaxing anywhere in Europe. Yet, my home-sickness had nothing to do with Miss Grable, the pin-up actress from Hollywood. What I saw on the screen did not represent the America for which I was longing—the forests, the mountains, the beaches of Oregon. Only a day or two there would have satisfied my greatest desire.

One of our headquarters had been established in the small town of Hal, outside of Brussels. Since Belgium was now liberated, most of our work connected with rescuing Allied soldiers there was finished, so we had some time off for ourselves. I decided to go on my usual "inspection" tour of the local churches, one of which served as a chapel for a Catholic monastery (or "monkery" as my buddies called it). I arrived there just in time for mass. After the service, the officiating priest gave me a very warm welcome, and he asked me to meet the other Fathers in the inner sanctum. I had mixed feelings because I really did not want to get involved in what I thought might be a difficult religious discussion, but I half-heartedly agreed. I had hardly consented when the Father unlocked the door, ushered me in, and very carefully locked the door behind us. This was a precautionary measure, he explained, for the part of the building we had just entered was definitely out of bounds for women.

I had a very interesting experience there. The monks were all liberal, young Dutchmen who were assigned to the monastery in Hal. They were willing to listen to anyone's point of view, although, of course, they were always prepared to explain their side of every question. Even though their native language was Dutch, we got along very well in French. Whenever we had to stop our conversation because no one knew the right word in French, we used a word of German, English, or Dutch. I had some very delightful discussions with these priests. We talked about the Marxian doctrine, about the powers of the papacy, about music, about fourteenth century church history (of which I considered myself an expert), about architecture, about the books that were on the Index (forbidden by the Catholic Church), and about many other topics. I was so impressed with them that I asked for and got permission from my officer to spend three days in the monastery where I was given my own cell—dedicated to St. Bernhard. The bed, which was not at all other-worldly, was already made when I arrived, and I slept between white sheets on a very comfortable mattress. For three days I played monk—went to their services, prayed with them, sang their old Latin chants, ate with them, drank "ersatz" beer with them, and walked together around the cloister, discussing philosophy and the world's woes and our solutions for them.

A young priest, Father Albert, became my special companion. He was a gentle, loving, and attentive man who did not like the Nazis and also did not like many of the edicts coming from the papacy. We walked around and around the cloister walks, talking about everything from the Avignonese papacy in the Middle Ages to the books on the Index and the Church's neglect of the Jews under the Nazis. We listened to each other, and this was a special experience for me after the strain and all the painful feelings I had experienced in the war. Father Albert and I became friends and we corresponded for some time after the war. The time I spent in the monastery reawakened my desire to become a minister.

Since our team's specific mission in Belgium to liberate Allied personnel had been accomplished, and since there were no longer Allied soldiers to be liberated, we were ordered to return to Paris. Before we left Brussels, we visited a Belgian partisan who had been our agent there, and he gave us an excellent dinner and some interesting souvenirs. I received false Belgian I.D. papers, a camera, and a bottle of cognac. When another soldier from our team and I climbed into the jeep, we made a solemn promise that the bottle of cognac was to be empty by the time we arrived in Paris. The weather was cold, and riding in an open jeep was no fun. We stopped every forty-five minutes to switch places, to fill up the jeep with gas, and to taste the cognac. When the jeep was finally traveling at the rate of 60 MPH (the official maximum speed for a jeep was 40 MPH), we were feeling extremely happy. We had only to keep pushing the accelerator against the floorboard; the engine provided the rest. When we arrived at the city limits of Paris, we had used up the last drop of cognac, as well as the last drop of gas.

October 31, 1944

Dear Mom,

If, after reading three letters in one evening one does not get a strong case of homesickness, one is not normal. Three days ago I received two month's worth of mail. I stayed up half of the night reading it. So, while you may have to wait a month going without any news, I have to wait longer and believe me, I suffer just as much if not more. All your letters were most delightful, particularly when they came from the heart. Your excuses about English are unjustified; or are you fishing? Anyway, I am sure that people no longer say about you "she makes the same mistakes with much more ease". Al did plenty of work in the transport of letters and packages, but I missed his letter in the bunch. What do I have to do to get into Dr. Levy's good graces? Chris's letter was enthusiastic, and was a sincere effort in trying to boost my spirits. More of that later. Jean's letter was as welcome as any of the others; it had on the face of it "To be read by Tom L. Frazier only, please"—a rather odd way of counter-censorship. The candy, honey cake, or what have you is always welcome in these backwoods. The New Republic arrived en masse. Thanks for the stationery, the envelopes arrived here slightly stuck together, and the erasers were a trifle too big.

Concerning the book by Van Paarse, it looks very interesting in spite of the fact that it deals with something that is somewhat out of the ordinary. I never read any of his books. Since when do you have to pay eight cents for an airmail letter? I am enclosing nine snapshots. It's all I could dig up.

I liked Chris's letter very much; a sincere effort. All the news about Reed College interested me tremendously; I hope he'll keep it up. Also Chris, would you give my very best regards to Mr. Chittick and to Mr. Arragon? I should like to know whether the pre-med has been dropped completely. Chris says that I have a wonderful and exciting time. Well, I have recently tried to make my letters as cheerful as possible, for there is no use to be sob-sisterish about this d--- war. Let me remind you, however, that this material life, this useless existence, makes one rot from within. It's not a pleasant feeling, and one never knows what one will and won't be able to do after the war is over.

Well, "Cheerio," as the English say.

Chapter 7

•

October-March 1945

Into the High Alps Behind the German Lines

We did not spend much time in Paris, which was probably just as well. There were too many GIs, including some WACs whose drinking and carousing were giving the U.S. Army a bad name. Our team was next assigned to the city of Grenoble in France on the Isère River, where there was a strong partisan presence. From Grenoble, our mission was to get into the villages and valleys of northern Italy, which were still held by the Germans. Scattered throughout this land (Piedmont) and behind enemy lines were a great many brave partisans who risked their lives daily to help in the liberation of their country from the Germans. They also managed to protect the Allied soldiers who had somehow gotten separated from their units, or had escaped from prison and made their way into northern Italy. We drove through Besançon (a very beautiful, fortified old town), Bourg, and Voiron, to Grenoble. On the way, we met the long motor columns of the French and American troops (the Third Army) who had just embarked into southern France.

We had to find a way to get into the valleys of northern Italy, where most of the men to be rescued were hiding. Grenoble is situated at the foot of the Alps, on the main thoroughfare leading to France's best winter sport resorts. The few highways that led from Grenoble over the high Alps into northern Italy were all blocked by the Germans; thus, somehow, we would have to get to the escapees and bring them out the hard way—scaling the high mountains. For this we would need special equipment.

In Grenoble we were given one or two pairs of skis from the stores of the U.S. 10th Mountain Division. We still needed special boots. A partisan who owned a shoe factory offered to custom-make some boots that could be used for skiing as well as for scaling the rocks or steep, snowy slopes. The boots were semi-flexible, with a groove in the heels for the steel bindings of the skis, and they had big hob nails to help us hold on to the slippery slopes when we were climbing. We also needed heavy jackets. The French had some very heavy, green waterproof material left over from some military use. They lined this with thick, white goat fur and made it into very heavy jackets for each of us. We sewed the American flag insignia on our left upper sleeve. We had fur-lined ski hats with ear protectors made from a shelter-half (tent material) and goat fur, and we each bought a huge Basque beret, ski mittens, and a pair of fur-lined mountain gloves. The French manufactured steel-frame mountain packs that fit around our thighs for support. We were indeed a sight—looking more like vagabonds than soldiers. (Fifty years later I still have much of this equipment.) What we needed next were two more vehicles to commute between Grenoble and

Val d'Isère—about four hours driving time. Uncle Sam had given the seven of us only two jeeps, one three-quarter ton weapons carrier, and a motorcycle. There was no way we could use the motorcycle in the high mountains, so we "requisitioned" two jeeps from the French (who were using U.S. equipment). Now we had a four-wheel drive vehicle for each one of us, so that we would have enough room for some rescued GIs.

Once we were fully equipped, we had to find some way of actually crossing the high Alps. At first we tried Briançon, which is the highest city in Europe (approximately 4,300 feet.) While we were driving up to Briançon, we passed some of the most beautiful scenery I have ever seen. We drove through beautiful valleys, passed over rushing torrents, went through many tunnels, saw numerous waterfalls and two big dams, and we took pictures of snow-covered mountains, glaciers, and overhanging cliffs. We passed through many picturesque mountain villages, and I could hardly believe I was seeing the gorgeous Alpine landscape that I had admired so often in books and on picture postcards.

Yet, as we drove up to Briançon, we also heard about and actually saw some ugly things. Our partisan agent pointed out several houses that had been pillaged and burnt by the Germans, who had suspected, but seldom seen, FFI activities in them. The Germans had killed innocent shepherds. In one village, they had cold-bloodedly murdered the father of ten children in front of his family. One grandfather (he must have been in his eighties) told me that one of these "salots" (bastards) had approached him one day to find out the time. The old man obliged, and so did the German—he took away the Frenchman's beautiful, old gold watch. In a village close

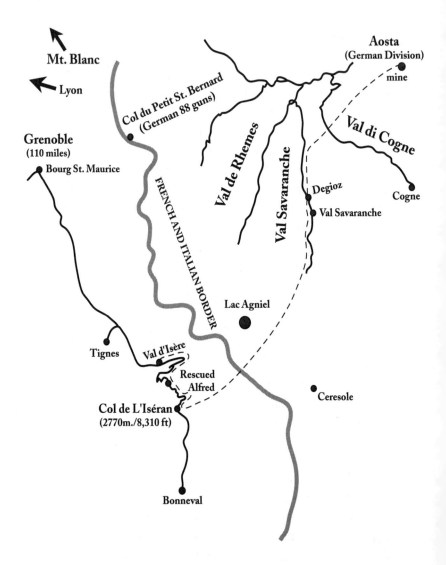

MAP OF PIEDMONT - FRANCE/ITALY

- - - - - - *Hiked and Climbed*
Val d'Isère to Val Savaranche (Degios) about 30 miles
Cogne to Aosta about 16 miles

RAY PELLETIER, TOM, DANTE (A PARTISAN LIEUTENANT)

to Briançon, the Germans cut off a woman's breasts. They also killed a pregnant woman and cut out her unborn baby with a bayonet. As Americans, we frequently found it very difficult to believe these things— even though the same story was told by many people again and again. We half-suspected that the French were telling us tall tales in order to get more attention and more cigarettes from us. Up until this time, I had believed that the atrocities said to have been committed by the Germans in Belgium during World War I had been grossly exaggerated by the British press. What we experienced later in the Alps, however, proved to us that the tales the French were telling us now were indeed true.

Briançon consisted of two parts: the new town in the valley, and the fortified, older part, high on a rock. The partisans and the French colonial soldiers from Africa were the only troops in Briançon.

The regular French army had an artillery unit there that consisted mostly of Moroccans. They seemed to us

STUCK IN SNOW

to come from another kind of civilization entirely. They wore part of their native uniforms, which included white and brown turbans; and when the weather was inclement they slung hooded cloaks over their shoulders. Most of their equipment was either American or antiquated French. We always tried to remain in their good graces. When they came too close, we either shooed them off politely, or got rid of them by passing out some cigarettes. We did not know them and were somewhat afraid of them.

Briançon came under shellfire from the Germans. We were established in the neighboring mountains. Every now and then, an 88 mm shell would come over,

BESSANS BURNT BUILDINGS
(SEE FRONT COVER)

and we were prepared to hit the dirt at any moment. Most of us remembered the 88's only too well from Normandy, and we knew that all of our lives were in jeopardy when those shells bombarded an area. That same day, we heard from experienced mountaineers and local partisans that it was impossible to cross the German lines at or near Briançon. Later, an Allied major and his men tried to get

LT. WOODS

through to Italy at Briançon, but they were taken prisoners within sight of the town. We decided to return to Grenoble.

We began to investigate the area around Val d'Isère for a possible route over the mountains. We drove from Grenoble through Moutiers, Bourg-Saint Maurice, and Tignes to Val d'Isère (Valley of the Isère River). In Val we received encouraging news about the possibility of crossing the mountains on foot, and we immediately requisitioned one of the big winter resort hotels. We would need it for our team and for the many partisans who had been enlisted to help us, as well as for the Allied soldiers whom we hoped to find and bring back. That same day we drove from Val d'Isère to Bonneval, where the last partisan outpost was located. Beyond that point, we were behind the German lines in German-controlled territory. In order to get to Bonneval we had to drive over the Col de l'Isèran, a pass finished in 1939 which is 2,770 meters (8,448 feet) high—the highest road in Europe. Just as we entered Bonneval, a rugged-

LT. WOODS & COL. DANIELS

looking Englishman was carried past us on a stretcher by some French and Italian partisans. He had been wounded during his activities with the Italian Maquis (the underground), and we heard later that he had to have one of his legs amputated just below the knee.

The partisans urged us to drive to Bessans, which was about five miles down the valley. "If you really want to know how the Germans operate, you go down there and find out for yourself," they said. We climbed into our vehicles, and ten minutes later we saw what they had been warning us about. Bessans had been almost completely burned down by the Germans. The black ruins with the ashes still smoldering made a frightful silhouette against the snow-covered mountains. The civilians were desperately digging in the ruins with their bare hands to try to retrieve some of their possessions. There was absolutely no military advantage in setting fire to Bessans. It was further evidence of the sadism of the frightened Nazis.

One time in Grenoble I came upon some partisans who were in shock because they had just witnessed the results of German torture of their friends. The German Gestapo Headquarters was in Lyon, which had just been taken over by the Americans. When the Gestapo fled, they left behind tortured partisans in their coffins. In some cases, women's breasts had been cut off, and some partisans had been made to bite on a pencil pointing toward their throat while facing a wall. They were then hit so that their necks were pierced. Two men were made to kneel on the ground with their hands tied behind their backs. Their feet were raised and held about ten inches from the ground by a rope that was thrown over a tree branch, then tied around the other man's neck. When one man could not hold his feet up any longer, he dropped them to the ground, thus choking the other man, who in turn let his feet drop, and hung the first man.

There were signs of other gruesome tortures, but for the most part, the partisans had remained silent, and little information had been given out. I took many pictures of the tortured partisans in their coffins. This was a turning point for me. I never felt the same about Germany again. At the same time, I remembered that this had been my country, which I had left only seven years before, and I wondered what my role would have been if I had remained.

We knew we would be spending the winter at Val d'Isère, in partisan territory in southeastern France high up in the Alps, provided that the road remained open to automobile traffic. Winter came early. The roads were crowded with herds of sheep and cattle being driven down to the warmer valleys, and everywhere we could hear the ringing of cow bells. The days were getting shorter and the nights colder. The peasants brought in their last wood for the winter, for they knew the coming winter would be a cold one. Most of the coal was reserved for the partisans, and all food was rationed.

The first snow had already fallen on the pass of

TWO MEN WERE MADE TO KNEEL ON THE GROUND WITH THEIR HANDS TIED BEHIND THEIR BACKS. THEIR FEET WERE RAISED AND HELD ABOUT TEN INCHES FROM THE GROUND BY A ROPE THAT WAS THROWN OVER A TREE BRANCH, THEN TIED AROUND THE OTHER MAN'S NECK. WHEN ONE MAN COULD NOT HOLD HIS FEET UP ANY LONGER, HE DROPPED THEM TO THE GROUND, THUS CHOKING THE OTHER MAN, WHO IN TURN LET HIS FEET DROP, AND HUNG THE FIRST MAN. (PHOTO SOURCE: UNKNOWN)

FRENCH PARTISANS TORTURED

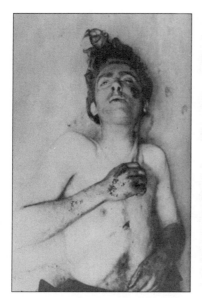

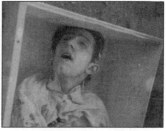
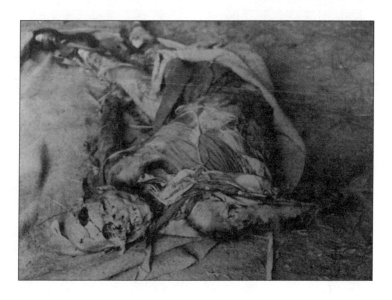

PHOTOS TAKEN BY TOM FRAZIER

FRENCH PARTISANS TORTURED: NONE TALKED

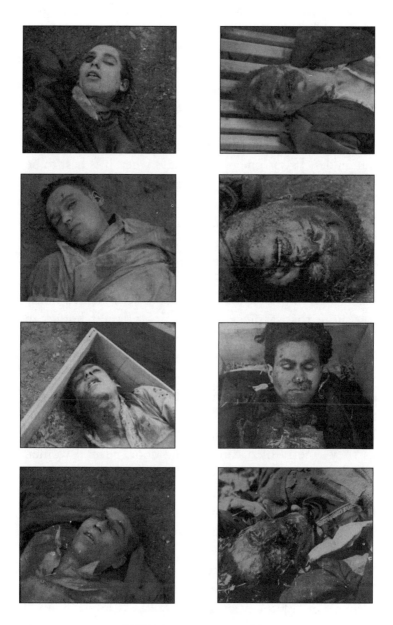

PHOTOS TAKEN BY TOM FRAZIER

Isèrans, and we knew that the road to Bonneval and Bessans would soon be closed for the duration of the winter season. We were responsible for the evacuation of the population of the sacked and burned Bessans village before winter set in, and some safe place had to be found for these refugees. They arrived in the valley late one afternoon in the middle of October. Wet snowflakes were blowing into our faces, and the slush came up to our ankles. It was one of those days when it is best to be standing near a warm fire drinking hot tea.

It was almost completely dark when two or three hundred of the refugees arrived. We saw their bent silhouettes walking slowly, step by step, through the puddles and the slush. Many of them were bowlegged (from inbreeding, it was said). Some were carrying small bundles containing their only possessions. Others had nothing more than a piece of the ruins of their homes in Bessans. They could stay only one or two nights in Val. The refugees from other villages were scheduled to arrive soon, and Val d'Isère did not have the facilities to absorb all of them. The Hotel du Dome was responsible for their food, while the other hotels offered cots and beds. I was at the hotel to meet the first of the refugees as they quietly filed through the door. Several women were over ninety years old, and one of them had never before left her native village. The men were proud but bitter. Some of the younger women were pregnant, others had small babies in their arms. One fellow had an epileptic seizure just as he was about to sit down at the table. A middle-aged woman knelt on the floor with her hands folded in prayer while being spoon-fed by her father. Few of them smiled or talked. Only the small children would cautiously approach the big Americans, grab of piece of the K-ration chocolate or hard candy that we offered them, and say "Merci Monsieur," then happily hurry back to their mother's apron. A week later most of these refugees had somehow been placed at temporary quarters away from the high mountain ranges.

The next day we had to return to Bonneval, which was really in "no man's land." We heard that fifty Russians had arrived there, and that they wanted to be evacuated by the Americans. Since we were the only Americans in the area, we were obliged to take care of them. They had been captured by the Germans on the Eastern front, and held in Germany where they had been treated cruelly. One day a German officer approached the ranking Russian officer, a colonel, and said, "If you and your men want to receive better food and lead a more comfortable life, you only have to consent to do some work for the German army." The Russians were ready to do anything in order to get away from their miserable living conditions, so they agreed to work. They were shipped to Italy, where they did menial tasks, such as guarding railroads and constructing roads, and they also fought against the French and Italian partisans. When the Italians capitulated to the Allies, these Russians decided to stop working for the Germans, and somehow found a way to escape. Many other Russians had not agreed to work for the Germans, but rather stuck it out in prison, in armament factories, or in concentration camps, and they naturally had some bad feelings toward those who had agreed to work for the Germans. The fifty Russians we were to deal with were in a peculiar situation. In addition to the animosity from the other Russians, they were not liked by the French and Italian partisans, even though they were now willing to fight alongside them. Naturally, they could not afford to return to the Germans, who were on the other side of the mountains, so they literally had no where to go and no group to join.

When we arrived to meet the Russians in Bonneval, they jumped up, clicked their heels, and stood at attention. They had some weapons and explosives with them, but nothing of interest to anyone looking for a souvenir—such as a Luger, for instance. I was put in charge of these men. It would be my job to get them to Val d'Isère, and from there to Bourg, or even Grenoble. My lieutenant promised that he would send up some buses from Grenoble.

These Russians became quite a problem for me. They did not know one word of English, and very little French. Finally I found out that the commanding officer spoke German, and thus communication was established. First, I had the Russians march all the way to Val (15-20 miles), while I went ahead by jeep in order to make arrangements for some transportation for them; but in Val, nobody was willing to cooperate. After considerable talking, and waking the wrong people a number of times, I finally procured an old bus, one open truck, and two drivers. The drivers took the Russians to Bourg, where a unit of the regular French army was stationed. That evening, after losing most of my patience speaking endlessly into the mouthpiece of a French field telephone, I made arrangements for a special train. People thought I was a bit out of my mind to make such an unusual request! It had never been done before.

Eventually, a train arrived, but only one that ran from Moutiers (18 miles from Bourg) to Grenoble. Now I had to find transportation from Bourg to Moutiers.

Nothing was forthcoming. Meanwhile, the Russians lived on water and air and meager rations in the French caserne (military barracks), which was constantly under shellfire from the Germans. They were becoming understandably impatient. Every time I looked at them they snapped to attention. It seemed that the whole house would shake with the resulting vibration. Finally, after two days of what seemed endless waiting, two buses and six cases of GI ten-in-one rations arrived from Grenoble. I was very relieved to see the Russians leave.

On November 25 I wrote:

Dear Mom,

Four letters, four rays of light from a sunny country. In the last few days I have been taking many a mental trip back to Portland. Concerning letter writing, I must have a firm word with you. I was a bit surprised when you asked me whether you should keep on writing as often as you do now. Of course you should, even though your letters don't arrive here in a short time. For the last twelve days I have not had a single chance to send off any letters at all. Believe it or not, I was completely snowbound and there was no way of getting through to civilization, neither by telephone, nor on skis, nor on foot. So don't fret when you don't receive any news for two weeks at a time; I have had to wait as much as one and even two months for letters from home.

You should like to know why I conceal myself in my letters?! Well, I don't mean to give that impression. First of all, everything we do and don't do in the army is highly secret and must be kept from the public. Secondly, I don't feel like writing about how difficult life is in the army any more. That's why I prefer to write about the beautiful scenery I saw, about a book I read, or what have you. In a life such as ours, those things have come to be more real than the twenty-four hours of a soldier's day.

You must know that I write as often and as much as I can. But you must remember that I don't run a letter-for-letter exchange service. So if you feel that you sacrifice by receiving fewer letters than you send I wish you'd do me one favor: SACRIFICE.

I am enclosing a picture of mine. It's nothing spectacular except that the holy ghost is again floating midair over my head (that's a flaw in my camera).

Yesterday I found a lovely poem by A. E. Housman. Perhaps you know it:

Be still, my soul, be still; the arms you bear are brittle,
Earth and high heaven are fixt of old and founded strong

Think rather call to thought, if now you grieve a little,
the days when we had rest, O soul, for they were long.

Men loved unkindness then, but lightness in the quarry
I slept and saw not; tears fell down, I did not mourn;
Sweat ran and blood sprang out and I was never sorry:
Then I was well with me in days ere I was born.

Now, and I muse for why and never find the reason,
I pace the earth, and drink the air, and feel the sun.
Be still, be still my soul; it is but for a season:
Let us endure an hour and see injustice done.

Ay, look: high heaven and earth and from the prime foundation;

All thoughts to rive the heart are here, and all are vain:
Horror and scorn and hate and fear and indignation –
O why did I awake? When shall I sleep again?

This reflects many of the feelings that I have at the pre-
sent time. They are mixed feelings of destruction and decay.
Life in the army is still about the same. There have been
days when I went skiing in the morning, played the village
organ in the afternoon, and read Bacon's essays in the
evening. Of course these days are rare. Then there are those
horrible days when I waste my time doing practically noth-
ing, getting annoyed with myself, and hoping that there will
be a change in the food at the next meal. There are those rare
days when I work hard, and a poem or a piece by Mozart
over the radio are most refreshing because they are
deserved—and I have worked in the last week. I've fought
the elements in the mountains and seen the tragedy which
comes to pass in the mountains.
Love,
Tom

When we returned to Grenoble, I met Colette. Her
father was the sort of capitalist Marx enjoyed describing.
During the Vichy regime he had evaded taxes. He was
very hard on his employees, and had the Gestapo billeted at his hotel. Like a number of seemingly respectable
Frenchmen, he was very active in the black market.
Because of these activities, the new Communist-influ-
enced government tried to put him in jail. His wife was
extremely shrewd and tough. She watched her daughter
Colette at every moment. Consequently, Colette and I
officially met in the main lobby of the hotel, and we
talked about French literature from Ronsard to Verlaine.

COLETTE

We also managed to meet outside of Grenoble, however, and we talked in the hallway, and whispered quietly in my room. This went on for several weeks until her mother became suspicious. Colette had come to recognize every footstep, all the elevator noises, rattling of keys, and closing of doors. When it sounded to her as though her mother was closing the door of the elevator four floors below us, Colette would suddenly disappear and I would be standing there quietly talking to no one.

One evening we were in my room busily conversing, when suddenly there was a loud and definite knock on the door. Colette immediately recognized this as her mother's knock, and with no escape route for Colette, her face turned whiter than a bed sheet. After two seconds of suspense I roared out in English, sounding very annoyed, "Who's there? What in the hell do you want?" Apparently, her mother was either satisfied or scared, and she walked off. This incident brought an end to my friendship with Colette, who was too frightened to see me again anywhere.

While I was in Grenoble I had an interesting conversation with a peculiar student of history. He may have been a disciple of Pythagoras, or of a nineteenth century school of mathematics, which taught that all historical events are based on mathematical relationships. He showed me a chart which not only proved (to him) a certain numerical coherence between past events, but which also gave a prognosis of the immediate future. It was called *Predictions 1944*:

1.	The German revolution took place in	1918	
	The French revolution took place in	-1789	
		129	yrs.
2.	Hitler came to power in	1933	
	Napoleon came to power in	-1804	
		129	yrs.
3.	Hitler attacked Russia in	1941	
	Napoleon attacked Russia in	-1812	
		129	yrs.
4.	Napoleon was finished in	1815	
		+ 129	yrs.
	Hitler will be finished in	1944	

According to this scheme, Hitler had two months and sixteen days left to live. Actually, he died a year later.

When we returned to Val d'Isère, I met Marie-Louise, the FFI nurse of the local Chasseurs Alpine Company (mountain troops). My buddies called her the "Gebirgsmaus" (mountain mouse), in contrast to Colette in Grenoble, whom they called my "hotel mouse." Marie-Louise had been in the French mountain Maquis for two years. She was said to have saved many FFI soldiers from falling into the hands of the Germans. She ran up those hills like a mountain goat, and she could out-climb me any day. It must have been amusing to others to see, me, a city-slicker, chasing up the hill behind her, totally out of breath and scarcely able to keep up.

MARIE-LOUISE

Yet Marie-Louise was more than just a storehouse of energy. We spent many hours by the waterfall two miles up the valley reading French poetry or talking about our favorite nineteenth century painters. She claimed she did not know much about music. One evening we were passing a rushing creek, and I asked her to listen with me to the various sounds of the creek and compare them to the notes of a symphony. We leaned over the railing of the bridge over this little mountain stream, and we listened to the "Creek Symphony." At first we heard the irregular clicking of the small pebbles constantly being pushed on by the rushing waters. Then there was a continuous hissing of foam, and an occasional bursting of a big bubble. The larger the rock, the deeper the note its fall produced. Not one sound was repeated. The music in the creek bed was accompanied by the rustle of the weeds and trees, or by the whistling wind. We listened as long as possible, but finally had to return to the hotel, for we were tired and our feet were getting cold.

We talked about social work and she explained the many ways one could serve the world and people who were in need. Social work in France was not a respected work, and yet Marie Louise made it sound deeply necessary and inspiring.

By the middle of
October, our team was fairly well established in Val
d'Isère. Contact had been
made with the Italians in
northern Italy, and it was
about time that we took a
little tour to the other side
of the high mountain range,
behind the German lines.
Since such a trip required
mountain experience, six-
teen Italian partisans made
the expedition with us.
Only two of the seven
Americans on our team—
that is, our lieutenant and
I—decided to go with them. The area we were about to
visit was full of Axis soldiers, mostly German, who were
constantly being driven northward by the U.S. Fifth and
Eighth armies. They were more or less stuck where they
were because they could not easily escape over the
Brenner Pass.

JEEP IN VAL D'ISÈRE

Our chances of being captured were high. Lt. Woods
had heard that the Germans treated their officer-prison-
ers much better than their "non-gentleman" prisoners
(apparently only officers were regarded as gentlemen),
so, to further protect me, we decided to break all army
rules and regulations and pin two silver bars on my
shoulders. I borrowed another lieutenant's name and dog
tags, and quickly memorized his serial number; thus, I
became a lieutenant. Twice we started out for Italy, but
both times a storm drove us back. Those two experiences

ITALIAN PARTISANS. DANTE AND HIS BROTHER IN FOREFRONT

were trying: wading through snow up to our hips, the wet snow whipping our faces, the heavy load—a carbine, .38 caliber revolver, and forty-pound pack—made our hike next to impossible, and we had to give up. Finally the weather cleared, and we were able to start again.

We set out at five o'clock one morning with a group of partisans. My pack still weighed forty pounds. As long as we were in the hotel it did not seem too heavy to carry. This was not the whole load, of course. In addition to the weapons, each of us carried a carbine, a pistol, ammunition, a compass, a rope, and an ice ax or alpenstock. We also usually took a pair of skis and ski poles. We had heard that when partisans were captured by the Germans, they were often shot on the spot, without being questioned. In consideration of this, we all wore big American flags on the left sleeve—even the partisans who did not speak a word of English.

It was pitch dark when we left. The lead man had to use a flashlight in order to stay on the path. I knew that the trip was going to be rugged, but I thought I was prepared for it. For the first four miles we followed the road bed. At first the snow was only about ten inches deep. I soon realized that my pack was very heavy, and that I should be quite proud of myself if I carried it all the way into Italy. At seven o'clock we left the road, and here the snow reached up to our knees, and the straps of the pack were slowly beginning to cut into my shoulders. By this time my only thoughts were to wonder what fraction of the route we had already covered. Was it a quarter or only one-fifth?

At least now we could see where we were going for the rays of the sun were already touching the high mountain peaks. The lieutenant and I followed the Isère riverbed through the Gorge Malpassant (Gorge of Difficult Passage). Our Italian guides walked along as though they were not exerting themselves at all, while I was catching my fourth or fifth wind. At about that time, my lieutenant ("the other lieutenant") taught me the rest step. Whenever I had completed a step, I was to let my foot rest on the ground for just a split second. Up to then, I had kept both of my feet and legs working and moving all the time. Now I rested my weight on one foot while the other foot did all the work. This new pleasure lasted only twenty minutes however, because the pack cut even more into my shoulder and into the small of my back; my arms fell asleep, and I had to shift the load constantly.

For a moment I thought perhaps one of the Italians could help with my load… but I quickly let that thought go, feeling that the reputation of the entire American nation depended upon my being able to carry my share of the burden. I thought of eating some of the food and thus distributing the weight more evenly over my body.

ON THE PASS OF THE GALISE

That would not work though, because we never stopped long enough to catch more than "twenty breaths." I wondered what the others were thinking. I finally managed to say very nonchalantly to one of the Italians, "Think you're getting a good workout?" "Ah, oui! Ça va bien" ("I'm doing great"), he replied—a remark that did not boost my morale, but only reminded me of the load that was torturing me. On this hike, I had long ago forgotten that there were Germans in the area. I was far less concerned about them than about the pack on my back. War really had become ninety-nine percent discomfort and one percent danger.

Finally, I realized that I had a fellow-sufferer. My lieutenant was beginning to swear at everything under the sun. Our French and Italian guides paid little attention to him. Shortly thereafter, my pack reminded me again of my woes. We had now reached the approach to the pass. It was very steep and we had to use a rope. Every step seemed like my last effort. Now I could not fall behind anymore. In fact, several times I was obliged

VIEWS FROM GALISE

to pull up the fellow behind me. There were times when I was ready to lie down by the side of the path and give up.

We arrived at the Col de la Galise (a pass 9000 feet high), at about one o'clock in the afternoon. For the first time in my life I stepped on Italian soil, and the view was magnificent. All around us were the snow-capped mountain chains of the high Alps. In the distance, we could see three Italian valleys that joined each other at the plateau below. Yet, even at 9000 feet there was to be no rest for us. I quickly took some pictures, had a swallow of "aqua" (Schnapps), which put me into another state of awareness, grabbed a bite to eat, and re-tied myself to the rope. The slope on the Italian side was much steeper than the one on the French side. We were told to walk very carefully and to avoid all shouting, for even one sound could have set off an avalanche. I was so

ONE FOOT IN FRANCE
AND ONE IN ITALY.

SLIDING DOWN ON MY SEAT

concerned about the abyss, which extended several hundred feet below me, that I completely forgot the agony of the pack.

Finally, the inclination of the slope became more gradual. We could free ourselves from the rope, and coil it up and make our way down into the Piedmonte Valley. When we could, we sat down in the snow and slid down rapidly on our seats. It must have been a sight: all of us sliding down the mountain with our packs on our backs, guns and other assorted things sticking out on all sides. I remembered sliding down Mt. St. Helen's in Washington with a stick, years before. At about two o'clock the Italians assured us that the rest of the journey would be on fairly level ground. From then on it was just one continuous grind, one constant agony. I had stopped looking at the beautiful surroundings. I saw only the tracks of the man ahead of me, and he watched the tracks of the man in front of him. Whenever I missed his track I sank into the snow up to my waist, or even slid down the bank off the path a few yards, always with the heavy pack and gun and skis. I had no easy time pulling myself out of such a mess. The Italians still walked along easily and merrily.

DEGIOZ VAL SARVARANCHE

I asked many times, "How much further is it now?" but they only answered vaguely: "When we get to the top of that small hill it won't be long," or "About nine more kilometers" (always "nine more kilometers"—about six miles). By six o'clock it was completely dark. It began to snow and we had to use the rope again. Finally, we arrived at Val Savaranche—four more kilometers and we would reach our goal. Apparently they said this to raise our morale, because these four kilometers turned out to be seven. At eleven o'clock at night, we got to Maisonasse in Val Savaranche. One of our Italian guides owned a hotel in the village, and we were to spend the night there.

We had marched or climbed thirty-four miles in

about sixteen hours. Sometimes it had taken us as much as an hour to hike just one mile. I was so tired that night it seemed as I slipped between the fresh sheets, I was asleep before I had a chance to close my eyes.

The following morning we began establishing a "rat line"—line of communication or underground railroad—with the Italian partisans in Val Savaranche and Val di Cogne. We needed to develop a system of finding the partisans in the area, and to set up a means of communicating with them. We had to develop plans with them for rescuing the Allied soldiers who were hiding in these valleys. The partisans who had come with us had left behind the weapons that they had carried over the high mountains in one of the refuge huts for later use, and we promised to get more weapons into the region.

At about nine o'clock the next morning, an Italian partisan stormed into our room. He was out of breath, but he managed to deliver his short message in his best French: The Germans were coming up to Val Savaranche from Val d'Aosta. This was, after all, German territory, well behind the enemy lines. We were told to grab all of our equipment and "beat it up into the hills and stay there until the Tedeschis (Italian nickname for Germans) have returned to Aosta." Ten minutes later we received a more favorable message: The Germans were just reconnoitering, and had gone only as far as the mouth of Val Savaranche. The Italian partisan troops seemed to have an effective G-2 (intelligence service).

Later that morning we hiked on to Degioz, the most important village in the valley. In Degioz, we were royally entertained by the partisan chiefs. They dug into their food reserves, for we were the first Americans whom they had seen. The first dish they served was risotto—a

ITALIAN PARTISANS AT DEGIOZ

rice dish that is prepared with rice, broth, grated cheese, and some cayenne and paprika. As had happened so frequently, I ate too much of the first dish, and thus was unable to enjoy the main course. However, after having tasted a few of the best Italian red wines, and then wait-

ed awhile, I was ready for the polenta with fondutta sauce. Fondutta is one of the principal dishes of food among the poor in Italy. It is a hot sauce consisting of grated parmesan and Fontana cheese melted in milk. Red wine is mixed into this concoction just before serving it, and the sauce is then poured over polenta. We loaded ourselves to capacity. The Italians were certainly

LAUNDRY IN DEGIOZ

artists at cooking all kinds of grain dishes.

Degioz, like so many of the Italian mountain villages, was poor and dirty. The natural resources were few. The pastures looked like the terraced fields of a rice plantation in Southeast Asia. They were small because the valley was too narrow to permit any big fields. The houses were all white-washed and had brown roofs. After we left the village, we passed the valley's defense system—of which the Italians were very proud. All we saw were a few observation posts, and several piles of rock to be used for cover and concealment. They sadly lacked arms, of course, and ammunition. These Italians were not very good organizers. This was one of the main reasons why the Germans and Fascists had a rather easy time in re-occupying Val Savaranche and Val di Cogne after we had left them.

Wherever we went we thought that we were being seen by German spies. I am sure that we must have talked to many Italians who were spying for the Germans. As we traveled further down Val Savaranche, the road suddenly stopped. It looked as though the whole mountain had caved in and blocked the valley. During the previous summer the partisans had placed land mines into the side of this mountain. A few weeks later, when twenty-five German, Ukrainian, and Fascist soldiers tried to come up to Degioz, a partisan set off the fuse, and all twenty-five of the Axis soldiers were buried under a huge mound of dirt. We walked around it.

We walked fifteen miles further to the neighboring valley, the Val di Cogne. We went over the Col de Poignon (Col meaning crest), and at five o'clock we arrived at the bottom of the valley. Here we were received by some Italian Communists who looked rather

CAPITALIST VILLA HEADQUARTERS OF GENERAL ARNAUT

rugged with their shabby uniforms, beards, and an assortment of modern and ancient weapons, all bearing the Communist insignia. They took us to the town of Cogne in one of the few partisan vehicles in northern Italy. When I asked the driver how he procured gasoline, oil, and spare parts, he answered casually, "Oh, we capture them from the Germans."

We spent two nights at Cogne. Here we met the Italian partisan general in charge of the whole area. He was on the German black list, of course. So, whenever the Germans occupied his valley, he took a vacation in Switzerland. His headquarters were located in a very luxurious modern house that had belonged to a former industrialist who had collaborated with the Germans. This building had noiseless light switches, and lights that could be controlled from various places in the room, and also could be dimmed or brightened—features that were highly unusual for that time. Each room was decorated in a style of its own: the living room was rustic, the dining room contained all sorts of rare art treasures, the

DIRECTOR OF IRON MINES

bedroom had plain surfaces and was modern, the stairwell was decorated with Chinese art, and the bathroom contained all the modern gadgets and fixtures one could imagine.

In Cogne, we visited Italy's largest and most famous iron mine. The director of the mine was an extraordinary and very colorful man. He looked very serious, tired, and sad. We learned later that on the previous day, his only son had been killed in a skirmish with the Fascists. He was very well read, and on his library shelf were books by Goethe, Byron, and Shakespeare, among others. He spoke French without a noticeable accent, and he also

spoke German and Spanish fluently. People who knew him told me that he was one of the greatest mining experts in the world. The mine, located on a high rock, was inaccessible by road or path, so we had to take a funicular (cable car), which climbed the 2,700 feet in twelve minutes. The building at the entrance to the shaft was five stories high, containing a general store, dining

VAL D'AOSTA - GERMAN DIVISION

rooms, dormitories, recreation rooms, and showers for the workers. In order to get into the mine itself, we had to walk several hundred feet through a tunnel to board a steeply inclined elevator, and finally, climb some slippery stairs.

When we returned to the valley, the director proudly showed us his Sten gun factory, where the workers were just putting the finishing touches on the first two guns produced there. To end our sightseeing tour, we decided to look at some Germans soldiers. We climbed onto a narrow-gauge small train and started off for the neighboring valley, Val d'Aosta. We spent most of our time traveling through a tunnel which, before the war, had facilitated the transport of iron ore from Cogne to Aosta. Now it was a link between Cogne and a partisan observation point. As soon as we left the tunnel we could see Val d'Aosta directly in front of us. This valley had a permanent German garrison—an entire German division of 12,000 troops—and we saw the German soldiers and their barracks right in front of us. (The Germans learned we were there, and came looking for us the next day, but we were long gone.) In the distance, we saw the Swiss Alps—Monte Rosa and the Matterhorn—as well as two valleys in which the partisans were said to be very active. To the east we could see Mont Blanc, Europe's highest mountain.

When we returned that evening, I was invited to say a few words over the clandestine partisan radio. The manager of the station was an intelligent young woman who spoke Italian, French, English, and German fluently. I was introduced to the radio audience by the "chimes" of a huge cowbell. Then a chorus of Italian partisans joined in: "Attenzione! Attenzione!" they said,

"Voce Americano!" (Voice of America), and some other, more complicated Italian phrases. I made my message short but cheerful: "The Americans are here. The Germans are losing the war, and Piedmont will be free." Then the big cowbell put the finishing touches on my "Voice of America."

Later that evening, we visited the aristocracy of Cogne. It was interesting to see their wealth in the midst of the poverty in the Italian valleys. We were served Ceylon tea, small sandwiches, pies, cakes, and cookies. The ladies were well educated, of course, and we were able to speak English most of the evening, but these women did little to help win the war. They lived there with their wealth, complaining about the shortage of good flour, while the poor peasants had no flour at all. After this tea party, we visited the director of the mine in his elegant study. On his white-washed walls he had painted in black lettering, in the original languages, quotations from Voltaire, Goethe, Milton, Virgil, the Koran, and the Jewish scriptures. We spent most of the evening listening to Beethoven's Seventh Symphony, and to some of Vivaldi's orchestral music, while we sampled our host's outstanding collection of Italian wines.

The next day we walked back to Degioz. When we got there my tired and blistered feet were about ready to give out. Yet I had enough energy left to spend an hour playing the organ in the local church, while a partisan vigorously pumped the bellows at the rate of one cigarette per chorale. My first impression of Italy had been a very good one. We had been well received. I thought the Italians in those alpine valleys very trustworthy. I met several partisans who had been doing undercover work against fascism, since Mussolini had come to power in

1922. The French partisans, however, thoroughly disliked the Italians. They still could not forgive them for some old wounds of betrayal at the beginning of the war. For us Americans, it was difficult to comprehend that a gang of FFI (French partisans) would severely beat up a "partizane" because he was Italian, when they were both fighting a common enemy. The Italians made sour faces when we dealt with the

LAC AGNIEL

French, and the French were suspicious of us when we employed Italian agents.

The following day, because the Germans were still occupying the roads, we set out with about ten Italian partisans, hiking over the mountains to return to Val d'Isère in France via the same route we had come. I had two blisters as big as silver dollars on my feet, but otherwise, I was in good physical condition. As soon as we were out of Val Savaranche we encountered a snowstorm, and the tracks that we had made on the way a few days before were now covered by two feet of snow. The wind was blowing ceaselessly, but fortunately our Italian partisan guides knew every square foot of the terrain, and we were able to continue, even if it was at a very slow pace. At about 1:30 p.m. we met a column of partisans going in the opposite direction who were carrying weapons from Val d'Isère to Val Savaranche. These were the weapons we had gathered earlier. They told us that it was impossible for anyone to get to Val d'Isère because a storm was raging on the Col de la Galise (the high pass).

We were not going to risk our lives unnecessarily, so we spent the night in a shelter at Lac Agniel. Throughout the Alps, these refuge shelters, built of stone and cement, gave skiers and hikers a place to rest or be protected from storms. We were warned that this particular hut was visited occasionally by a patrol of German mountain troops, but apparently the weather was too inclement that night, because the Germans never bothered to leave Val Ceresole, where they were stationed. Just the same, we cuddled up with our weapons that night to be prepared for anything.

The next morning at about five o'clock, I saw the first real Alpengluehen, (Alpine-glow), in my life. I described it in a letter to my mother:

November 1944

Dear Mom,

Yesterday a strong blizzard prevented us from going over a high pass, so we spent the night in a lonely refuge. At about half-past five the stars were still sparkling. The silent winter landscape with its grayish and vague color was all around us. Then comes a change from the all-covering shadow to the all-pervading light. The sun is not yet up, but its first rays have come to rest on the rugged, snow-covered mountain peaks, tinging the white snow with a delicate rose, a gentle color. At a lower altitude the snowfields are slowly beginning to display their glaring white, as the lake, which they surround, is taking on a darker and darker color, until it appears as a mysterious black hole. In the valley, the brilliant and varying colors are just awakening: bright yel-

lows and reds of dying leaves, and the dull and moist green of the white clouds are reflected. And as the sun keeps rising, we can see the works of man: the white house with the red-brown roof, the church towering over the village, the herd, the bridge, and the narrow gray road which is twisting itself through the valley like a snake through the green grass. It is a definite part of the beauty of the universe, of the whole, or—if you wish—of God.

DESCENT FROM COL (CREST)
DE LA GALISE

The climb up to the Col de la Galise was not easy. Again we had to use the rope, and every now and then we heard the rumbling thunder of an avalanche, and we became very uneasy. During the first stop we all received instructions on how to behave in case one of those "babies" did come down, and before long, an avalanche did start rolling in our direction. Fortunately, it was not a very big one. It was started when the Italian partisans we had met earlier laid down their weapons in the snow in order to take a brief rest below the pass. While they were piling up all this war material, the snow suddenly gave way, and all the Italian, German, French, and British grenades and guns came sailing down the steep grade at a terrific speed. As soon as the first bit of snow had started to move, one of our Italian guides—who apparently had an excellent sense of hearing, feeling, or vision—

shouted "Una lavina! Una lavina!"—Italian for avalanche. High above me, the partisans in our group were flat on their bellies, ready to swim across the current of snow. Fortunately, this turned out to be only a small snow slide, and we were able to continue our climb without any considerable losses. We even recovered most of the weapons. For a few minutes, however, I was scared out of my wits.

We finally arrived at the crest, and it was a great relief to see Val d'Isère in the distance. At least now our journey was downhill. We walked down, easily, and when we could, we sat down once again in the snow, with our packs on our backs and our guns sticking out, and slid down the mountain. When we finally arrived in Val d'Isère, people were glad to see us back, and they greeted us with polenta, red wine, and many partisan songs. We were happy to know that, at least for a while, we would travel by jeep.

During the next few months we were to make this trek over the mountains many times. It was never easy, but it was the only way we could get weapons into the small Italian Alpine towns that were still held by the Germans, and it allowed us to organize the partisans in order to keep the "rat line" to them, and to Allied personnel, open. We were able to get much ammunition to the partisans, and, with their help, to bring out many Allied soldiers who had been caught in these valleys. We had rescued hundreds of Allied soldiers, sometimes in enormous groups like the Russians, sometimes individually, and often we just set it up so the partisans could get them to us. It was much hard work yet deeply satisfying to realize what we were able to do. I was not always so happy though, and this was reflected in a letter I sent home:

November 7, 1944

Dear Mom,
   *One is simply not in the mood to write a decent letter.
Right now I am angry—angry at myself, angry at the
army. Stupidity flourishes everywhere, and as long as I have
this damned uniform on, I am completely powerless to
improve on anything. In face of all this frustration I can try
to compensate, but compensation often produces abnormal
situations, and that won't work either. Thus I sit tight and
decay.*
   *I am sending along the one and only Christmas present
this year: two lousy, posed photos. At least you can see my
beautiful teeth and the fact that I need a haircut badly.*
   *Last week we had to go to XXXXX [censored]. This
time we took along skis. Of course we couldn't use the boards
all the time. Well, that was quite a load with a heavy pack,
a rifle, and the skis on my shoulder. I have my own skis with
ski bindings and steel poles. All I need to have now is
knowledge of the art of skiing.*
   I shall keep on dreaming of home.
Love to all of you,
Tom

As soon as we could, we took off for Grenoble,
where a big batch of letters was waiting for me. For the
past two months I had not received a single letter. And
now, there were all sorts of cheerful messages from the
States, Canada, England, and France. It took me nearly
three hours to wade through all that correspondence.
That night I dreamt of a big welcome home party.
   Our last jeep ride between Grenoble and Val d'Isère
was difficult and memorable. This trip normally took

END OF TRIP

TOM AT HOTEL IN
VAL D'ISÈRE

LONGCOAT

three hours, but this time we had one continuous fight with the elements from two in the afternoon until ten at night. The roads in the French Alps had become more and more hazardous because of increasing snowfall, and the French snowplows were either broken down or their drivers did not know how to operate them. We barely managed to get our jeeps through because of the snow. And after we did, the road was closed to all but skiers and pedestrians, and even they had a difficult time avoiding the avalanches and snow slides.

Only a few of us remained at Val d'Isère. We took turns managing the big hotel, supervising the kitchen crew, and keeping those forty to fifty Italian "partizane" occupied and happy. There was not much else to do. Outside of our hotel a bitterly cold wind was howling. For days it kept snowing steadily, and every morning we had to dig ourselves out of our hotel, for the wind had blown a huge pile of snow right against the entrance. Soon the electric current went off for good, and we had to improvise all sorts of gasoline and oil lamps, which would invariably fill our rooms with clouds of smoke.

The evenings, however, were always very pleasant. After supper we gathered together by the flickering lights and listened to the beautiful songs sung by the partisans. All the Italians, with their colorful uniforms and full beards, were sitting at one table, and the FFI (French) mountain troops in their blue uniforms at another. As soon as the Italians had finished one song, the French came in with another. Whenever we could, we joined in at the refrain.

After an hour or two of continual singing, laughing, and drinking, we went down into the kitchen to eat fondutta. The fondutta I described before is prepared with wine and is of a much more chewy texture than the French fondue. The French cook had already gone through the initial preparation by the time we arrived in the kitchen. Everyone was armed with a fork in his right hand and some croutons in the left. As soon as the cook gave the word, everybody stuck a bread crouton onto his fork and plunged it into the cheese sauce, which was kept hot by a flame.

As I pulled out the piece of bread a string of cheese followed all the way to my mouth, and this could have been embarrassing if all the other people had not had the same experience. The heat of the fire under the pot was causing big cheese bubbles to pop off; this made the dipping procedure more hazardous. Again our partisans sang, only this time the songs were more bawdy. Among the songs we sang was the famous Italian mountaineering song, "E la penna que noi portiamo son disciplina di noi soldat" (The feather we wear in our hats reflects the discipline of our soldiers)!?

Because of the weather, our chances of returning again to the villages in the Italian Alps were very slim. Additional snowfall increased the avalanche danger in the Gorge Malpassant. The owner of our hotel told us that it took at least two days of good weather before the snow settled down firmly enough to ensure a safe passage through the gorge.

High Alps Rescue

ENTRANCE TO
THE GORGE MALPASSANT

One day when the snow had let up a bit, our lieutenant and I decided to take advantage of those two days of good weather to practice skiing. By two o'clock I was tired and returned to the hotel. Just as I was taking off my skis, one of the Italian partisans who had left for the gorge that morning came running up to me exhausted and out of breath. He barely managed to break the bad news: "twenty-four English soldiers—and thirteen partisans—frozen at the entrance of the Gorge Malpassant—two Italian survivors on way to Val d'Isère." I told the partisan to rest a bit while I went for the lieutenant, and when I returned the Italian had rested enough to tell us his story.

He and his pal were just about to enter the Gorge

Malpassant that morning, when they noticed two black figures at the bottom of the gorge. One of the figures was stumbling along through the snow, and the other was crawling behind him. The two partisans immediately lowered their ropes into the gorge and pulled the men out. They then helped the two to the nearest refuge hut, which was half a mile away in the direction of Val d'Isère. Since one of the men was in very bad condition, one of the partisans skied at top speed to Val d'Isère, which was five miles down the road. On the way he stopped at a chalet and told the farmer to take a sled, get the two men at the refuge cabin, and transport them to Val d'Isère.

There was no time to waste. Someone had to interview the two Italians who had been found that morning, in order to find out what had happened to the thirty-seven men who were still in the snow at the other end of the gorge. The lieutenant immediately organized a rescue team and started off for the gorge. I was to be in charge of getting thirty-nine beds ready, gathering up all the first aid equipment, and preparing some food. Practically the whole village eagerly cooperated. Only the wife of the owner of our hotel gave us some difficulty. When I told her that some of the men who were to be brought in would be incapacitated, and that some might be dying, she immediately became enraged and told us that she would not have any dead people in her beds. She later changed her mind and with the help of the villagers and the partisans I reserved thirty-nine beds in the various hotels, got bandages together, had a huge pot of hot soup prepared, and told everyone to stand by.

Shortly after four o'clock, the sled with the two rescued Italians arrived, pulled by two skiers. A crowd of curious and silent people had gathered by the roadside. The two men on the sled were wrapped in blankets up to their chins so that we could see only their heads. One of them had black hair and dark eyes, and the other had blond, curly hair and blue eyes. Both were unshaven and looked emaciated and pale. We lowered them carefully onto a stretcher, carried them into the hotel, and put them to bed. Everybody wanted to come to the room where the two casualties were lying; so finally we had to post a guard at the hotel entrance with instructions not admit anyone who was not on business.

We expected to find that both of these partisans were very badly frostbitten. The Italian with the dark hair seemed to be the most severely injured, so we took his blanket off first. We saw that his hands up to his wrists had swollen to about twice the normal size. The palm and the back of each hand was a bluish red color. All the fingertips had shriveled to half their normal size and were completely black, as though they had been charred in a fire. Big blisters had formed on the backs of both hands. The skin had opened up in several places, and a yellowish liquid mixed with blood was oozing out and dropping on the white sheet.

We all stood around in awe while the Italian partisan doctor smeared sulfadiazine salve over both hands, and then bandaged them with the gauze that we had gathered from the various first aid kits in the village. Then the doctor took some scissors and very carefully cut open the shoes on both sides so he could take them off without having to pull. He cautiously took off both socks, and again we saw the same condition. Both feet were severely swollen up to the ankles. They were red and blue with big blisters. Again the doctor applied the ointment and then bandaged both feet. It looked as though the partisan was going to lose both feet as well as both hands.

When the doctor was ready to work on the other man, we found that he had been standing behind our backs all this time, looking over our shoulders, and watching what was happening to his friend. He told us that he was perfectly all right, he merely wanted to get a good meal and sleep for a day or two. We granted him his first wish and then before he went to sleep, we asked him to tell us about what had happened before he went to sleep.

He said that he had been with a party of twenty-four English soldiers and fifteen Italian partisans who were attempting to get over the mountains with a Lieutenant Vittorio. They had been caught in a storm and he and his friend had been left behind with two badly injured Englishmen. When no help arrived, the Italians decided to leave and go for help themselves. On the next day, the eleventh of November, the storm let up a little, and the two partisans were able to find the entrance to the gorge. They got through it, but with great difficulty, narrowly escaping a large avalanche. Late in the morning of the twelfth, they were found. The partisans were afraid that the two Englishmen they had left behind would be frozen to death by now. None of us could understand how the blond Italian partisan had lived through the ordeal, apparently totally uninjured. He went to bed and did not wake up until the afternoon of the following day.

At six o'clock that evening the partisan lieutenant and his rescue team returned to Val d'Isère. They had been able to get up to the mouth of the gorge, but the bad weather and the constant avalanches kept them from going on. This rescue was clearly our responsibility, since it was our job to bring captured Allied personnel back to our lines.

By the following morning the weather had turned for the worse again, and it was impossible to evacuate the injured Italian partisan into an area where he could get needed medical care. We were certain that the thirty-seven men in the gorge had frozen to death, and that we would not be able to reach them, even to evacuate their bodies. Since we were unable to continue our work, and since it was very difficult to bring supplies into Val, the lieutenant decided to close down our CP (command post), move to Grenoble, and await further orders from headquarters in Paris. I was told to remain alone at Val for three or possibly four days, in case any rescue effort could be mounted. I was to take care of any unfinished business and emergencies that might arise, and to distribute the remainder of our supplies to the Italian partisans.

The bad weather persisted. On the morning of the fifteenth of November I talked to a Moroccan lieutenant who was in charge of twelve mule drivers and their teams. He desperately wanted to have a GI flashlight battery, so I made a deal with him. I promised him the two batteries, if he would take most of our equipment and pack it as far as Tignes. (The road from Grenoble to Val was open as far as Tignes.) He accepted, and twenty minutes later twelve mule drivers and their mules came to a halt in front of our hotel. We loaded all our equipment onto the mules, and were glad that we did not have to go along with them. It was still snowing very hard.

Around noon the Moroccan lieutenant came into my room and told me that all the equipment was piled up in front of the hotel. His men had been stopped by a big snowslide one hour earlier. They had almost lost two of the mules in the ravine and decided to postpone the trip to Tignes.

On the afternoon of the sixteenth the weather began to turn for the better. It cleared up quickly—we were able to see the Col de la Galise that same evening—and the Moroccans took off for Tignes again with most of our equipment and most of our men following in jeeps.

The Italian partisan officer, Colonel Bellandi, told me that he would send four of his men to the Col the next morning to find out if the Germans were in Val Ceresole. He said that he and his men had developed a simple but very effective code system of communication: the partisan who stayed at Lake Agniel, the refuge hut at the head of the valley of Ceresole, always put his black blanket on the clothesline whenever the Germans were around. This blanket showed up very well against the snow, and could just barely be seen from the Col. When the area was free of Germans, he put up white sheets, and, on this day, the sheets were indeed white. Colonel Bellandi's four men took off early the next morning, the seventeenth of November.

Since this was to be my last day at Val, I went skiing in the morning, played on the church harmonium right after lunch, and read Francis Bacon's essay "Of Truth" to a French partisan.

At quarter of five that afternoon, an emergency phone call came through from Fournet (the shelter), which is the only settlement between Val d'Isère and the Italian border. One of the Italian partisans who had left that morning to search for survivors offered amazing news in a very excited voice; they had found one of the two Englishmen who had been left behind by Lieutenant Vittorio. He had been buried over his head in the snow for nine days, but he was still alive! I could hardly believe that, so I asked the partisan, who spoke very broken French, to repeat the story in Italian. He seemed to be telling the truth.

As soon as I recovered from the shock, I ran to Dr. Petri's house on the other side of the valley. Dr. Petri was a bone specialist who, before the war, made a living setting the bones of injured skiers; he was also an excellent skier. He immediately volunteered to go through the gorge that evening and take the Englishman to the nearest refuge hut. He took three French mountaineers with him, as well as food, equipment, and medical supplies. These four men left Val d'Isère forty minutes after I received the frantic phone call.

Then I dispatched one of the Italian partisans to Tignes, and asked him to request an ambulance from the regular French forces who were stationed at Bourg St. Maurice (nineteen miles from Val on the road to Grenoble), and to have the ambulance ready for the morning of the nineteenth.

After the Italian was dispatched to Tignes, I went to Monsieur Diebold, the local sports director. He had already heard the news about finding the Englishman, and I asked him whether he could evacuate the injured man the following morning. He not only accepted immediately, but also put all of his mountain equipment at our disposal. He suggested that we take along several of his ten-foot poles, some of which were red and some green, so that if we found any frozen bodies we could mark their locations. He also volunteered to pull a light sled up to the mouth of the gorge to carry the Englishman.

I spent the rest of the evening packing and making arrangements so that we could transport the Englishman to a place with better medical care after we had gotten him back to Val d'Isère. The Italian partisan with the frostbitten hands and feet who had come down earlier with his partner could be taken with him. There was so much to do, and I was so excited, that I scarcely slept that night.

The next morning at 4:30, after a hearty breakfast, we left Val on skis to head into the mountains through the gorge. We hoped the Englishman was by now resting in the refuge hut. It was pre-dawn and pitch dark, so we had to use a flashlight to see where we were going. At around six, it became light, and at about seven we arrived at the gorge, just as the sun was rising and its rays were striking the high mountain peaks.

Again, we were hoping there would not be any snowslides. We left the sled at the mouth of the gorge, which we managed to get through without either slipping down into the gorge or being hit by an avalanche. When we had almost reached the other end, we noticed a piece of black fabric far down in the ravine under an overhanging cliff. We had to use our field glasses to recognize it as an old jacket. Around this piece of clothing were foot tracks, some of which led a short distance up the steep incline and suddenly stopped under a big cliff. Someone had evidently tried to get out of the ravine but had had to return because he could not scale the rock. We also discovered some spots of urine scattered about in the snow. And then we suddenly realized that probably most—if not all—of the thirty-seven people down there were covered by five feet of snow. We knew it was of no use to climb into the gorge to start looking for them. It would have been far too dangerous. There was no way we could have reached them, and we also knew it was hopeless to expect that any of them could still be alive. Even so, it was a difficult and painful decision to pass beside a place where we knew there might be so many people buried in the snow.

When we got out of the gorge we breathed a sigh of relief. The going had been tough and we were tired, but there were no avalanches. The snow came up to our knees, and the tracks were not yet firm enough so that we could walk without slipping.

We finally arrived at the small refuge hut called Prarion. It was completely covered by snow, and we had to crawl through a hole in the snow in order to get into it. The first thing Dr. Petri told me was that the four Italian partisans had found the Englishman only two hundred feet away from the refuge hut, and that the other thirty-six who were all now dead must have passed within a few feet of the refuge hut. They had left two Englishmen and two Italians behind.

I was surprised at the cheerfulness with which Alfred, the Englishman, replied to my greeting. Dr. Petri had placed him on a ladder that he had found in the refuge. We intended to use it as a stretcher until we got to the sled at the other end of the gorge. The doctor had already wrapped Alfred's hands and feet, and put several blankets around him. We very carefully set him down on the ladder and then tied him down, so that he would be secure during the transport.

It was now eleven o'clock. The sun was shining brightly, and since it was quite warm outside, we set

Alfred on the snow in front of the refuge. It was then that I was able to get a good look at him for the first time. He looked more like an East Indian than a Londoner. His unkempt hair was so long that it covered his ears, and he had large brown eyes and very dark skin. His face was emaciated—he had not had a good meal for the past two weeks. I was reminded of a picture I had seen in the papers a few weeks before showing a starving Indian in the streets of Calcutta.

As soon as we put him down, Alfred asked me for a cigarette. The doctor said he could have three drags. Fortunately, I had along some English Players cigarettes. Alfred actually refused American cigarettes preferred by most Europeans when he realized he had a chance of getting English ones. He told me that he was a heavy smoker, and that he had not seen a "fag" in several weeks. I lit a cigarette and let him have three drags. He was so hungry for a smoke that it looked as though the insides of his emaciated cheeks touched at the end of each drag.

We had no time to waste. The longer we waited, the greater the avalanche danger became. The two French mountaineers were, as the doctor said, "built like steers," and they did not seem to mind carrying Alfred. We picked up all the equipment, and ten minutes later we arrived at the beginning of the gorge. We were on the sunny side, and we were very much afraid that the avalanches would soon come down. Monsieur Diebold and I felt that we should relieve the two French mountaineers, who were puffing like steam engines. The going was tough even for them. The men had to test every bit of ground first with every step they took and then put their whole weight down carefully in order not to slip.

We volunteered to change places with the two mountaineers. At first they were somewhat doubtful about our ability to carry the ladder with Alfred on it, yet they needed to rest for a while. I took my place behind the last rung of the ladder and in front of the Frenchman, who had been helped carrying Alfred; Diebold placed himself behind the mountaineer in the lead. I had hardly told the second mountaineer that I was ready, when he let go of the ladder and the enormous weight came to rest on my shoulders. I was so surprised and overwhelmed by the weight that I let out a strong, "Oh my God!" Since no one present except Alfred understood this exclamation, nobody came to my rescue. The two side pieces of the ladder came to rest on the bones of my shoulders. I immediately tried to shift the ladder to the right and then to the left, but each time I did this, the ladder slipped off on the left or right side. Then I tried to lift the ladder in order to relieve my shoulders, but that was too much of a hardship on my wrists.

All this happened in only a few seconds. Diebold soon asked me whether I was ready, and I managed to pronounce a very unconvincing "Oui." (Yes.) Cautiously, I put forward one foot, tested the ground for a split second, and then put my full weight on that foot. Then came the next foot, and so on. Down to our left, the abyss was constantly in view. High above on our right, topped by a cornice, were hanging snow fields. One slip of the foot on an icy or slippery surface to the left or one small avalanche from the right would have sent Alfred, Diebold, and me into the abyss. The load on my shoulders seemed heavier and heavier. I became so tense that I began to make faces, and to shake all over. I even tried holding my breath for three to four seconds at a time to ease the pain.

At the end of four minutes I felt that my strength was coming to an end. I was so exhausted that I whispered to the man behind me, "Je ne peux plus!" (I can't go on). The two mountaineers relieved both Diebold and me immediately. Diebold was also completely exhausted. Ten minutes later we took over once more. Alfred had begun to suffer quite badly. He told us that he had severe pains in his arms and hands where the healthy flesh met the frozen flesh.

Finally, we arrived at the mouth of the gorge where we had left the sled. There we met forty Italian partisans who were climbing the mountains on their way to Italy. They had loaded their packs with ammunition, weapons, food, and equipment. I was later told that quite a few of these fellows carried packs that weighed as much as one hundred eighteen pounds.

We placed Alfred on the sled, and the two French mountaineers pulled him to Val d'Isère, where he was to stay with Dr. Petri until he was ready to be transported to the FFI (French partisan) hospital at Aix-les-Bains. My main task now consisted of looking after him. I fed him, helped him smoke his cigarettes, and I talked with him. Dr. Petri and his family were most generous in giving him special food and in making him comfortable.

Alfred told me that he had been a radio scriptwriter before the war. He was drafted, sent to Africa, and taken prisoner by the Germans at Tobruk in June 1941. He was sent to a prison camp in Italy, where he stayed until September 1943. Italy surrendered to the Allies at that time, and before the German army was able to take charge of the various prison camps in Italy, many of the

Allied prisoners escaped because the Italian guards neglected their duties or some even simply went home. It was at that time that Alfred had escaped.

He had gone north and worked for a partisan farmer in the Italian Alps. This was in an area held by the Germans, and several times he was almost caught by them. He had learned to speak Italian fluently in just a few months, however, and he was able to talk himself out of several dangerous situations with the Germans. In October 1944, he heard a rumor that an Italian partisan lieutenant would pick up all the English soldiers who were hiding from the Germans and take them over the high mountains into France. He soon found Lieutenant Vittorio, who worked for us, and who had already gathered up several other English soldiers. That is how he came to be part of the disastrous and tragic climb over the mountains.

Lieutenant Vittorio was bringing these men into France against the orders of his superior, Major Bellandi, as well as against the orders of our lieutenant, who would have been responsible for such an undertaking.

Alfred said that on the morning of November 7, 1944 a party of thirty-nine men—both partisans and English soldiers—left Val Ceresole under Vittorio's leadership. Since there were supposed to be K-rations in the refuge hut at Lake Agniel, and since the trip normally took only a day, the men had eaten a meal in the village of Ceresole in the Val Ceresole, and then proceeded without taking along any provisions. That evening, the thirty-nine men arrived at Lake Agniel, situated at the head of Val Ceresole. In the hut they found the K-rations (each of them food enough for one meal), we had left on our previous trips, to be used in case of an emergency. Unfortunately, there were only about twenty cartons of these rations, so the men decided to leave them until the following day and had nothing to eat that night.

The next morning, everyone ate one half of a K-ration. The party was ready to leave the hut at five o'clock, but they decided to wait awhile because it was snowing so hard. Finally, at around ten o'clock, the snow stopped, and Lieutenant Vittorio decided to start out for the Col de la Galise. The steep climb to the crest was very difficult, and the men were poorly clad. After two hours of climbing, they were also very tired and hungry, and most were bothered by the cold, especially in their hands and feet. After a seven-hour struggle, they finally arrived at the high pass. The weather on the French side was worse, with several big snow clouds drifting right toward the pass.

Instead of returning to the nearest refuge hut on the Italian side, Lieutenant Vittorio decided to continue in the direction of Val d'Isère. The group walked right into the snowstorm, and before long, they were enveloped in total darkness. Although they were going downhill most of the time, the men soon began to feel that they were getting nowhere. After they had dragged themselves through the snow for two hours, Lieutenant Vittorio told them they would spend the night in the snow and continue the next morning. It was a miserable night, with cold gale winds blowing snow into their faces. Alfred and another Englishman had frostbitten hands and feet. Some of the Italian partisans kept jumping around and rubbing their cold limbs until they fell asleep from sheer exhaustion.

The following morning the weather changed for the

worse. Lieutenant Vittorio spurred his men on, telling them their goal was not very far away. Alfred and another Englishman were unable to walk any farther, so two Italian partisans were left with them, and Vittorio promised to send help that same day.

The four men stayed behind, trying to get as much shelter as possible by resting under a big rock. When no help had arrived by that evening, the two Italians became impatient. The next morning, on the tenth of November, they left the two English soldiers, promising to send help as soon as they got to the valley.

Both of the men left behind were completely covered by snow. Alfred said that his friend stopped moving on the fourteenth. On the morning of the seventeenth Alfred heard some men's voices not very far away, so he mustered his last bit of strength with his elbow; pushed away some of the snow, which was completely covering him; raised his head as high as he could; and yelled for help. The Italians who were searching for him heard him immediately. They lifted him out of the snow and carried him to the nearest refuge hut, only two hundred feet away. Alfred had been lying in the snow for nine days. He had been without food for ten days. His friend had died next to him three days before Alfred was rescued.

Lieutenant Vittorio had made the most crucial mistake a mountain climber can make. He did not feed his men sufficiently, nor clothe them properly. He had no guides, and in that part of the country, nobody ever travels without a guide. Instead of starting at five o'clock in the morning, he had left at ten. The sun had come up, which caused the jagged crystals of each snowflake to melt and become rounded, increasing the possibility of avalanches. Vittorio did not return to the nearest Italian refuge hut when he encountered the storm on the Galise pass. An old French mountaineer told me later that this was certainly one of the most tragic mountain accidents that had ever occurred in the Alps. He also said that it was fitting that Lieutenant Vittorio had died. He never could have survived with the deaths of thirty-six men on his conscience.

After hearing Alfred's story, Diebold told me that we needed to evacuate the bodies immediately. The longer we waited, the more difficult it would become to reach them, and if the bodies were left until the following spring, they might contaminate the drinking water of several villages, including Val d'Isère. He had been told by the various town mayors downstream to start working on this project right away, and I promised him some Italian partisan volunteers to help. However our team had to leave the area long before they were able to get to the bodies and we never heard what happened to them.

In a day or so, when Alfred could be transported, we loaded him and the Italian partisan onto two sleds and departed on foot to pull the injured men to Tignes, where an ambulance was waiting. All of our friends turned out to bid us farewell. In keeping with the French custom, we had to drink all sorts of toasts and embrace many people. When we got halfway to Tignes, two French farmers met us with their mules. We tied the two sleds to the mules, and twenty minutes later arrived at Tignes. There we found an ambulance, which one of our Italian partisans had arranged for by skiing thirty-five miles to Bourg St. Maurice and back in one day.

In Bourg we reported to the French regular-army doctor, who treated both of the injured men. He pierced several blisters on their hands and feet, and removed a good deal of dead skin and tissue. Contrary to the experience of many American soldiers, we were extremely well received by the regular French army. They gave the two sick men medicine and bandages, they fed all of us, and most important, they gave us transportation to Aix-les-Bains.

When we arrived at Aix-les-Bains, I left Alfred in an FFI (partisan) hospital. I was told by the doctor that both of the men would lose their feet. He hoped to save both of Alfred's hands, except for three-and-a-half fingers on the right hand, but he was afraid that he would have to amputate both of the Italian's hands.

In the hospital, Alfred asked me to write to his mother. I took dictation, then copied the letter in what I hoped was more readable script. The original follows:

November 1944, France

Dearest Mother,

You may be surprised to hear that I am in France at the present time and that I am in a French hospital on the way to recovery. As you can guess, I am no longer a prisoner, which was the main reason I was not able to write for such a long time.

I had an accident in the high mountains and got my hands and feet a bit damaged. Anyway, I hope to come back to London before long. I won't be able to write with my own hand for a while, but I shall be with you always in thought.

I would like you to do me a favor, however, and that is, don't worry about me, because I am quite well here. I shall

try to send you my address as soon as possible.
With all my love,
From your most affectionate son,
Alfred

(I saw Alfred eleven months later, during a visit to London. He had two artificial feet, with which he managed to walk around nearly like a normal person. His left hand had healed almost completely; the first three fingers on his right hand had been amputated. I never again heard of the Italian who lost both of his hands and feet, and who had a big family awaiting his return in an alpine valley in Italy.)

After this, I was recommended for the Silver Star medal, but since the action did not take place during combat, the commendation was reduced to a Soldier's Medal. It was later awarded to me in Paris, and the boys on my team were a bit perturbed because they had to polish their shoes and buttons, and wear ironed clothes for the ceremony. It was supposed to have been presented at the same time as Glenn Miller's Soldier's Medal. (The well-known orchestra leader was lost in a plane crash over the Spanish Sea.) At the time, I could not write to my mother about this experience or where I was because of the censors, but I wrote later:

December 1944

Dear Mom,
  I have just received one of the most delightful letters you have ever written. I am sending along a sermon by Niemoeller. The latest I have heard on him is that he is in a

concentration camp north of Berlin (what is left of Berlin after all the bombardments). They do not know whether he is still alive.

You have already asked several times how I got that medal. I guess now it won't do any harm to tell the story. First of all, the thing was not pinned on by Eisenhower. I got it for organizing the rescue of an English soldier who had been given up for dead. Of course I don't deserve all of the credit... the man who really deserves a medal is the

FORMATION FOR SOLDIER'S MEDAL

English soldier himself. I have never seen anyone with so much courage, with such excellent morale, with such high spirits as this most delightful chap from London. For nine days he had been lying covered by snow two feet over his head, and he had not eaten anything at all for twelve days. I definitely think it takes an Englishman to survive such horrors. I could not have written about this at the time it happened because of the censors.

December 9, 1944

Dear Mom,

I received two very nice letters with two more pictures...

AFTER RECEIVING
MEDAL OF HONOR

one of them of Madam Levy, toto solo, positione intelligen-
tia pensato, con collina Willamette au fond (try and figure
that out). I'd give my right hand to be able to wear civil-
ian clothes again. Alas, c'est la guerre. All the family pic-
tures seem to be taken in front of the church, while Mrs.
Levy prefers the front porch for her snapshots. I'd appreci-
ate it if you wrote to the New Republic tout de suite and
notify them of my change of address. Received a New
Yorker; had a great deal of fun with it. I would like to
receive more of these, and I repeat my request for candy.

Last week I received a catalog from London
University; the whole program sounds very intriguing. I
still hope to study one year in England, possibly before
returning to the States. I should like to return to the States
first, but that would be a big financial problem. I spend a
great deal of time being with you in Portland [in my
thoughts].
All my love,
Tom

After leaving Alfred at the hospital, I spent the
evening in Aix-les-Bains, and I took my first and last
ride on a French bus, which was certainly not one of the
latest models. The tires were treadworn, and the whole
thing looked as though it would fall apart any minute.
Of course we had to pay black market prices for the bus
ticket. I got on when the bus was already full, but with
the help of the dispatcher more people kept getting on
for the next ten minutes. The driver had had one drink
too many, and he had reserved all the seats around him
for the good-looking young girls. When we finally got
under way, his girlfriend, who had also indulged in a
good deal of "bon vin," sat on his lap, put her arm

JUNIOR AND THE ALPS

around his neck, and began kissing him, quite often blocking his view. We almost went off the road several times. Most of the passengers were appalled, but they did not dare speak up for fear that they would be asked to leave the bus. Somehow, three or four hours later, we arrived in Grenoble intact, and I was so tired I slept for two days.

While we were headquartered in Grenoble, we had a good deal of spare time on our hands and expected to be there a few weeks. Some of our team spent their time in the bar of our big hotel, some went in heavily for entertainment with the opposite sex, some went skiing, and others spent their time reading American mystery stories. I asked the lieutenant for permission to take a course or two at the University of Grenoble. He agreed under one condition: that I should leave the coeds alone.

Since I was an Allied soldier, I did not have to pay a single franc for tuition at the university. I signed up for a course in "Économie Nationale," which seemed to be the only interesting subject in the bulletin.

When classes began, I arrived a little early and took my seat in the amphitheater. Shortly after the bell rang, the doors opened like sluices, and a horde of young men and women streamed into the room. Most of them did not bother to walk down the aisle. Instead, they climbed on the first table, and then jumped from one table to the next, until they got to the front row. Since many of them had wooden soles on their shoes, the noise was terrific.

Most of the students appeared to be very mature for

their age, in spite of their noisy behavior. The girls were beautiful and tastefully dressed. If it had not been for the ersatz frayed cotton material that they were wearing, and for their hollow cheeks, they could have been mistaken for American coeds. The boys were poorly clad and pale because they had either been hiding from the Germans for the past four years, or they had been deemed unfit for slave labor in Germany.

Suddenly, a small door near the podium opened, and Monsieur le Professeur made his entry. Over his worn-out suit, he had thrown an academic gown that was made of beautiful black pre-war material. His academic hood was a brilliant red color and had white fur around the edge.

After the class gave him a big ovation—this seemed to be an academic custom in the French universities—he set out to cover the field of national economics—from the eighteenth-century physiocrats down to the nineteenth-century Marxian school. Like so many Frenchmen, the professor spoke exceedingly fast. I had no easy time following him. I tried to understand everything he said, thumbed through my dictionary, glanced surreptitiously at my neighbor's notebook to get the spelling of some French names, took notes in English, and watched the blond by the window two tables ahead of me. I was exhausted after the first lecture.

During the second lecture I started taking notes in French, and had an easier time understanding the professor. In general, I was not very impressed with these lectures. They seemed quite superficial. For instance, when he discussed the English Utilitarian school, he never once mentioned James Mill or John Stuart Mill, who so greatly influenced the U.S. constitution.

The war had certainly left its mark on the university library. I did not find one book that had been printed after the war broke out in 1939, and I wasn't very impressed with the collection of pre-war books. Since I knew more about history than any other subject, I checked the historical section, and found that some of the great French historians were only partially represented, or were not represented at all. After a few lectures I decided to quit school. I had studied most of the subject matter in the United States at Reed College already, and I also needed to return to the mountains. I was supposed to be fighting a war.

Stationed in the High Alps—Landry

Two weeks after we left Val d'Isère, the orders to continue our work arrived from Paris. The lieutenant decided to move our advance post to the village of Landry, situated off the main highway, just before Bourg St. Maurice. Bourg was still under observation and artillery fire from the Germans, who occupied the pass of the Little Saint Bernard in the hills above the town. Yet our little village was safe, even though we were the only Allied troops there.

I expressed my changing philosophical view to my family:

December 1944

Dear Mom,

Got a lovely picture from you of the whole family. You with your cheeks well nourished, with the new dress, smiling enthusiastically and looking at something or somebody other than the lens of the camera. Al being spic-and-span as ever, with a youthful smile, and the younger generation being like they are ... that is, expanding even while the picture is being taken ... and they have grown. It was good to see the whole family together and smiling.

Speaking of pictures, I am sending along the snapshots. That shadow around the lower part of my physiognomy represents ten days of neglect.

Let me quote from your last letter: "Chris is so idealistic, so Puritan, that the clash with reality will be quite unpleasant." Well, I wouldn't worry so much. I, too, was inclined in that direction. You remember my reactions toward the world in the first letters I wrote in the army. Reed is surely not the place where one finds out about the real world.

I spent some very happy months in Landry. Except for my army clothing, I was more of a civilian than an American soldier. We all had individual rooms, slept in feather beds, ate the most wonderful food, and were even served breakfast in bed occasionally. The

LANDRY DINNER TABLE WITH MELCHIOR FAMILY

proprietors of our little hotel, who were from Belgium, were very charming people, and I thought that Madame Melchior was one of the greatest cooks in the world. We ate like kings. When we left Landry, she told us that she had never once repeated the same menu, and that she had produced these meals using our GI rations and bartered goods from the village.

The following is a menu for an average day: Breakfast: fruit juice, porridge, fresh eggs, homemade raisin bread, fresh butter, jam, and coffee. Lunch: wine, pickled meat, potatoes au gratin, steak, cream puffs, and coffee. Supper: soup, coldcuts, peas, homemade ice cream (made out of our B-rations from the quartermaster in Lyon), cake, and tea. Whenever we had too many cans of sauerkraut or chili, we traded it for fresh meat, eggs, wine, fruit, etc. Thus, we were able to keep the best part of the American rations, and also get the best of French civilian food. Even with all the good living there, we were still kept very busy keeping open the lines of communication, some of which were located behind the German-held lines.

I spent Christmas at Landry, where we had a "White Christmas"—in the middle of the Alps. The Melchior family tried to make it as pleasant as possible. I was even entertaining thoughts of marrying the Melchior's daughter. All of us in the army would rather have been at home with our own families, of course, even for just a few hours. But we had only to think of the boys in the Ardennes and in the Bulge, and we counted our blessings and didn't allow ourselves to dwell in feelings of homesickness very long.

On January 1, 1945, I wrote to my mother:

Dear Mom,

Today is New Year's Day. I started to reflect on things past and things to come in a very uncertain future. Nineteen forty-four was surely one of the most eventful years in my life. I am grateful that things came out just the way they did. I should say that I learned more in this one year than I did in any of my college years. Most interesting was meeting people of various countries under the strain of war. Although it is commonplace to classify people into economic classes, races, and nationalities, and although people in general put themselves into one of these categories, I have seen that one can transcend such classifications.

The new year looks to be more interesting than any year ever has. One would surely think that the war in Europe will be over by this coming fall, if not sooner. But again, one must not be overly optimistic. Many of the German prisoners told me that they'd defend their Vaterland to the last drop of German blood. The damned fools! But what will happen after the last drop of German blood has been spilled? I might have to go to the Pacific. This would involve six months vacation in the States. I might stay with the occupation troops in Europe. Secretly I hope to be back in civilian life by the end of the year. I am surely going to try to spend some time in England for two reasons: one, I know an awfully nice person there; two, I hope to go to school there. But that's just between us and the future.

Well, I wish all of you my best.
Tom

That evening I wrote to our Unitarian minister:

January 1, 1945

Dear Dick,

I was delighted to receive your letters. Thank you and Deborah for the Christmas gift. A report on the book will follow later. I have asked my mother to pass on all my letters and I hope you pass this on to my mother. I just didn't have enough six-cent envelopes.

You asked me about one year conscription for the eigh-
teen year olds. In general I'm for it. First, it brings the vari-
ous sections of the country together. Second, it gives a certain
type of discipline to the younger generation [I was twenty-
one at the time I was drafted]. I feel this is sadly lacking in
the States. It'll give the young folks a broader outlook before
they go on to a job or continue with college. If this post-war
army is more or less an international police force, it'll give
the boys a chance to see other nations and form a more inter-
nationalist outlook. I also think that the girls should be
drafted for farm work (as in England) or other essential
jobs. Or perhaps I've just got an ax to grind with those fel-
lows who didn't have to "waste" their time in the army.
    I hope that you are all well.
With my very best wishes,
Tom

During the first part of January 1945, Lieutenant
Woods and I made a trip to Paris, which is about four
hundred fifty miles from Grenoble. It was midwinter
and the roads were in bad condition. There were several
detours, and on one of them I had a small accident. The
roads had not been sanded and were icy, and when I
went around a big curve in the middle of the village, our
truck kept going straight ahead, and there was nothing I
could do to control the vehicle. We ended up hitting and
demolishing the stairway leading to a restaurant. I hit
my lip on the steering wheel and began bleeding profusely. A minute later the owner of the restaurant looked
out of the window and said, "Never mind that! Come in
and have a drink." When we were ready to turn all our
financial resources over to the innkeeper in order to pay
for his stairs, he said, "Oh, don't let that worry you!

That's all right! Just bring me two or three packages of cigarettes when you return from Paris!"

After twelve hours of almost continuous driving, we arrived in Paris, which had drastically changed during the past four months. The city was overrun with GIs, and the Parisians had lost a good deal of enthusiasm for their liberators, many of whom were making a bad name for themselves and for the United States. If it had not been for my Parisian friends, I would have felt unwelcome in this town, which I had entered on the shoulders of its citizens only four months earlier.

Paris was dark and cold. Electricity was turned on for just a few hours every day. There was little coal, and people sat in their homes shivering. The food shortage was drastic, and only the rich could afford the black market prices. Although I had a nice room in our headquarters hotel, I preferred to stay with my friends, Jean and René Mauger, whom I had met in Chartres. They showed me parts of Paris that had not yet been discovered by the Americans, such as a few exclusive nightclubs and black market restaurants. They also introduced me to many of their friends from Montmartre.

We spent one evening at the opera to see a ballet performance that included a work by the French choreographer, La Grisi. It was cold in the opera house, and the audience wore their heavy coats and gloves and hats. Even the dancers wore all sorts of heavy woolen underwear that sometimes showed through their tights.

While in Paris, I decided to seek help for my left knee, which I had twisted while skiing at Landry. It was hurting constantly, and I was walking with a limp, so I decided to go to an army sick call. There were two long lines of soldiers waiting—I chose the left one at random.

When I got to the medic he said: "All right, what is her name? And address? When did you sleep with her, and what are your symptoms?"

With surprise I said, "What are you talking about? I hurt my left knee skiing behind the German lines." He said I had gotten into the VD line and referred me to an M.D. captain who bandaged me up, and sent me limping on my way.

The evening before our departure from Paris, I had an interesting experience with an American MP. A British sergeant and I were on our way to a show. The Englishman had on his regular British uniform, and I wore a French beret and a British battle jacket with a SHEAF patch (Supreme Headquarters of the Allied Expedition Forces). By this time I had been promoted to Sergeant and my sergeant stripes were sewn on the sleeve; I also wore GI pants with my custom-made mountain shoes. My .38 caliber revolver dangled openly from my hip.

Just as we were about to enter the theater, an American MP hailed me over: "Hey bud! Come 'ere!" I knew I was in for some trouble. We were not allowed to carry revolvers in a rear area such as Paris, and most of my uniform was against all army rules and regulations. Besides that, I did not have a pass, and so I quickly told my British buddy that he should introduce me as his French friend, Pierre. The MP looked at my revolver and said, "Let's see your pass!" I replied in my best French, "Pardon?" The MP became impatient, "Where is your goddamn pass?" I immediately started sputtering off in rapid-fire fashion, "Mais, qu'est ce que tu veux? Je suis français moi, et je ne veux pas avoir d'ennui avec vous americains. Va-t-en, ou autrement je vais appeler la police!" The MP looked stunned. Yet he insisted on showing off his French. He pointed his finger at me saying, "Ah—vous ... français?" I responded immediately, "Mais bien sure je suis français," and we hurried to the window to buy tickets. The MP looked at us with mouth and eyes wide open.

A week after our arrival in Paris on leave, we were told to return to Grenoble. I was given a few rather short farewell parties by my Parisian friends, and after I found my lieutenant—in the apartment of his friend, the movie actress—we left for Grenoble at half past nine one morning in a quarter-ton GI truck. We were both somewhat exhausted from the Parisian nightlife, and the weather was terrible for any kind of driving. The snow came down in thick flakes, and the fog was heavy. I felt as if I was fumbling my way through a dark clothes closet. I could not see where I was going, nor where I had come from. Every fifteen minutes we had to get out and clear the windshield; and even in spite of that effort, I had to hold one hand against the inside of the glass to keep it from freezing and cutting off what little view I did have.

On both sides of the road were French civilian vehicles that had broken down or gotten stuck in the snow. Before long, we were followed by a whole convoy of French trucks and passenger cars taking advantage of the tracks our truck had left behind. Every now and then we got stuck in a snowdrift blocking the highway. Each time this happened, some twenty Frenchmen immediately jumped out of their vehicles and came up to our truck with shovels, chains, rags, and jacks, as well as all sorts of suggestions. After a short parliamentary debate as to the correct procedure, the Frenchmen usually agreed that they would have to push. While ten of them talked using their hands to explain the procedure with wild gesticulations, the others helped us push. Along the way, we did stop at the restaurant where we had demolished the stairs and delivered some cigarettes, which were enthusiastically received.

The bad weather continued for the rest of the day, and by eight o'clock that evening, we were still fighting the elements. Since there were no decent hotels in any of the villages, we decided to continue on until we got to Grenoble. At about two o'clock in the morning I became very tired, despite six or seven cups of coffee, as well as the excessive cold. My eyes were already half-closed, and in order to see the road, or at least the stretch immediately in front of the truck, I leaned my head back against the seat. After awhile my head got tired and I slumped forward. I came to my full senses again when I felt the truck leave the main roadbed and head for the trees. I repeated this process of dozing off, heading for the trees, and waking up again, several times. When I could stand it no longer, I woke up the lieutenant, who had fallen asleep long before. He agreed to take over and I fell asleep immediately. About thirty minutes later, I half-opened my eyes to find that the lieutenant's head was resting on the steering wheel. This really woke me up. I automatically grabbed the wheel, but when I looked out, I realized the truck was already parked peacefully on the side of the road.

I took over again, driving until we got to Grenoble at half past nine in the morning. Excluding the two stops for lunch and supper, and the half-hour sleep, I had been driving for twenty-two hours.

When we arrived in Landry the following day, I was

very ill with a terrible cold, and I made up my mind to stay in bed. Claire, the daughter of the hotel owners, played doctor, nurse, and waitress. I had all my meals served to me in bed. Claire did not believe that aspirin and hot tea would cure me, so she decided that she would try the famous local remedy, the ventouses, a cure-all for the most dreadful of diseases. The word ventouses comes from

CLAIRE

the Latin ventus—wind. The English term for the method is "cupping glass".

The next evening Claire came up to my room with a tray full of small glass cups, some cotton, and a bottle of some sort of fuel. I lay on my stomach, while Claire dipped a small piece of cotton into the fuel, put a burning match to the cotton, threw the flaming cotton into the glass, and put the glass upside down on my back. Fortunately, the cotton did not burn very long for lack of air. This partial vacuum caused the blood to be drawn to the surface of my skin, thus extracting all the "evil" toxins. When Claire got through with me, I had about ten of these vacuum glasses distributed evenly over my back. After the glasses were removed, it looked as though I had just emerged from a tattoo shop. I did immediately recover.

January 17, 1945

Dear Mom,

*   I simply must drop a note before you put me on your missing-in-action list again. I had a chance to go to Paris recently, and so I did not have much time to write long letters. I'm still with the same people and with the same job (whoever and whatever that is). Also have a slight advance in pay ... and was promoted to sergeant!*

*   I've also been "awarded" the good conduct medal. This is about the equivalent of saying: the chap hasn't slept with a diseased woman for a year now, let's give him a medal. This ribbon isn't worth anything, except perhaps bluffing the French.*

*   A hasty kiss from Sgt. Frazier.*
Tom

The innkeeper had an excellent radio, which he had concealed from the Germans during the years of occupation. Since Landry was at a fairly high altitude, we were able to hear most of the Western European stations. We listened to the BBC for news, to Radio Paris for French lessons and amusement, and to the German stations for good music and propaganda. On February 2, 1945 I was able to tune in Adolf Hitler. He was making a desperate appeal to the German people. There was nothing positive in the entire speech, and everything he said was based on fear and hatred. He told the Germans that they would all be killed if Germany lost the war. He told them that the Allies could never promise anything without breaking their promise. "It's just as though one sheep promised another to protect it from the tiger," he said. I never knew exactly who the sheep and the tiger were, but I was sure that Hitler's days were numbered. I had not heard him speak for several years, and it seemed to me that the morale of the German people must have been very low to have listened to such talk. How could a nation believe such obvious lies, and be driven by so much fear and hatred? And if I had remained in Germany in 1937 what would I be doing, what would be my state of mind?

After Hitler's speech we heard a beautiful little Mozart symphony from the same German station. In the middle of the third movement, the music suddenly became very soft, and the announcer said: "Achtung! Achtung! There is a squadron of fast enemy attack bombers over the Reich. They are coming from southeastern Belgium, and flying in the direction of western Saxony!" Then the symphony was resumed at full volume.

On February 27 I wrote home again:

Dear Mom, Chris, and Reed [College],
I haven't heard from you in three weeks. I often find that I don't get enough letters from home. I liked Professor Chittick's picture. Unfortunately he very rarely writes, so I wrote to Mrs. Chittick. Enfin ... received five very nice letters. Very proud of Chris. After I have made somewhat of a mess out of my college career, he has at least saved the family's reputation. I never gained as much from Reed as I should have. Judging from his letters Chris is becoming a real Reed student: an idealist, with the right kind of ideals, who needs to get a whiff of the outside world; and I don't mean out of the pages of a sociology book.
One more thing about Chris: I met M., who thinks that he is very cute—mon dieu, from all over the world I hear

MULE, SLED AND DRIVER FOR TRANSPORT

SGT. EDDY, PVT. JOHNY
AND ICICLE

about his love life.

What on earth is going on? I was amused to hear that my letters were read in church—I certainly don't hope for any divine inspiration or intervention. Unless these letters are highly censored, I should not like to have every Tom, Dick (not Richard of course), and Harry listen to the confessions of a young soldier to his mother.

Got a nice package with the cake, candy, and scarf. Thank you ... still waiting for underwear. New Yorker's are most welcome. Please raise hell with New Republic. Spatz [Al's sister] sent me some lovely Lebkuchen for Christmas. There'll be some changes made in my life rather soon. Future looks very uncertain. Stand by. In the last five months I've had in many ways the best time of my life. Personally, I am turning out to be rather leftist, though never Communist. I might say that I've been around to see all classes of people. As to your discussion concerning my profession ... I shall wait some time yet.

All my love,
Tom

Chapter 8

•

Return to Paris - March 1945

On March second, our pleasant vacation at Landry came to an end. We were told most emphatically to stop our work in the region and return to Paris. Since there was no more work for us behind the enemy lines anywhere in Europe, except in Germany, we were all having nightmares about what would happen to us. Whatever happened, we were sure that from now on, the journey would be downhill until we hit the shores of America.

Some of my feelings were revealed to my mother in the following letters:

March 7, 1945

Dear Mom and all,

Why is my morale low? Well, I've just finished a dream that lasted three months. I've never given you much detailed information about my lady friends. How would you like to be a mother-in-law to a French girl?—but take it easy— it'll probably never happen. Now I am separated from her for I don't know how long. I am no longer in the high mountains. Within a few days, I'll probably have a new job, and perhaps a new address. But no matter how good the job, or how good the chances for promotion, I'm pretty much fed up with the army, and I dread the thought of staying in one more year.

Perhaps all this is the young lady's fault. Politically she is even more to the left than I (she used to belong to the Communist Party). I am writing this because you are my mother, and I got to know you pretty well. I don't want you to share this with anyone.

Tom

March 17, 1945

And so I have a new job. It is with regret that I left the last assignment. I know there are few men in this army who have had such an interesting job. I am not comparing army with civilian life. I was sorry to leave my good friends in Paris and my little girlfriend in the mountains. Now I'm back in the army. But perhaps it won't be as bad—after all—I am now the senior noncommissioned officer in my little group, which leaves a little room for personal initiative. If I am a good boy, I'll eventually become a master sergeant (three stripes above and three below). The only drawback with this little deal is that there is quite a possibility that I will have to stick around Germany after the armistice. If the war in Japan is over by then, I'll be greatly annoyed, for I have no interest in sojourning in Germany.

A week ago today I was finally decorated. They had a big formation, at which a colonel pinned the Soldier's Medal on Sergeant Frazier. This entitles me to two dollars extra in my monthly pay.

I have some very charming friends in Paris: a young couple with two babies (who are undernourished). Although there is very little food in Paris, practically no heat, etc., they have taken me in as though I was their brother. Half of my mountain equipment, and a lot of rather personal papers and letters are with them. So in case I shouldn't come back, and that is always possible, write to them after the war. (Send them some money and goods, and they'll be only too happy to ship my stuff to the States.)

You might be interested to hear that right now I speak French with more ease than I do German.

Now, I may not be writing every day, but you may rest assured that my thoughts take me back to you almost every hour. (Sob, sob!)

Ever yours longingly,
Tom

In Paris, our lieutenant told me that he had chosen me and another enlisted man on our team to go with him to China. He wanted us to jump behind the Japanese lines to do the same type of work we had done together in France, Belgium, Luxembourg, and Italy. I definitely did not want to go to the East, even though it meant getting home sooner.

I knew there was an acute shortage of German-speaking personnel, so I informed the authorities that I spoke German. Two days later, I received word that I was being transferred to another organization. I was sad to be leaving our team. We had worked so well together and accomplished so much. We had depended on each other for our very lives and lived through danger, hard work, adventure, good times, and bad times. I genuinely liked our entire team in a very deep way. (After I left them, I never saw them again, except for a brief visit with Lieutenant Wood.) Now I would have to get used to a completely new team.

Rosière was our staging area—the last stop before entering Germany, and the place where we would be briefed about our job. Since we had a good deal of free time, I caught up with my letter writing, and I took the opportunity to record some of my impressions of France and send them home. This is the way I saw France at that time. It was my personal farewell to a country that had meant so much to me.

French Impressions

France had been going through hell for four years. The population had been starved by the Germans, who took eighty percent of the country's agricultural produce. Five million young Frenchmen were prisoners of war or served as slave laborers in Germany and were starved physically and morally. These were the men who would shape the future of France. In addition, a good deal of French machinery had been carried off to Germany, or had been destroyed by the bombardments.

Now that France was liberated, material life was not much better. Some 1,800,000 homes were left uninhabitable, and roughly 2,500,000 people were left homeless. An estimated 100 million land mines (targeting vehicles and personnel) had been left behind by the Wehrmacht. Food was scarce, and although many of the communities were expected to be self-sufficient, they did not have the means to do so. Communication channels had been badly disrupted. As many as nine hundred bridges were destroyed, and most of the big highways had either disintegrated during the German occupation, or had suffered under the heavy bombardment.

The morale of the French was very low. They had hoped that most of their problems would be solved soon after the arrival of the Allies. As their memory of the German oppression began to fade, however, new worries appeared. They anticipated another cold and hungry winter and were worried about runaway prices supported by a feeble food-rationing system. And they worried about the fact that there was no more food coming from the Allied storehouses.

The French hated to admit that they had been defeated by the Germans in 1940. This was hushed up in the French press and radio. A Parisian friend of mine seriously argued that the liberation of France had been a cinch for the Allies, because the FFI had done most of the work. They failed to realize that the time had come to an end when they could waylay German trucks or live off the rations their fellow patriots managed to acquire and give to them.

The French were trying desperately to assert themselves as a nation. To me it looked like they were at the point of a national nervous breakdown, largely because other nations failed to share the French view that France was still a mighty and prevailing power. Deep down, the French felt the certain humiliation of having been liberated by someone else. France wanted, and even expected, charity from these liberators, but they wanted the gift labels removed from the articles, and the goods marked "paid in full," even though they had not paid a cent.

We once spent a week in the sector of the French First Army. One day we were stopped by a French soldier, who asked us for our passes. After a while, he said, "Oh, you are Americans! Well, why in the dickens are you wearing French uniforms?" We did not bother to tell him that his complete uniform (as well as the ones we were wearing) had been made and paid for by the American taxpayer. Most of the French war equipment was either American, British, and sometimes French. Yet, it was all exhibited as being French.

Although there was a healthy political trend toward the left, I found that political thinking in France was quite disorganized. The Communists I met had little idea of Communism. They only wanted to deprive the rich of their wealth. The French Socialists seemed to move in the same direction, as did the Socialists in several other European countries. They, too, advocated the nationalization of the public utilities, of the banks, and of transportation. Many people looked to DeGaulle for national salvation, but they also felt that his major job of rallying the French against the Germans had been accomplished. In fact, De Gaulle had swung to the right politically.

Many of the old factions and political parties were being revived. This was because the Germans had succeeded in decentralizing and splitting up France, and because the majority of the French people wanted to return to the "good old days." Yet, because of the strong pressure from the left, there was little chance that France would return to the same type of conservative government that existed in 1940. The French voter soon had to decide which political, social, and economic direction his country would go.

By this time the American troops had become quite unpopular with the French, since few of the Americans spoke French, and some were mostly interested in liquor, women, and cheap entertainment. The Frenchmen were quite disgusted with the GI way of gulping down vast amounts of liquor quickly rather than the French way of savoring their fine wines. Seldom did one see a truly drunk Frenchman. Many of my Parisian friends believed the Americans took advantage of the French women, and that they were too hedonistic in their approach to them. Most of the entertainment was geared for the GI trade: prices were high and the quality of entertainment low. It was quite evident that Paris would not regain its sophisticated pre-war sparkle for some time to come.

Many GIs complained that the "frogs" (the GI nickname for the French) cheated them right and left. Some of my educated friends told me that France had certainly lost her august place among the great nations long ago. According to them, France had reached her peak in the seventeenth and eighteenth centuries, and the French were still basing their greatness on the Age of Enlightenment. But Voltaire's and Rousseau's world would not return, and their philosophy needed to be enhanced.

When I landed at Normandy Beach, I shared many of these prejudices about the French culture with my fellow GIs. Yet, after traveling through most of France, meeting people of all sorts and in all conditions, working alongside the Maquis (partisans) and watching them fight, and having been made most welcome by so many French families everywhere and at any time, I modified my ideas and became very favorably impressed with the French. Of course, the French partisans I had known were a special, heroic breed.

It is true that many of the French were perhaps more casual and relaxed in their personal hygiene than are most Americans, and that they have some habits—such as relieving themselves in some of the most public places—that are hard for us to sanction. (I wondered, though, whether they put gum under movie seats or drugstore counters.) I felt it was wrong to condemn a people for their different habits and ways. They have a somewhat different cultural background than the Northern nations—more bon vivant, certainly less rigid.

It is important to remember what the French had gone through in the previous four years. I was often surprised to see how well they had withstood the Nazi tyranny. Although I agreed with many of the negative remarks made by my fellow GIs about the French, I also found much to admire and respect. It seemed to me that the French showed little of the cruelty displayed by the Germans. Although I found a good deal of class distinction in France, it did not seem as deep-seated and entrenched as in England or Germany. The French attitude toward sex seemed to me more natural and less hypocritical than our own. The French also struck me as being artistic, or at least interested in and appreciative of the fine arts. I spent many an hour discussing ballets, famous painters, sculptors, and composers with all kinds of people—street sweepers, nurses, secretaries, and bakers.

What impressed me, possibly the most, was the French cuisine, which they have made into a high art. My experience was that every French woman I met, rich or poor, was able to prepare a delicious meal, if she had the material. For instance, after having eaten C-rations for several weeks at a time, we came to despise them so much that we could not even look at the cans. Yet, when we gave these rations to a French woman, she would make a very delicious meal out of them. Of course, eating off regular plates made quite an improvement in the taste already. And then there was the wine! It took me several months to learn how to enjoy a good wine, which we often had with our meals. Usually a good, balanced dinner, which took two to three hours to consume, had five or six different types of alcoholic drinks on the menu. First we were served an appetizer. Then we had red as well as white wine with the main course, followed by a glass or two of champagne with the dessert. Before, after, or with the coffee we had some cognac or Calvados, and then a digestif, which gave its final blessing to the whole meal.

France had been a wonderful experience for me. I felt the pain of leaving that country, and I planned to return there as soon as the Army would permit it. I was not, however, looking forward to moving into Germany.

Chapter 9

•

March-July 1945

Now that the lands formerly occupied by the Germans—Belgium, Luxembourg, Italy, and France—had been liberated by the Allies, our work there was over. Moving into Germany would be a different story. Without the help of partisans and in the midst of an enemy's population, it would be too dangerous to attempt to rescue prisoners. Our assignments would change, and we did not know what they would be.

On the fifteenth of March 1945, we left Paris and drove all day until we got to Rosière, close to Lunéville in France. The whole American Army seemed to be on the move. The roads were cluttered with motorcycles, quarter-ton pick-ups, seven-ton trucks, ducks (amphibious trucks), tanks, motorized artillery, ambulances, refrigeration trucks, ordnance vehicles, amphibious jeeps, engineer trucks carrying pontoons, and many other vehicles. Everything, it seemed, was moving east. The dust and heat were unbearable. Little French children, dressed in torn clothing, were standing by the roadside. Some of the soldiers who could still see despite the dust threw bits of their K-rations to them.

I was now the senior non-commissioned officer in a

DOCUMENT TEAM - LT. SCHRANK ON LEFT

new team originally organized to interrogate German prisoners of war. At Camp Richie we had gone through the training to prepare us for that job. In what seemed to me typical army fashion, however, we were soon told that we would have nothing to do with the German prisoners. Instead, we were assigned to move with the forward infantry into certain German cities of 400,000 or more and locate, evaluate, and evacuate the important documents we found there.

In Rosière we found the headquarters of our new outfit, which went by the name T-Force, or Target Force. Usually the term "target" was used by the artillery or air force as something to be aimed at and destroyed, but in our case, it meant an intelligence target, such as Gestapo headquarters. Our job would be to search all the assigned targets from the basement to the top floor, if there was a floor left above ground level.

Naturally, all of us in our newly formed team were more or less acquainted with the German language. Our

RUINS IN ST. DIE, FRANCE

commanding officer, a first lieutenant, came from Texas where he had lived in a German community, and he spoke German fluently. The second in command was a lieutenant from Vienna, who had the Viennese charm, and he was very proud of being a lieutenant. One enlisted man had also come from Vienna, where he had practiced law before the Anschluss (annexation). One man had come to the United States in 1929 from Hamburg and spoke English with a very heavy German accent. His German was quite faulty; he was one of those unfortunate foreigners who cannot make themselves clearly understood in either language. The fourth man was a refugee from Austria. Unfortunately, few men on our team got along well with each other. Luckily the CO (commanding officer) and I had a good working relationship. One thing we had in common was that we both knew how to drive, while the others either did not drive, or drove so poorly they should have had their licenses taken away from them. To go into a large city and search through many buildings without being able to drive around was a hindrance and an inconvenience, and did not speak very well of the army's system of personnel placement. I missed my old team of "real Americans" who understood each other and worked together so well.

We had two jeeps, one trailer, two chairs, one table, a field desk, two field telephones (none of us knew how to install or operate them), all kinds of tools, and the baggage of the two officers and four men. After everybody and everything had been loaded into the jeeps, we looked like Barnum and Bailey's Circus on the move. I had my own jeep, and on the front panel I had stenciled in white Mein Krampf (my cramp), after Hitler's tome, Mein Kampf. I watched the German reaction: many gasped at this sacrilege, and some looked away. Only a few laughed.

A New Mission in Germany

On March 24, 1945, we entered Germany. Immediately after we crossed the border, I noticed two things that made Germany and the Germans different from anything I had seen in other European countries. All the villages and towns had taken quite a beating in the bombardment and shelling, and at the same time, all the civilians were well fed and well dressed.

The destruction wrought by the war was terrific. No matter where we went, we seldom saw a building left un-

GERMAN AUTOBAHN (FREEWAY) DESTROYED

touched by the war. The clouds of dust and the dead
German soldiers as well as civilians lying by the side of
the road, the stench, the rubble, and the endless columns
of dusty vehicles all passed in front of our eyes like a
nightmare. On some of the walls still standing, there
were the familiar, crazy slogans about loyalty to the
Führer or promises of revenge.

We were given detailed and specific instructions
about our targets. Long before a large German town was
taken, our headquarters made up a dossier or list of targets in the town. The information came from German
prisoners and civilians, telephone directories, and secret
directories that had fallen into American hands. As we
were going through a town, many changes and additions
to these lists had to be made. New targets were discovered, and old ones had to be located at a new address
because, as we so often stated in our reports, the buildings had been completely bombed out.

One of our target lists for the town of Esslingen follows:

List of Targets Sent to First Lt. Schrank—member of
U.S. Army document section near and in Esslingen, a
town outside of Stuttgart, April 1945

- 46 NSBO, NSDAP (Nazi party), HJ (Hitler youth),
  BDM (Hitler youth for girls), DAF
  (German labor front)
- 146 NSDAP Kreisleitung,(District Headquarters
  for Nazi Party), Bahnhof St. Weiblingen. Some
  records of general nature remaining.
- 290 NSD STB, at the Staatliche Ingenieur
  Schule (State college of Engineering)

- 292 NSLB (NAZI TEACHER'S LEAGUE DISTRICT HQ.)
- 336 SA STANDARTE 247 (STORM TROOPERS #247)
- 338 NSDAP KREISLEITUNG, (NAZI PARTY DISTRICT HQ.) OBERESSLINGEN, ESSLINGEN
- 340 KRIPO (CRIMINAL POLICE), HAFENMARKT 2, SA PLATZ, ESSLINGEN
- 341 SD AUSSENSTELLE, (SECURITY OFFICE OUTER DISTRICT), ESSLINGEN
- 352 HJ (HITLER YOUTH), BANN, ESSLINGEN, BLOCHINGER ST. 13
- 356 NSKK MOTORSTAFFEL (NAZI MOTORIZED CORPS) IV OTTILIEN PLATZ, ESSLINGEN
- 359 SA STURMBANN, (HQ STORM TROOPERS #1247) WAGNER ST. 22, ESSLINGEN
- 360 SA STANDARTE 246 (HQ STORMTROOPERS #246) AUGUSTINER ST. 2, ESSLINGEN
- 361 SA STURM 1-247, (HQ STORMTROOPERS #1247) BAHNHOF ST.35, ESSLINGEN
- 362 AD STURM 2-247 (HQ LABOR SERVICE #2247) ESSLINGEN 8 ESSLINGEN
- 363 SA MARINE STURM (HQ NAZI PARTY, NAVAL BRANCH) 318 GOETHE ST. 8, ESSLINGEN
- 366 NSFK (HQ NAZI WOMEN) STURM A/101 ZOLLWERK ST. L, ESSLINGEN
- 367 NSFK (HQ NAZI WOMEN) 9/102 ZOLLWERK ST. L, ESSLINGEN
- 371 DAF KREISWALTUNG (HQ GERMAN LABOR FRONT) ESSLINGEN, KANAL ST. 29, ESSLINGEN
- 374 NSF KREISFRAUENVERWALTUNG (NAZI WOMEN LEADERSHIP) WEBER ST. 12, ESSLINGEN
- 376 RDB KREISVERWALTUNG (HEADQUARTERS) OTTILIEN ST, 53, ESSLINGEN

Others: Maschinen Fabrik Esslingen, Locomotive and airplane motors, Esslingen Machine lathe factory, Esslingen, vicinity Indexwerke, KAHN & KOLB, lathes, etc. Esslingen Glass factory, making A/C silencers, Esslingen, vicinity Factory making hydraulic presses, 5 80t presses, Esslingen, vicinity Factory Carl Mahr, Wienometer and gadgets, Esslingen. Factory Dr. Dick, cutting tools, Esslingen Boley & Linen, machine factory, Esslingen Daimler-Benz, Untertürkheim I.G.Farben, Ziegelwerke-Endersbach, Endersbach.

Each target was rated in priority. When we moved into a town, we covered all the number one priority targets first. These targets usually consisted of important political institutions like the Gestapo headquarters, Hitler's residence, the party headquarters, concentration camps, and so on. Second-priority targets were of less interest, and third-priority targets were usually covered only when we did not have much to do.

Our sole job was to find documents and confiscate them, if appropriate. Therefore, even if we found an important Nazi at one of the targets, all we could do was to report him to the Counter-intelligence Corps, who were usually so busy that they did not have time to pick him up, and he would go free. Once we found the man who had formerly been the sole publisher of Mein Kampf, and who had been in charge of the biggest Nazi publishing house in Munich. Since he had no documents with him, we had to let him go. The Nazis or the Russians would have handled that differently.

Our targets consisted of a large variety of buildings, ruins, and institutions. There were army barracks, headquarters of Nazi organizations such as the Gestapo, the Nazi Party, the Hitler Youth (boys as well as girls),

German Labor Service, Kraft durch Freude (Strength through Joy), Nazi women's organizations, SS, and the German Labor Front. There were also factories such as I.G. Farben, university libraries and laboratories, post offices, museums, broadcasting stations, banks, federal and local government offices, police stations, jails and prisons, geodetic survey institutes, railway stations, botanical institutes, a suicide-plane factory, hospitals, underground factories, mines, and castles. We found many interesting articles, from canned pickles to Hitler's stationery, which had been stowed away by the Germans, and was now available for "liberation." Therefore, instead of calling us T-Force, the other GIs began calling us "loot-waffe," after the German Luftwaffe.

When we first started doing target work, we went through every file (the Germans kept many files), tried to open every safe, and examined every piece of furniture. This was very tedious and time-consuming, yet, after a week or two we developed an intuition or special sense for locating important documents. I suppose that we had come to understand the German mind a bit better, and had come to know just where the German bureaucrats might hide the important documents. In most instances they locked their empty safes, hoping that we would waste a lot of time looking for the keys or trying to break in. An example was Hitler's safe in Berchtesgaden, high up in his Bavarian mountain palace. When we finally got it open, we found two autographed copies of Mein Kampf and nothing else. It felt eerie to stand in his living room—the man I saw with trepidation in 1934, and who was responsible for such destruction upon the world.

VIEW FROM HITLER'S LIVING ROOM
IN BERCHTESGADEN

SS BARRACKS BOMBED
(NEAR HITLER'S HOUSE)

While I was doing this work in Germany, I went through the personal effects of hundreds of people, broke open hundreds of desks and cupboards, and read many love letters of the Fräulein secretaries. We found loads of office supplies and files on each Gestapo member, as well as those they arrested. Occasionally we found weapons such as pistols and daggers, and often we found nothing of any interest whatsoever.

The Germans were extremely orderly. Every eraser, every paper clip, had an assigned place in the desk. Every piece of paper was filed somewhere. Therefore, it was always fairly easy to find whatever I was looking for. I wondered: Did this extreme neatness, as exemplified by orderly desks, contribute to Germany losing the war? Were they so busy keeping things neat and in a rigid structure that they had not enough time to do other things? Or did they put all their energy into being so orderly that they did not see the overall picture?

When we first arrived in Germany we carried carbines and hand grenades. Now we lugged around a flashlight, a small sledgehammer, a crowbar, and some dynamite. We were finally being taught a trade. In the army we were specialists; in civilian life we would have been called thieves and robbers. Naturally there was a good deal of looting, which was reluctantly tolerated as the spoils of war. After two weeks of this kind of operation I was sick of it, but some of the people connected with us developed a regular looting complex. In fact, they were often looking for loot rather than for the important target documents.

In many of the party headquarters we found thousands of German reichsmarks, most of which was turned over to our military government. Most of the GIs, having little idea about the relative value of the mark, often overpaid the Germans because they had a lot of this extra German money on their hands. For instance, when we first got to Germany, I paid one mark for a haircut. (Although the mark had the exchange value of forty cents before the war, it had about the same purchasing power as the dollar.) When I left Germany I paid five marks for the same haircut as a result of the way the GIs passed out money so freely. Some GIs made a lot of money in Germany, looting and bartering. Since the Germans did not quite trust the new Allied money, they were only too happy to trade it at considerable loss for their old marks. Some soldiers went on looting tours and sold their finds to their buddies at high prices.

Our first target after arriving was Frankenthal, a small town about ten miles north of Ludwigshafen on the west side of the Rhine. We stayed in the barracks, which had been occupied by the Luftwaffe (German Air Force) and was now occupied by our "Lootwaffe." Our living quarters consisted of an old two-room shack that shook down to its foundation every time someone tossed in his bed.

All around our encampment the U.S. artillery boys had placed their heavy pieces, and there must have been dozens of them. The following day at nine o'clock in the evening, one of those guns fired the first round, shaking the whole earth until we were afraid that our shack would disintegrate any minute. My bed jumped at least six inches toward the middle of the room, and my sleeping bag was covered with flakes of old paint, which had come down from the ceiling, and most of the windows did not survive the blast. We had hardly recovered from this first round, when another one came off, and then a third one. Before long the rate of fire increased. Our fragile shack was squeaking and moaning and knocking about. This went on all night. The next morning we learned that our boys had dispatched 2,500 ten-centimeter shells to Mannheim, on the other side of the Rhine.

Our first target in Frankenthal was the local office of internal revenue. We went through all the papers, even though we were told by some of the German civil servants that this institution was "of course" a non-political organization. On the third floor we found a big safe. Since none of the Fräuleins on duty could produce the key, we decided to let our combat engineers blast it open. They stuck some plastic explosives on the lock and hinges, set the fuse, and told everybody to run as far away as they could for safety. The blast took off some of the paint and filled the room with smoke, but did not open the safe. The engineer lieutenant then decided to give it the works, and he plastered the whole safe with explosives. The second blast turned out to be even more exciting. Bits of furniture came sailing through the win-

dows, to be followed
by a big cloud of
dust and smoke.
This time the safe
door was bent open
halfway. Although
we still were unable
to open the door
because the hinges

LUDWIGSHAFEN RUINS

were jammed by the blast, we were able to shine a flashlight inside and get the contents out with a long wire.
All we found was an antiquated revolver and some literature of the Nazi organization Mother and Child.

After we had covered Frankenthal, we went to
Ludwigshafen, also west of the Rhine River. There were
snipers throughout the town, and the Germans on the
east side of the Rhine were still blasting at us. One day
we were looking for the Nazi party files in a big building
by the wharf in rooms that faced the river. We saw a GI
looking out of the window, and when we had passed by
him, we suddenly heard a short, whistling sound, followed by a click, and then a dull thumping sound of
something hitting the floor. We rushed into the room
and found the GI lying there dead. He had been shot
through the head, and the bullet had left a very neat hole
in his helmet.

After working in Ludwigshafen for three days, we
crossed the Rhine at Worms and then went south to
Mannheim, which was very badly damaged. Most of our
intelligence targets had been destroyed. Only the basements were intact, and even they were often burnt out.
In many instances our guards were guarding only a pile
of rubble. The various infantry divisions had received

NAZI HEADQUARTERS-WÜRZBURG
BOMBED-OUT

copies of our target list and they posted a guard at each one.

According to our dossier, the Gestapo headquarters was located at 137 Adolph Hitler Street. As soon as the Americans had moved into the town, guards were sent there and told to let nobody in or out until our target team arrived. This was to prevent both the GIs and the civilians from looting and to protect the important records, yet it sometimes caused major discomfort for the German civilians who occupied a part of the building.

One time we got to a target seven days after the town had fallen. The building was in fairly good shape. The Allied guard had been ordered to keep everyone away from where the important documents were until we got there. He took his orders seriously and was so strict that he had told the civilians to get into the basement two stories below the ground floor and to stay there. They had been confined there seven days, and every time they wanted to step out of their basement room, a guard pointed his rifle at them and chased them back. By the time we finally arrived the civilians were crying, and they begged us on their knees to let them go one floor above, where they had stored some canned goods. And we did give them permission.

After we had finished with all the targets in

Mannheim, we drove through Wertheim to Würzburg on the Main River. The larger part of Würzburg was located on the east side of the river, and the Germans were still holding it. Our own forces had not been able to cross the river because of the German 88 mm guns and the snipers. All the four bridges were down, and the Germans and Americans were having duels across the river. Finally, after a day of dilly-dallying around, the American division commander gave the Germans an ultimatum: Surrender or we will blast Würzburg! The German mayor was willing to surrender in order to save his beloved town and his people, but the German Army commander refused to give up. So—the shelling intensified. Before long, Würzburg, which had already suffered from repeated Allied air bombardments, was totally ruined, and, of course, many civilians were killed. I had grown accustomed to the fervor with which Germans were willing to give their lives for their ideal, but it was still a shock to witness someone, such as the German Army commander, willing to let the Americans annihilate hundreds of people as well as their whole town. I was often told that Würzburg had been considered one of Germany's most beautiful towns.

Before crossing the Main River, and still under siege from the Germans on the other side, we were stationed in a brewery that had been in operation until recently. Although I seldom drank beer, I certainly enjoyed this Würzburger Bier, especially since it was "on the house." Once in a while a bullet came whizzing through my room, or a German fighter-plane swooped low over the valley. My particular room was facing the Main River and the Germans on the other side of the river. Whenever the spraying of machine gun bullets became too heavy, I moved across the hall into the room of a buddy where there was more security and more champagne.

We were finally able to cross the Main River, even though under enemy fire. The town was dead. All the civilians were told to remain at home or in the public shelters. All the buildings were either partially or wholly destroyed, and it was difficult to imagine where the 90,000 civilians had gone. Many of them were still in their basements, some had fled to the country, and some were lying in the streets dead. I had never before seen so many dead people. They were lying everywhere—in the middle of the street, in the gutter, on the lawns, leaning on windowsills, and one had even been blown up into a tree. No one in sight was alive. Soon after we had crossed the river we came upon a 15-ft. high pile of Germans—all dead. The stench was so strong that it overpowered all other senses. Then came the mortal fear that death could come to us at any moment, and then there was a terrible and confused feeling of disgust, sickness, terrible sadness, and even physical pain. These were sights that never left me, and I don't think that anyone who has seen such sights can ever be the same. One alternative is to completely block out these scenes—to literally not see them, or not recognize what one is seeing. I often thought that many Germans must have found this solution of not seeing.

Once in a while we heard the sharp ring of sniper fire. In the chapel of the royal residence we found a dead woman in a German Army uniform stretched out by the altar. Her face was swollen from the blows of a rifle butt. The guard who took us through the building said, "This bitch killed three of my buddies before we were able to get to her."

Würzburg was full of historical monuments, most of which were badly damaged or demolished. The church of Saint Burkhard, which dates back to the eleventh and twelfth centuries, now consisted of only three walls. The roof and the apse had been destroyed, and the famous university, which had been founded in the first part of the fifteenth century, was almost completely demolished. Ironically, only the French and English library halls on the second floor were intact. Since the stairway had collapsed, we had to scale the walls to get up there. The rest of the building was one big, burnt out mess of books, telescopic lenses, biological specimens, chairs, and charts. A civilian later told me that this university used to have a student body of nearly 3,000 and a library of 600,000 books. All the many, many buildings, which dated back to the Middle Ages, were burned or demolished. When I saw all the destroyed churches, I was reminded of Bristol, England, where the Nazis had destroyed 30 churches and cathedrals in one night during the Blitz in 1940. What did these universities, libraries, and cathedrals have to do with the war? Because one was destroyed, did that make it right to destroy another in retaliation? My mind reeled. I had no answer.

In Würzburg we came upon the food stores of the Wehrmacht (the German Army). I never had such a feast in my life. Most of the food had been stolen from the occupied nations, and thus we had no scruples in keeping this food from the Germans. We found Norwegian sardines, preserved fruit and vegetables, all kinds of canned meat, and many cases of the most delicious French champagne. For one whole week we drank champagne as if it were water. On Easter I wrote to my mother:

April l, 1945

Dear Mom,

Today was Easter, but it could just as well have been Christmas, and nobody would have known the difference. I was thinking of our nice Easter service in Portland this morning. Even the churches here are destroyed. Life is strictly army. We are not allowed to talk to civilians unless it is on business. But I have no desire to do so anyway. I am still daydreaming about the French mountains. Right now there is some Handel on the radio, a German station. I hope one of these days we will hear some Russian music from the station of "Berlin-ski."

Yesterday I sent you two packages. One contained an SA dagger, a swastika flag, a German mother's medal (for you), and some pamphlets. The other consists of nothing but music for the recorder. I found a recorder the other day "somewhere in Germany," an alto. Good luck has it that there is a lieutenant in my outfit who owns and plays a C-soprano. So under the noise of the adjacent artillery, we got together and tootled our way through some German songs while the fragile shack was moaning and knocking under the strain and stress of war. Do you remember Mac G.G. (Lieutenant) from Reed? He went to the Odenwald school where Anni taught. I met him again the other day, and did we have a bull session! We covered almost the whole Reed college student body since 1937.

Just another reminder to tell you how lucky you are to have a home in America. Germany is almost completely destroyed. I have already been in several of the larger and better known German cities. It is rare to see a building that has been untouched. You will look down the street and see the whole facade of every house there, but once you look through the window, you don't know whether you are inside or outside of the house. Apparently this destruction was necessary. I couldn't help feeling sorry for these old people who now live in their basements or air raid shelters. Unfortunately, the worst criminals moved with the German troops. And now you find a somewhat bewildered, embittered civilian population. Yet many of them are still arrogant, materialist, pseudo-martyrs, in spite of this defeat.

I have now gone four weeks without mail. That's probably why my morale is a bit low. I have been writing at least once a week, and hope you have done your share. Please give my regards to old friends.

My love to you,
Tom

April 7, 1945

Dear Mom,

It is evening. In front of me are two candles shedding their flickering light on this piece of paper, which will eventually be 6,000 miles from here. A little way down the path, a soldier is producing some hair-raising sounds on a saxophone he got today. And beyond, we see the artillery shells coming from the Germans' positions and the tracer bullets sailing with a fiery speed through space. I finally got the letters I waited for. Concerning my love life, you needn't be worried.

The news from father struck me just as much as it did you. [Max was in Berlin, but I could not get permission to see him]. Naturally I cannot write to him nor send any food.

Concerning the latter, don't worry. The Germans, even now, are not as badly off as the French. They still have enough foodstuffs stocked up in the basements of their bombed-out houses to get along for a while. Since I might have to stay in Europe with the occupational troops, there is a good chance that I'll succeed in seeing him [Max] as soon as the actual fighting is over.

* The war! One lives and sees destruction, fear, death, hatred, and disgust all day. One revoltingly gets used to destroyed buildings, and I haven't seen one for a long time that was untouched. One avoids the dead soldiers strewn all over the streets. One walks and drives over rubble, reads the slogans of hatred and fear smeared on the walls, thought up for the mind of a ten-year-old kid. "We follow our wonderful Führer into death, and yet we shall be victors." One sees civilians here and there haunting the streets, and wonders whether Christ died to save the sinners. Is there anything Christian about the dead civilian twenty yards away with his face blown off? Perhaps it's normal to have a reaction against war. But it is not just a common reaction like after the last war when everybody turned pacifist. I am beginning to dislike Germany and the Germans at the same time. I compare this destruction with the tortured FFI partisans in Paris. I read German contemporary lit, and talk to hypocritical Germans. The old, ever-present conflict between "love thine enemies" and "kill or be killed" is still very vivid. "Between the ideal and the reality falls the shadow," as T.S. Eliot put it so well. Believe me, if only it were over....*

* Well, to come down to earth. Occasionally we find things left behind by the enemy. That's why that case of champagne, the thirty pounds of bon bons, the canned cherries, apricots, and pickles are standing over in that corner.*

* I will close now. Don't ever accuse me of not writing for*

three weeks. That is not true. Also, keep on writing. We are
still not fighting machines. We still worry our heads off if
there are five letter-less weeks. And we still get excited when
two letters from home finally arrive.
    A bientôt.
My sincerest love,
Tom

    On April 13, 1945 we heard what seemed to many
of us the saddest news of the war: President Roosevelt
was dead. At first, we refused to believe it, hoping this
was enemy propaganda or a rumor started by German
civilians. We did not turn on the radio for fear that we
would hear that it was true, and when the news was
finally confirmed, we knew we had lost a friend. Many
of us felt that the worst reverses on the field of battle
were not so tragic as this death. It seemed as though the
common man had lost his greatest spokesman. Only my
lieutenant from the German community in Texas said,
"It is very bad to stake all of your hope on one leader;
there are plenty of others who can take Roosevelt's
place." We wondered.
    That evening I sent home a modified version of part
of Lincoln's Gettysburg address:

It is for us to be here dedicated to the great task remain-
ing before us; that from the honored dead we take increased
devotion to that cause for which he gave the last full measure
of devotion; that we here highly resolve that he shall not have
died in vain; that this nation, under God, shall have a new
birth of freedom; and that government of the people, by the
people, and for the people, shall not perish from the Earth.
    One afternoon I visited an American field hospital,

where the wounded and dying lay next to each other in one big tent, men with bloody bandages across their eyes, a soldier whose leg had been shot off. There were also quite a few wounded German soldiers there. Many wounded were under heavy sedation, and some were moaning and crying. Nurses and doctors were scurrying from one cot to the next. There was a radio in one corner of the tent and I heard the new president's voice. Truman was now president of the United States, and his voice did not move me. I was still in mourning for Roosevelt.

While we were stationed in Würzburg on the Main River, we also covered targets in the town of Schweinfurt, which was twenty-six miles northeast of Würzburg. Since Schweinfurt was an industrial town where ball bearings were made, it had been heavily bombarded, and most of our targets had been completely destroyed.

From Würzburg we were to drive to Stuttgart, but got only as far as Thalheim, which is about three-quarters of the way, when we were caught in a rather peculiar situation. This sector had been evacuated by the Americans, who wanted to give the impression they were retreating. According to the plan, they hoped the Germans would then return to occupy Thalheim, at which point they could then be surrounded by American troops and taken prisoner. However, we were not aware of this complex strategy when we moved into the town, and so we were welcomed by small arms fire from the Germans, who were entrenched in the surrounding hills. We posted guards all night, but fortunately the Germans never dared to descend into the valley, where we were waiting for them with our guns ready to shoot.

The next day we packed our stuff in a hurry to get

away from the shooting and drove to Maulbronn, twenty-seven miles northeast of Stuttgart. Maulbronn, a small town of 1,400 inhabitants, had hardly been touched by the war. Here we saw one of the most beautiful monasteries in Europe, founded in the twelfth century and still well preserved. The town center consisted of a big, square market place with surrounding medieval buildings. Three sides of this forum were occupied by very beautiful, medieval, half-timbered houses. On the fourth side, shaded by big trees, was the monastery, with a vaulted cloister walk. The cloister garden contained a few ancient trees and the famous Faust tower, where the legendary Dr. Faust in Goethe's story is said to have spent the last hours of his life.

In Maulbronn we took over civilian housing after giving the owners an hour's notice to move out of their homes. This seemed a rude way of asking people whether we could move in, but we had been told to treat the Germans with a firm hand. The man whose house we occupied was typical in his reaction toward us, the conquerors. He hated all of us, and yet he became very obsequious in his efforts to serve us, providing linens, food, heat, and everything else he could think of that we might need. After he had given us the usual story about "those Nazi swine," he proceeded to malign the French who, he said, were uncivilized and dirty. I found my own anger rising, and I told him about my experience with the conduct of the German soldiers in France. I showed him my pictures of tortured partisans, and I told him about the many French villages the Nazis destroyed, and about the innocent women and children whom they had mowed down with machine guns. He just looked at me, and with firm conviction he said that he did not believe

me, "Ein Deutscher tut so was nie!" (Germans would
never do those things!)

I was angry at him because I was angry at Germans
in general; he was angry at me because I was the "conqueror" and was taking over his house and saying bad
things about the Germans. We did not hear each other.
He was a solid citizen, a "gute Bürger," probably a good
man with a good wife; (I did not know at the time that
for many years I would remember him and wonder just
what was going on in his mind at that time and how he
dealt with it.)

While we were at Maulbronn, I visited Heidelberg,
the only German town I saw that had little damage. It
had been purposely saved by the Allies, some said,
because they loved that town. Heidelberg is situated in
the Neckar Valley, and its famous castle, which sits on a
granite hill high above the town, was open to visitors.
The guide who took us through it had already brushed
up on his English. Among other things, we were shown
the biggest wine barrel in the world, a barrel so big that
people could folk dance on top of it.

The town of Stuttgart finally fell to the Allies, and
we were able to begin our target work there. We continued to live in Maulbronn, which meant that we had to
drive sixty miles back and forth every day on very bad
roads.

In Stuttgart we met long columns of German prisoners that were being marched to the prisoner of war
camps by the French colonial troops. Day after day we
saw thousands of "supermen" marching by. Some of the
civilians waved to them or gave them some of their meager rations, while others wept bitterly.

There were thousands of DPs (Displaced Persons)

everywhere. People were stealing everything they could lay their hands on, and the presence of French as well as American troops added to the confusion. We were in the French sector, but the Americans wanted to take over Stuttgart, so to keep us from having that honor, the French put up barricades and gun emplacements. On the second day in Stuttgart we heard the rumor that there was an abandoned wine storehouse in the freight yards near the modern railway station designed by a famous architect. In the past the Germans had stored great quantities of liquor there to be easily loaded onto the trains. As soon as we got near the freight yard, we saw people coming from all directions with empty paper bags, carts, baskets, packs, and buckets all converging on one small door in a big freight storage house. A heavy-set, rough-looking French sergeant had placed himself right in front of the door, with his right hand leaning ostentatiously on his American forty-five caliber pistol. With his left hand he was gesticulating wildly trying to control incoming and outgoing traffic. Every now and then he took out his pistol, held it in front of a German's nose, and forced him to turn over the bottles which he had taken from the basement. Since he himself was fairly drunk, I was afraid that he would start shooting any minute, and no one else spoke enough French to persuade him to let us by. Cautiously, I went up to him and he immediately tried to push me off the ramp. When he recognized me as an American, he said "OK," slapped me on the shoulder, stepped aside, and ushered me downstairs into the darkness. Since I had not brought along my flashlight, it took my eyes a few minutes to get used to the dark. After I groped my way carefully down a cement stairway from one step to the next for two-and-a-half stories, I finally arrived in what seemed the midst of the underworld. Dante's Inferno or Goethe's "witches' kettle" in his Walpurgis Night scene were respectable institutions compared with this scene. There was no electric light, and only here and there among the streaming dark shadows was a flickering, dim candlelight. People from many nations seemed to be down there: Ruskies, Francais, Popolskis, Italianos, Deutsche, Moroccans, Norweger, and one American (me!).

There was liquor stored in huge barrels or in bottles stacked loosely against the wall. Every now and then a drunkard took a bottle, pulled it from the middle of the stack, and thus brought twenty more crashing to the floor. Everybody was walking on broken glass or wading through puddles of wine, cider, champagne, or fruit juice.

The stench was frightful. People were perspiring in spite of the cold and damp atmosphere. The odor of the liquor had fused with the smell of those who wash themselves only twice a year, or who compensate by sprinkling themselves with cheap perfumes. One drunken Pole insisted on shaking hands with me and giving me a drink of rum. He had just slipped and fallen on a broken bottle, and his hand was bleeding profusely.

Out of the dark corners, away from the milling crowd, there came all kinds of sighs, moans, expressions in many languages, and nasty snickering. I never went into these dark places, but I saw several women whose clothing was torn or badly arranged, and I saw men coming from there who were adjusting their pants. All people, from twelve-year-old children to seventy-five-year-old grandmas, were busy gathering bottles or emptying them down their throats.

When I finally emerged from what I thought must have been Hades, I noticed that two smart-looking French officers had joined the sergeant in relieving the Germans of their bottles as they left the building. While I was watching the three, one of them turned his head in my direction and said, "C'est la guerre, hein?" (That's war, eh?)

Dachau and the Search for SS Files

On April 29, 1945, the first peace rumors started to come over the radio. We heard that Hitler and Mussolini were both dead and that the German Army chiefs were ready to capitulate. Munich, however, the birthplace and capital of the Nazi movement, had not yet fallen, but French, American, and Russian divisions were all racing eagerly toward the town from three different directions. We had left Maulbronn (northwest of Stuttgart) on the 18th of April and drove through Nordlingen and Dachau on our way to Munich. As we were passing Dachau on the night of its liberation, a cold wind was blowing through the open jeep and mud was splashing into our faces. I wondered if by chance Pastor Niemoeller was still there, so I decided to try and get in to see him. We asked a German civilian who was standing by the roadside for directions to the concentration camp. "Concentration camp? Concentration camp?" he said, "I'm sorry but I never heard of it." We had become accustomed to that typical German denial of having any connection with the Nazis. About four miles beyond, we found the sign: Dachau-Umschulungslager (Rehabilitation Camp) Next Right. Beautiful modern

MUNICH FRAUENKIRCHE

buildings lined the road on both sides. These were SS barracks, one of the many things built with the sweat, blood, and very lives of the prisoners.

We had heard many rumors about the camps and knew that people who went there oftentimes disappeared, but we had no idea of the kind of systematic, well-organized horrors that went on there, or the tortures committed by the SS. Since the camp had just been liberated, the first sight we saw were the bodies of several SS men who had been killed by the inmates. As we turned into the courtyard we saw the prisoners on the other side. They all looked the same with their worn striped suits, and emaciated, pale faces. There were hundreds of them who were unable to leave the camp because they had typhus. All of those who could possibly be moved had been moved. Some of the prisoners immediately joined us. They laughed heartily when we told them about the sign—Umschulungslager, the "re-education" camp. There was a building for the

FELDHERRENHALLE MONUMENT
WHERE SIGNATURE BOOK WAS FOUND

ADOLPH HITLER
ORIGINAL PHOTOGRAPH

ADOLPH HITLER
ORIGINAL PHOTOGRAPH

H. HIMMLER
HEAD OF SS AND
CONCENTRATION CAMPS

NUREMBERG PHOTOS FOUND IN MUNICH: SS OFFICERS

VON HINDENBURG
GERMAN PRESIDENT UNTIL 1934

RUPPEL
SURGEON GENERAL

LUDWIG ROSELIUS
INVENTOR OF DECAFFEINATED COFFEE

HERMANN GOERING
ASSISTANT TO HITLER -HEAD OF AIRFORCE

MEISSNER
SECRETARY OF STATE

DR. GURTNER
HEALTH SECRETARY

LUTHER
LAST AMBASSADOR TO WASHINGTON

ALL OF THESE MEN WERE ON TRIAL

TODT
HEAD OF GERMAN
FREEWAYS

ARTHUR SEYSS INQUART
NAZI GOVERNOR OF AUSTRIA

LORD HAW HAW
(HARRY PIEL)
RADIO PERSONALITY

KONSTANTIN HIERL
HEAD OF LABOR SERVICE

BLOMBERG
HEAD OF GERMAN ARMY

AHREN
CAPTAIN OF THE LARGEST
GERMAN CRUISE SHIP: BREMEN

ROEHM
HEAD OF
STORMTROOPERS

PAUL LINKE
COMPOSER OF "GLOWWORM"

Umschulung, they said, but it never served that purpose.

It was apparent that Niemoeller was not in the camp, so we soon headed for Munich and arrived there at 3:00 in the morning. The city had not yet fallen and we had to be very careful as there was still sniping going on.

One day in Munich, I came up to the Feldherrenhalle, where the Nazis had placed the coffins of their heroes who had been killed in 1923, and which had been a shrine to the fallen Nazis. I decided to explore the whole monument. As I climbed down a steep stairway (the Germans have deep basements in many of their buildings), I realized this had also been the headquarters of the ADAC (the German Automobile Club). As I was rummaging around, I found a thick, pigskin leather-bound album with a big swastika embossed on the front. I had wanted a photo album for my growing store of pictures so I "liberated" it for myself. When I got back to my living quarters the landlady said, "You've got something there!" It was the ADAC guest book, which had been at the Nazi shrine since 1934. In it were the signatures of Hindenburg, Hitler, Goering, Himmler, and Blomberg (head of the German Army), Paul Linke (composer of "Glow Worm"), Seykss Inquart (Nazi governor of Austria), Hans Frank (Nazi general of Poland, later executed), Von Brauchitsch (race car driver of Porsches), and many more. I turned the book over and, with the empty pages starting from the back, made a photo album of it, eventually putting in photos of my trips behind the German lines in the Alps, the tortured French partisans, the dead in Dachau, and many of the people I had come to know.

Shortly after we got to Munich, I also heard the

rumor that the complete files of the SS personnel and their families and their assignments, were stored in or near the concentration camp at Dachau. This would certainly be one of the most important finds of the war and invaluable for use in the war criminal trials to be held later. I was determined to get these files before they were destroyed.

INMATES-DACHAU

While we were searching a big SS camp outside of Munich, a Yugoslav captain, who had just been released from Dachau told us that he used to work with these files when he was in Dachau. He said they contained all the information about all the SS

WATCHTOWER-DACHAU

men, officers (up to generals), and enlisted men and their families. So, after getting as much information as we could from him, we dashed off to Dachau to search.

When we got to the camp, we found that it had been placed off limits because the typhus danger apparently was too great to allow any visitation. Since we were determined to get in, we insisted on seeing the authorities who, after much persuasion, finally gave us a special pass to visit the camp for three hours and forty five-minutes. However, before we were admitted, a GI gave us a typhus shot, while a former inmate took down our pants, opened our jackets and shirts, and sprayed us all over with DDT powder.

Immediately to the right as we entered, there was a U-shaped building, which contained the kitchen, clothing rooms, and workshops. Hidden behind that was a large building without any windows or furniture—a prison within a prison. Over to the left of the large courtyard were man-sized boxes standing upright that looked like footlockers. A man could barely fit in there and would be forced to stand inside for punishment, unable to bend his knees or move any other part of his body. The prisoners were forced to stand inside of these boxes for up to eight days without food or drink.

Dachau was the first large concentration camp the Nazis built. There were fifteen barracks on the right side of the center walkway, and fifteen on the left. Each one had been originally built to house two hundred prisoners, but before long, there were a thousand men jammed into each building. This meant six prisoners had to share only two beds. Of the thirty-thousand men from seventeen nations who were held there, two were English and five or six were American.

To try to escape would have meant certain death. The inner camp was surrounded by a strip of lawn five feet wide. If a prisoner just barely touched this lawn with one foot, he was shot to death from the tower with a machine gun. Next to the lawn there was a ditch, too wide to be jumped over. Beyond that was an electrically charged barbed wire fence, and finally the last barrier, the high prison wall, under constant observation from the watch towers. We wanted to know more about the camp so we asked some of the inmates to describe a typical day in prison to us. They wanted to talk about one particularly black day, January 22, 1939, one of the coldest days that winter.

As usual, wake up time was four o'clock in the morning with only fifteen minutes to wash up and make the beds. The bed-making drill was a favorite pastime of the SS. The smallest irregularity, like a tiny fold in the blanket, brought severe punishment. Either the prisoner was beaten twenty-five times with a heavy stick, or he got the "post." This meant that the prisoner climbed onto a chair and had his hands tied behind his back. A heavy rope was lowered from a scaffold and attached to the prisoner's bound hands. Then the rope was pulled up, and as soon as it was taut, the chair was pulled away, and the man was suspended above the ground for one hour. That is why so many of the prisoners had crippled fingers, hands, and arms.

Breakfast consisted of two pints of ersatz (substitute) coffee and a part of the daily ration, which included one loaf of bread shared between eight men. Immediately after breakfast came roll call. In rows of tens, the three thousand prisoners marched into the courtyard where they were carefully counted and then picked out for the work details. Those who were not chosen had to stand at attention all day in the same spot. It was absolutely forbidden to enter the barracks during work hours.

On that particular day in 1939, as the various details set out for their work, they passed a fellow inmate who had been shot dead earlier that morning. He had been walking along the barracks and had failed to notice the SS man who was following him, so naturally he had not tipped his hat as he was required to do. The SS man called him over and slapped him in the face. In an automatic reflex, the prisoner raised his hand in self-defense, and the Nazi pulled out his pistol, saying "I'll teach you swine not to raise your hand against an SS man," and he shot and killed the prisoner.

The work to be done was hard and included road building, shop work, building mansions for the SS, and so forth. One of these work details was particularly well-known. They were called the Garage Construction Gang. A prisoner, Karl Kapp from Nuremberg, had been in charge of the group. He cooperated completely with the SS and he beat his fellow prisoners to death any time there was the slightest infraction of the law. He would tell a member of his work crew to leave his tools behind during the noon hour, and when the prisoner would get to the eating area without his tools, an SS man would tell him to run back and get them. As he was running through the gate, the guards opened fire as they did for anyone who ran through that place. Several weeks later a relative of the man received notice that Mr. X had been mortally wounded while trying to escape. (As early as 1936 and 1937 in Berlin, we began hearing that our Jewish friends who had "gone east" had been wounded while trying to escape, or they had committed suicide.)

At half-past eleven the same day, a slow moving cart could be seen plowing, or dragging, through the snow. It carried those who had died that morning. The break at noon was short, and the food consisted mainly of turnips and cabbage. At half-past twelve, it was roll call again, and off to work again.

Later that afternoon, a siren sounded the alarm. A prisoner had escaped from an outside work detail. All of the inmates immediately lined up, giving no thought to how thinly clad they were. Some had no hats or gloves, and some were even without underwear. They stood at attention in a temperature of a mere 20°F. When the platoon leader noticed the slightest movement in line, he immediately walked over and kicked the guilty prisoner with his boots or beat him with clubs.

At nine o'clock that evening, the first man fell dead into the snow. The thermometer read 22°F. Tears of rage rolled down the cheeks of the men as fathers, brothers, and friends fell down right next to them and froze to death. By midnight fifty people had collapsed and died. By six o'clock the next morning, two hundred had been counted dead. All the while the prisoners remained at attention. At half-past two the following afternoon, the order "Dismissed" was finally given. The result of that day was about three hundred dead with hundreds more suffering frost-bitten noses, ears, fingers, hands, and feet.

This was only one day: there were many others in which the camp guards tortured their fellow human beings to death. We wanted to get out quickly. I simply felt I could not look into the eyes of these men without being able to help them. Yet, I strongly sensed that what they really wanted right now was to be able to tell their story, and to have it heard and then told to others outside. And so we listened.

There was more to see. As we walked through the gate, we noticed several tough-looking American front-line soldiers coming out of a building on the slope to the right. Some looked pale, and others went off by themselves and turned their stomachs inside out. As we approached the building, we encountered a horrible stench. Inside, hundreds of dead bodies had been thrown into large piles. Most of the bodies consisted of just skin and bones. We later found out they were supposed to have been burned in the four big furnaces. This winter, however, the Nazis ran out of coal, and so they piled the dead in each of the crematoriums or they had some of the inmates dig huge pits that held about five hundred bodies. I was told that there were sixteen holes like this all filled with dead prisoners. Most had died from typhus. In the last few months before the liberation, the typhus mortality rate had gone up to two hundred per day.

We tried to get away from all these horrors, but we were unable to avoid them. Some five hundred yards down the road we ran into fifty boxcars. As we looked closer, we could see that each car was filled with the dead. They were nothing but skin and bones. All of them seemed to be Jews judging by the yellow star sewn on their clothes.

These were the famous boxcars we had heard about from the prisoners and some of the foreign workers. About fourteen days before Dachau was liberated, these Jews were crammed into the boxcars to be shipped south, away from the Allies who were approaching. However, because of the destruction of the railroad tracks and bridges by Allied planes, the trains never departed. For fourteen days and nights the prisoners stayed in these boxcars without anything to eat or drink. One of the American guards told us that on this same morning of liberation they had found two prisoners who were still alive, though unfortunately they could not be saved. The Army said there were indications that some of them in their final agony had eaten their dead friends. I could not bear to look and so I tried to shut my eyes.

From a squint I saw something strange and barely describable—a sort of moving cloud or veil where the boxcars had been. I took out my camera and snapped some pictures, but when they were developed, the camera only recorded the railroad cars and bodies. (see photos).

We learned more about the camp as we continued our search for documents and interviews. There was one curious barrack. From the outside it looked like any other, but inside on the walls were paintings of delicate women from the eighteenth century wearing costumes of gay colors of that time. When we entered the building, we could see it was like a college dormitory with many rooms on the right and left. Our prisoner guide told us this was the "house of pleasure." Each door had a peephole so that the SS guards could look inside and see what was going on. They would invite male and female inmates to have sex inside those rooms. While the prisoners were being intimate, the SS guard would watch them through the peephole and, in the midst of intercourse, open the door and send the prisoners back to their barracks. Being coerced into having sex was a further humiliation the Jews had to endure.

In this same building was a huge room that could hold up to a thousand people. Hundreds of Russian prisoners of war had been sent to this room where they were gassed to death. Every three days, Jews, who were working in the crematoriums, vanished and were replaced by others. The Nazis had hoped that all the secret furnaces and gas chambers would remain hidden, and now they were being inspected by the outside world. These structures were carefully planned, and skillfully built and operated by the ingenious German engineers who had devised the most efficient way of killing.

That was Dachau. How anyone could have survived a year there was beyond my imagination. As one of the prisoners told me, "It is certainly not to the credit of the SS that we are here after eleven years of hell."

I later learned that Pastor Niemoeller had indeed been at this concentration camp in Dachau along with Chancellor Schussnigg of Austria, and Daladier and Blum of France. I also discovered that two weeks before my arrival at the camp, Niemoeller had been sent to another prison in the Alps.

Privately this was a turning point for me. My anger toward the Germans reached a climax while I visited Dachau. When I asked myself the question, were my people responsible for these indescribable cruelties?, I began to ask myself other questions as well. These questions had become so familiar to me even though they never produced any answers. I had been born a German. Could I have done this? I was not Jewish. I would have had to serve the Vaterland (Father land). What would have happened to me if I had stayed in Germany?...if I had focused my adolescent admiration on someone other than Niemoeller? Deep down, was I angry with myself? But why? Where did this cruelty in the Germans come from? Thanks to my Jewish stepfather and my mother I had managed to flee the Nazis, and now I was fighting them, and taking big risks in the process. I wondered what my German school comrades had done? At one time, we had been very much the same; had the same ideals and goals. I was beginning to feel I had to know the worst, and yet it filled me with terrible pain and disgust—two sentiments I could not integrate into my being. I felt accepted by America and I was sure I had done important work to help the Americans and the cause of peace and democracy. The conflict between the USA and Germany dominated my mind. Could I have been a guard in a concentration camp, or would I have been six feet underground on the Russian front? It was unbearable to picture so many dead young men, German or American. I still would not admit that in many ways the cultures were essentially the same, or that I was both German and American. If that were so, why were they fighting and killing one another? The only truth I knew was that I was an angry and upset soldier, but I kept these feelings to myself. When I returned to my room in Munich, I shut the door and cried bitterly for a long time. My mind simply could not comprehend what I had seen. Life seemed so unfair, and I felt so helpless in the face of all this horror.

We returned to the camp several times searching for the complete SS files. One day we arrived at a building where the files were reported to be hidden and we found the storage space empty. One of the Yugoslavs, who was standing around, told us that all the file boxes and their contents had been evacuated in two big trucks shortly before the Allies arrived in Dachau, and he had no idea where these records were now located.

I went immediately to the Yugoslav committee head-quarters, which were located in the former house of "pleasure" in the camp. Apparently, the Yugoslavs at Dachau knew more than anyone else about these records. For several hours, I interrogated one man after the other, but no one knew where the records had been sent. Finally, one of the Yugoslavs introduced us to a man who said he had taken the card files to a village somewhere in the Bavarian Alps. He had to make two trips, since one truck could not hold all the records. It took him some time to recall the name of the village, but he finally was able to point on our map to a small town in the mountains, Bayrisch Zell. He casually mentioned that the records were stored in the "Post," or post office.

Very early the next morning, armed with a .38 caliber revolver and a carbine, I left alone for the Bavarian Alps to drive about 50 miles to Bayrisch Zell. There I found the post office closed, so at that point I roused the postmaster and his wife out of bed and asked them to show me the whole building. Neither one of them knew anything about the records, they said. They became very worried and excited when I insisted on finding the boxes I thought the SS had stored there. I went through the garage, examined the sewer system, probed the lawn with my army knife and examined everything in sight. Finally, in despair, the postmaster suggested that I might look for the Hotel Zur Post instead of the post office. (In former times, the mail coach in Germany stopped in front of the biggest hotel in a town or village, and this hotel usually assumed the name Hotel Post Office, or Hotel de la Poste, as it was called in France.) The postmaster said that the SS had taken over the Hotel Zur Post as a sanitarium for their war casualties. I thought this was a brilliant suggestion, and although I had not completely exonerated the postmaster, the poor man breathed a sigh of relief when I left his building.

The Hotel Post-Office was full of SS officers, all of whom had allegedly been badly wounded while fighting for the Vaterland and were now recuperating. However, most of them managed to swagger and strut proudly through the building, still wearing their black SS uniforms with all the insignia and swastika decorations. The officers seemed to have trouble looking at me, let alone addressing me—a mere enlisted man—and also the enemy. There was an eerie silence in the room. There were twenty-five or thirty of them—very tall as most of the SS were. They all seemed well over six-feet, with their impressive uniforms, big black leather boots with the leather manchettes almost reaching their knees, the awesome SS lighting-strike insignia, and all the mystique that had struck fear and awe in me since childhood. It was clear that I was the conqueror and in charge, but it was also clear that I was totally alone and if anything happened to me, no one would ever know. It was only the carbine on my back and my finger on the trigger of a .38 caliber pistol that gave me control of the situation, and I was prepared to use either weapon. I was visualizing how I would pull out the pistol, if necessary, to become "the fastest gun in Deutschland."

It was obvious also that these proud and once powerful Nazis were frightened, and that they realized their pride was founded on an institution that had already disintegrated. These were the SS officers who might have committed the cruelties I had seen and who had sworn fealty to Hitler until their last breath. And I had to take immediate and total command of the situation and of them. I was aware that my knees were actually shaking, and I knew that my greatest challenge would be to keep my voice calm and firm. I pulled myself up to my full five-foot-seven-and-three-quarter inches as I asked the senior non-commissioned officer—the Stabsfeldwebel—who was responsible directly to the commanding officer, to show me the whole building. I told him that I was on a tour of inspection, and that I wanted to see every cupboard and every possible nook and cranny. I did not say that I was searching for the entire SS files, but I suspect-

DEAD INMATES ABOUT TO BE BURNED

INMATES WHO HAD DIED IN THESE BOXCARS AND HAD EATEN EACH OTHER

DEAD S.S. MAN   RE-EDUCATION CAMP

MORE BOXCARS WITH CORPSES

ed that they all knew that, and they also knew that if I found these records, it would implicate all of them and all of the German SS in terrible war crimes. The stakes for them were very high—and for me, too.

I was shown the whole hotel from top to bottom. I saw all the supplies they hoarded. There were big crates of cigars. The refrigeration unit was full of the best cuts of meat, and the two storerooms were stacked to the ceiling with fresh as well as canned foods. After I had seen what I thought was the whole building, I proceeded to ask some indirect questions concerning the SS files. The Stabsfeldwebel assured me that he did not know anything about any records of any kind. I then asked him whether there were any other SS buildings in the village, and he told me that there was a TB hospital high up in the mountains, in the Hotel Berghof (Mountain Inn). I was aware that he seemed very eager for me to go and search there at once.

I drove up a steep and winding road that took me to the resort. Again, a thorough search came to naught, but

GERMAN SS AND LABOR SERVICE WITH SS FILES

just as I was leaving the hotel, a man, who introduced himself as a former inmate of Dachau, and who had been detailed to work at the TB hospital, asked me what I was looking for. I told him that I was trying to locate some SS records. "Oh! You mean the personnel files of the whole German SS?" he said very nonchalantly. "I'll show you where they are."

He climbed into my jeep, and we returned to Bayrische Zell at full speed. I drove up to the Hotel Post Office, where I had left the SS men. The former prisoner-guide immediately took me to the back of the building. There he showed me a small concealed door, which led to a basement separated by a wall from the cellar I had seen previously. Here I found two rooms stacked to the ceiling with big, wooden boxes that contained the record of every SS non-commissioned officer and commissioned officer and their families in Germany. In a third room, an SS private, who looked about fifteen years old, was just about to burn the first batch of files in a big furnace. Apparently the SS men I had seen before had indeed suspected my intentions, and they were going to destroy all the records after sending me off on a futile trip to the Hotel Berghof. If I had returned much later, all would have been lost. I was so excited about this find that I pulled out one of the cards and kissed it.

The cards were arranged in a very neat and orderly manner. They were subdivided into groups: officers, non-commissioned officers, those who had been in the SS police, those who had been taken prisoner, those who had been wounded, and those who had been killed. Each card gave a complete description of the man: his hometown, his family background, his paydays, his various ranks, the date of his enlistment, and his functions in the

SS. I knew this was certainly a valuable find and I was not going to let these boxes out of my sight for one second.

The first chore was to get these files out of the SS hotel. I managed to get word to an American lieutenant, stationed nearby, who had a squad of infantry soldiers in the village. He gave permission to store the files temporarily in his living quarters and he lent us his truck for the transport of the heavy boxes. I ordered the SS officers to load the boxes, even though I was not sure I had the right to do that under international law. They obviously looked as though they thought this work was beneath them, and I took some private pleasure in seeing them struggle. I presume these documents were used in the Nuremberg trials and later stored in the underground bunkers in Berlin-Zehlendorf right near the home of my old recorder teacher, Cora Schröder.

On May 11, 1945 I wrote home:

Just a short note in answer to those three letters I received last night. So Chris is finally going into the army; perhaps he will still be able to finish his second year in college. I certainly hope that the war in the Pacific will be over by the time he is ready to leave the States. He should stress right from the very start that he knows German, and that way they will send him to Europe, if anywhere.

The only bad news you seem to send is about Al's relations with certain doctors who are excluding him from operating in any hospital, and about your cold and the condition of your back. I hope that will pass with the end of the rainy season. My physical condition right now is excellent; it has been for several months. This is rather rare. I think those four

*months of out-door life in the mountains have done the trick.
Perhaps I should go back there before I start disintegrating.*

*I shall write more often now that I have a typewriter of
my own, now that there is electricity, and now that I have a
little more extra time. I hope to send off two packages tomorrow. One contains a pair of honest-to-goodness Bavarian
leather pants with the suspenders, and the other is a fur-lined
leather jacket. There are also several books and pamphlets in
it.*

*I don't seem to be able to concentrate any more tonight.
They are playing the last act of Carmen on the radio, and
things are getting exciting in the opera.*

Hurriedly yours,
Tom

May 20, 1945

Dear Mother,

*At least there is some good news every now and then. It
pleased me to hear that we may give our location, and that
our officers won't have to read our mail any longer. This
enables me to write more openly to my folks and friends.*

*The news of Chris' rejection from the army really sur-
prised me. After all, I thought that such a big husky lad
would surely be in better shape than most boys who are in the
army now, and I am including myself. The army should take
men like Chris to replace those who have served for three
years or more. Believe me, I am not the only one who is only
too anxious to get out. Every soldier is talking about the necessary eighty-five points these days. I have sixty-two, which
means I would have to stay overseas at least eleven more
months to get out. In a soldier's life, which is not very constructive, it is easy to forget that we are giving away the best*

years of our lives. So much for the complaints department.

I sent a package of all kinds of junk. Three recorders may be turned over to Mr. Chittick. The flags I sent along more or less as a novelty. Since you have always asked me about my reactions to Germany, I am sending along a few "opinions" on the German people. I have called them opinions because I would not be 100 percent sure that I am right. I should like to hear what you think and whether you can recognize some changes in the German people, even in you.

Last week we had a little job to do in the Bavarian Alps. I was ever so happy to be back in the mountains. I saw the ruins of Hitler's hangout in Berchtesgaden, rode on the Deutsche Alpenstrasse to Innsbruck, thus getting a good glimpse of Austria, and on May fifteenth, my birthday, I took a motorboat ride on the Königssee. The German land-scape certainly is almost too well-ordered, too man-made, to be beautiful.

Concerning those gifts, don't overdo it. I have had a cam-era ever since Brussels. It is an Agfa 6 x 9 with an f8.8 lens. Now I would like to get some of the fancier shots, which is impossible with the Agfa. I think that the Allied troops have picked up all the fairly decent cameras in Germany. Do you think you can get me a lens better than f5.0 with a shutter a little faster than 1/100?

The rest of this army life doesn't look very pleasant from here. It will be mostly garrison life, and that involves reveille, inspections, correct uniform, and all kinds of restric-tions. And yet I'd rather swallow that than go to the Pacific. The further up to the front line I am (or even behind the enemy lines), the better my morale, even though the living conditions are no good. I hope to get a furlough to England one of these days. We may have to stay over here at least one more year. That is one thing I had not figured on.

June 17, Munich

Dear Mom,
    This letter may reach you on your birthday.
    *The army is slowly driving me nuts. If there were only
something to do. If I am not kept busy all of my waking
hours, I get very tense and nervous. I simply don't feel like
reading a good book. I am having a hard time concentrating
on anything that requires a bit of organized thinking. Those
articles on Germany have kept my mind a bit occupied, but
that is only a temporary affair. If things don't get better soon,
I shall attack something better: Memories from June 6, 1944,
to June 6, 1945. I had hoped to make photography my hobby,
but for that I need film and a good camera. I am enclosing
the third and last article on the Germans. I should again like
to hear about your reactions.*
    *I have not had any mail for a week now. This afternoon
I got myself some SS skis. I will store them some place in
Munich. In case I am still in Germany next winter, and in
case I happen to get ten days off, I'll be all set to go skiing.*
    *There is absolutely nothing to tell, except that I enjoyed
the cartoon in the New Yorker in which a Salvation Army
girl, marveling at the coins coming out of a public telephone,
says "Bless you, sister."*
    *I hope that you have a very happy birthday. Please say
hello to Al and to Chris and take a big birthday kiss from
Tom.*

After my experience in Germany I began to wax
philosophical about the Germans and the German girls.
Officially, fraternization between the GIs and German
women resulted in a sixty-five dollar fine. Yet, there were
so few girls from Allied countries—Polish, Russian,

Latvian, or French—compared to the demand, the average GI managed to have a Teutonic girlfriend or two behind the walls of many German homes. Personally, I was off women during my stay in Germany. I was having some strong feelings against the Germans by this time, and I had come to like the French and English girls very much, and I did not feel like getting rid of my pay in sixty-five dollar installments.

The morale of the German girls was quite low. Most of their young boyfriends were in prison camps, or they had been killed. The German girl was still our enemy, and she felt this more strongly than did the average GI; yet, the American soldier could offer many material things besides his innate masculine charms. Often I saw an American soldier sneak through the back door of a German home, with his pockets full of rations. The German girl had an ambivalent attitude toward her conqueror friends, appearing to be either very aloof, conceited and self-conscious, or overbearing, intimate, and ordinary. Usually, however, she accepted the GI's rations.

The GIs who had been in Germany and in England, France, Belgium, and Italy, often told me that they liked the German girls by far the best. Unfortunately, the GI had become quite unpopular in these other countries because of his ways of courting, and the ladies there no longer went out with him for a small K-ration or a package of cigarettes. The GI preferred the German girl because "she was clean in her outward appearance" and she appeared to fall very easily for the GI's line. It seemed to me that a daily bath did not make the German girl any better than the English or French.

A Parisian friend of mine once gave me his opinion of the German girls who were in Paris. First, he thought that they were too muscular and relied more on their breasts and short skirts to get attention than on character and charm. These German girls apparently tried very desperately to imitate the chic, little "Parisienne." Yet, no matter how many beauty parlors they visited, no matter how much money they spent on dresses, my friend believed that they always just missed that something special of the Parisienne.

I found that the German girls had very little sense of humor and were unable to laugh at themselves. Politically most of them were still leaning very much to the right. They had not been disillusioned by the Nazi Party as much as had the front-line German soldiers, and their political thinking was less developed than that of the average German man. With the help of Nazi ideology, they had become quite domesticated, and their main goal in life was the reproduction of their kind. I often wondered whether the preference, which the average GI had for the German girls, did not indicate some of his own weaknesses, his need to feel superior as a man.

June 10, 1945

Dear Mom,

I know this won't be a good letter. Last Wednesday was June 6 —D-day a year ago. I cannot help recalling those early days on Normandy Beach. What I have gone through since those days is impossible to describe, and too painful to remember. I have never passed a year with so many events, or a year that changed me as much as this one. Some day, if I have enough energy and time, I shall write my memoirs on just that one year: From Normandy to Munich, facing the enemy and being behind the enemy lines, sleeping in the fox-

hole as well as in Europe's best hotels. I might say that there are probably few soldiers in Europe who have seen as much in events and in excitement as I have. And now I feel tired. I want to go home—somewhere. A soldier does not have to think. He is mentally unemployed and that's why I want to go back. I simply refuse to face more than a year of Army life, especially when I am kept busy doing nothing.

Oh, yes, I was talking about June the sixth. Eisenhower gave us a day off. So another sergeant and I decided to go on a little trip in the jeep. We drove over Oberammergau to Schloss Linderhof. We saw Kloster Ettal (I believe you visited that with Chris in the early days), Garmisch Patenkirchen, and the Zugspitze. Germany is surely pretty around these parts. But I would not call it beautiful. The whole landscape is geared up for tourists and to the tourist trade. I have the idea that even the forests are being swept daily. Tourists cannot see anything without paying the proper fees. Of course as soldiers we don't pay anything, but that's beside the point. Personally I prefer the French Alps, even though the villages are by far not so clean. Or better yet, I'll take the rugged, vast, and overwhelming beauty of the Oregon Cascades any day. Meanwhile I shall stand by waiting for a furlough to England. Years ago I requested some good dental floss. I still need it badly.

Here is a morale booster for you: our meat ration has been cut by 10 percent. Food since the armistice has been more or less lousy. Yet, I do not complain. Those material inconveniences don't phase me anymore.

I am having an awful lot of trouble with my camera. Since August, 1944, I have taken some 350 pictures. I am sending along some news on Niemoeller. It comes out of the Münchener Zeitung, June 9, 1945, edited by the Twelfth Army group.

I shall finish now. Please don't forget that I might be going through the toughest phase of the war, that is personally. Many thoughts and a big kiss from Tom.

July 15, 1945

Dear Mom,
You are the third person who has suggested that I write some sort of memoirs. Well, I have been doing that for the past five weeks. Yes, it may be fun; but it has something negative about it. If I had a decent job, I would certainly never think of it. You are reading Myrdal's book, The American Dilemma, *and I would certainly appreciate if you sent at least the first volume. I probably have told you that I sent the* New Republic *a very juicy letter. I like that magazine very much, and I would very much like you to send it along after you are through with it.*

For the past few weeks, I have been trying to get to Berlin with my lieutenant [to see my father]. But he is very conservative, and although he is very decent with me, it just takes him too long to make up his mind. Besides that, it is extremely difficult to enter the Russian sector these days, and Berlin is now Russian. Two fellows wanted to look for their parents in Warsaw, but they only got as far as Prague, where the Russians stopped them.

Last week I went swimming for the first time this summer. I remember last year in August I went swimming in France right next to a forest that was teeming with Germans (and I don't mean prisoners). Right now we have two big swimming pools at our disposal.

I read today that the non-fraternization rule concerning the Germans has been lifted to some extent. Well, that doesn't make much difference to me or most of us. Whenever I felt like talking to a German girl, I did it anyway. Last week we had a dance with Estonian girls. As far as I am concerned, these girls are leaning strongly to the Right, one might call them Nazis, as many of the soldiers do. They fled from the Russians and now they do not want to go back because the Russians are there. Some of the German girls really appeal to one's Freudian impulses, if I may talk like a soldier. But somehow I don't seem to change my opinion of them.

Last week the two-hundred-year-old organ broke down while I was playing it. Fortunately this happened through no fault of my own. Now it is repaired, and last night I tried using the foot pedals for the first time. It's a lot of fun.

Cheerio,

Tom

Chapter 10

•

July-October 1945

I had been in Germany only seven weeks. But I observed the Germans at very close range and developed some strong opinions about them and of what was going on in their country. (The following statements have been compiled from various letters I mailed home from Europe. They reflect the ideas I had at the time, and not necessarily the observations I made after the armistice. I wrote this in 1945.) I was 24 years old, and after working with the French, Belgian, and Italian partisans, and having visited Dachau, I had some strong feelings.

To the average American soldier, who did not know them, the Germans appeared just as virtuous as any other European people, if not more so. They were clean, they worked hard, they seemed intelligent, and they were interested in music, art and lit-

JEWISH BUDDIES WITH NAZI TROPHIES

erature; they were well-mannered, generous hosts, and there were many other admirable qualities. But at the same time, they seemed to differ from people of other nations. Why was it, I asked myself, that the Nazis were able to stay in power for such a long time? Was there any justification in saying that the average German had been a good Nazi? This was the question that I and many other soldiers would begin to ask again and again.

Although the NSDAP (German National Socialist Labor Party—the Nazis) was among other things a labor party, it was not necessarily the common worker who profited by these twelve years of Nazi rule. It is true there had been little unemployment during that time, but there was more regimentation, money bought less every day, and there were fewer goods available. Most of the profits accrued to the party or to the big industrialists who financed the Nazis' bid for power. And when the big bombardments came, the homes of the laborers were destroyed first because they lived near the big industry; the mansions of the rich fell much later, if at all. It was the proletariat and the lower-middle-class people who had made most of the sacrifices in this war, and I felt that they were perfectly sincere when they expressed their gratitude for the end of this horrible war.

Although I had not yet been to Northern Germany, I met many German soldiers and civilians who came from the north, and it seemed that the Bavarians and Austrians of the south were somewhat more sympathetic, more easy-going, and less boisterous than, for instance, a Berliner Groszschnauze (big-mouth). The Bavarians still hated the Prussians. This seemed like a bit of hypocrisy to the Americans, even though the Nazis had tried to mix the populations. For instance, they never promoted a Bavarian civil servant unless he accepted a job in Berlin (or the Berliner accepted a job in Bavaria).

There were some people whom the Nazis had not changed; for instance, many members of the Protestant and Catholic churches who remained true to their Christian theology. Then there were those Germans who suffered most in the war, and were therefore disillusioned about the Nazis. Surprisingly enough, I found that youths between the ages of ten and seventeen had not become the arrogant Nazis that people in the States believed them to be. There was a definite chance to set them on the right path, away from Nazi ideals

Unfortunately, the Nazis had succeeded in making a bogeyman or devil out of the Russians and the bolshevist Jew. Also, they had succeeded in making the Germans more nationalistic-minded than ever. For instance, when I told a "decent German couple" about the torture of French partisans, or about the intentional sacking and burning of French villages by the Germans, they simply did not believe it.

I met very few Germans who frankly admitted that they had belonged to a Nazi organization. If one of them was forced to admit his long allegiance to the party because all evidence pointed against him, he came out with a statement such as, "Yes, I was forced to join the party in 1927 (Hitler came to power in 1933) because my boss belonged to it." They usually, however, denied their loyalty to the party. In fact, they were so sure of their denial that, at the moment, they seemed to believe it themselves. Most of these Germans underrated the intelligence of the average GI, due largely to the fact that the American did not speak German (or at least not well enough), and that he was not well acquainted with German ways and culture. Usually it was the German who betrayed himself, however, if merely by his arrogance. I had seen it again and again, that the ordinary GI, although he did not know any German language, was soon able to recognize those who had been devout Nazis. Perhaps it was their arrogance that gave them away, and also their depression, since Germany had lost an entire generation of men.

One day I had to do some business at the town hall, where the Allied military government was located. A big crowd of Germans with all kinds of papers, recommendations, complaints, and requests was waiting at the entrance. The MP was having a rough time trying to answer all their questions and to prevent people from sneaking in. Inside, on the desk of the reception clerk, a big sign in German reflected very well the attitude of the Germans as well as of the American military government personnel. It said:

We know —
1. *That you were forced to join the Nazi party.*
2. *That you have a cousin in Patterson, New Jersey, U.S.A.*
3. *That you were on the privy just when they set fire to the synagogue next door.*
4. *That the Poles said good-bye to you when they left.*
5. *That you had the closest relationship with the Jews.*
6. *That the uncle of your aunt was almost sent to the concentration camp.*
7. *That you collected the dues for the Nazi party because it was your turn.*

All this we know, and we would rather not hear about it any more.

It seemed to me that the Nazis had fully developed the most negative of German characteristics. What were these qualities? The Germans did not seem to be as independent in their attitudes as, for instance, the English, French, or Americans. They were not used to working with other people. They either worked for someone, or they had someone work for them. They were either a slave or a master. This is exaggerated to make my point. Therefore the German respected and feared authority as such (including his own). But once he had a little power and elbowroom, he became overbearing, didactic, and sadistic. He loved to indulge in destructive criticism (e.g., "I only want to tell you the truth."). He took his emotions and himself most seriously, lacked common sense, and he seldom laughed at himself.

The Germans were pedantic in ordering or pigeonholing things, ideas, and people. Every eraser, pencilsharpener, and paper clip had to have a certain assigned spot in the drawer. Even in their thinking, they were thorough about details: witness Rosenberg's Myth of the Twentieth Century or all of the Nazi propaganda. In these writings they jumped from isolated details to sweeping generalities without using the bridge of logic. They had an anti-rationalist attitude.

Although there were many problems peculiar to the Germans, it would not be right to isolate Germany from the family of nations after the war. The more we singled out Germany, the more we would have to control her, the more the German nation would become a nation of martyrs. Therefore, it seemed to me, our measures should be not only punitive and restrictive, but also constructive. The first two could very well have been taken care of by the armies of occupation, but the third had to be dealt with, as much as possible, by the Germans themselves.

We certainly had not done a good job with the punitive measures. Many SS criminals were living luxuriously in German hospitals sporting Red Cross armbands or going under the pretext that they were recovering from all sorts of wounds. Many German soldiers were still proudly adorned with Nazi medals and ribbons, including the SS insignia. It was quite common that, when the ordinary German went to the Rathaus (city hall), he encountered there one of his former Nazi superiors who was now a public servant under the Allied military government. The American public apparently was satisfied with the death or capture of important men like Himmler, Goering, and Streicher. However, the Russians had done by far the most thorough job of all the four Allies in regard to the capture and punishment of all the devout Nazis and of the worst war criminals. Their breaking up of the land-holding Junker (nobility) class was a good example.

I also thought that we should employ prisoners of war in areas (including Germany) that had been devastated by the war, to clear off the debris, to repair or construct essential roads, and to build homes for the bombed-out refugees and civilians. The non-fraternization policy seemed to be a punishment more to the American soldier than to the German civilian. Although the essential purpose of this policy was a good one, few of the American soldiers were sufficiently idealistic to ignore their civilian environment to such an extent. Besides that, the recreational facilities for the average GI were particularly poor at this time, and there was some advantage to having natural human contact and companionship with the former enemies.

As far as the restrictive measures were concerned, we would have made a great mistake by limiting transportation and food distribution to the same extent as the Germans did in the countries they had occupied during the war. It would not have been a wise policy to make the Germans starve as a retributive measure. We should have let the Germans produce their own food. When the Allies first moved into Germany, they found the basements well stocked with food. However by next winter these supplies surely would have been exhausted. It was also the task of the Allied armies to establish essential transportation. All the big German industries had to be strictly supervised. When Hitler came to power, German science was immediately geared to war, and this now had to be reversed.

And finally, the constructive measures: It was very necessary to tell the Germans about Dachau and the other concentration camps, about the cruelties and atrocities committed by the German Army in the occupied areas, and about the lies fabricated by Goebbels and others. The people needed first to face the truth. However, it was not enough to inform the Germans about all these evil deeds and prejudices; we had to put something more positive in their stead. We could not leave a vacuum, or the Germans would simply drift back to their old ways or develop new prejudices. Germany was off-center now. Before she regained her sense of balance, we had to be fully prepared to start her off in the right direction. Until now we had failed to a large extent, and it seemed to me that the Russians had proved to be much more successful in their administration of German territory. Unfortunately, they were also very dictatorial. We should have made better use of press and radio. We should have opened theaters, museums, and music halls, and we should have printed new books, especially those used in the institutions of learning. Many of the public school books, often dating back to the Weimar Republic, needed to be replaced. After all, it was the education of the young that would count the most eventually. We should have put more responsibility on the shoulders of the proletariat and of the lower bourgeois, for the most ardent and dangerous Nazis came from the middle and upper-middle class. Therefore, I was in favor of strong labor unions—stronger than those in the Weimar Republic.

After the conquest of Germany in May of 1945, most of the measures taken since had been negative or only half-hearted affairs. We had not made the least effort to fight German prejudice against the French or the Russians, and we had done hardly anything in educating the Germans to a more international outlook. I had talked with many Germans who were willing and capable of working for or cooperating with the Allies. To my surprise, their background was quite liberal and their outlook very progressive, yet the military government invariably chose reactionary Germans for the important civil service and political positions. They chose the people who had done very "nicely" under the Nazis. Most of our military government seemed to think that our main task was to prevent Germany from preparing for another war. Few of these officials realized that it should be our ultimate aim to bring Germany into the family of the United Nations as an equal partner.

The End of the War

Every morning our situation map indicated that the Germans had lost more ground; the thin black string that encompassed the area held by the enemy on our map covered a smaller and smaller area. It was quite apparent that the war in Europe would be over very soon. On the morning of May 9, 1945, a GI tore down the string and replaced it with a big sign: "It's All Ours."

THE SITUATION MAP

Europe was indeed "all ours." The war was over, and we expected to celebrate. However, few of the GIs that I was with were in a celebratory mood. VE-Day felt almost sad. We had waited for so long and with such hope for the shooting to end, but we knew that much of the excitement was over, too. Our team's job of looking for documents was coming to an end. Now there would be more regimentation, more garrison life, more "chicken" (the army term for useless orders), and we were still far from home. We no longer had a purpose. It's no wonder that during the next few months, many GIs went out to look for excitement and found trouble.

The constant topic among remaining GIs was ser-

vice points, adding them up, comparing them, and trying to figure out how to acquire the magic number of
eighty-five, which was needed to be sent home. The task
of shipping millions of Americans home seemed overwhelming, and we spent much time trying to guess from
which port of embarkation we might leave. The soldiers
were, of course, eager to get home and exuded confidence and plans for what they would do when they
arrived there, yet underneath this confidence was a real
fear of whether or not they would be able to fit into
civilian life. The lucky ones already had jobs waiting for
them, but most of them did not.

The end of the war was hard for me too. I had experienced much independence, and suddenly was caught
up in the minutia of rules and regulations that I had
always had a hard time accepting. The army offered to
fix some of my teeth, which had been lost during the
war, but I wouldn't even wait for that; I wanted out right
now!

C.B.I. (the China, Burma, and India theater of war)
became the scare word for many GIs, especially those
with few points. I didn't worry much about that; I was
one of the high-point men. Thanks to five battle stars,
for serving in five theaters of war (France, Belgium, Italy,
Luxembourg, and Germany) and two medals—the
Soldier's Medal for rescuing Alfred, and the Bronze Star
for finding SS personnel files, I had thirty-five extra
points. Most of us felt little interest in the Pacific; we
knew far too little about all those islands. C.B.I. was a
subject most GIs avoided, and although the West may
have been declining (according to Oswald Spengler),
world attention was still focused largely on the countries
that bordered the Atlantic Ocean.

There were no wild victory celebrations around me; instead, only small parties and quiet gatherings. A friend of mine, also a staff sergeant, and I decided to go up to my room to celebrate VE-Day over two bottles of champagne, a can of sardines, and a loaf of German rye bread. Sergeant Scott was a special buddy. Wherever the army had taken me there always seemed to be GIs who shared my inter-

Tom and Sergeant Scott

ests—cathedral hopping, playing music together, or hiking, etc. The Sergeant was also a "three-language man" and we had developed a system of making up puns and short sayings in the three languages. He was very quick and very funny, and we often roared with laughter at our play on words in several languages.

That night the officers next door were having a hilarious time with their German girlfriends. Two houses down the road, in the colonel's villa, a German accordionist was playing some old, popular folk songs. Occasionally, the colonel and his officer friends joined in singing American tunes, while the German songs were sung exclusively by women's voices. Ironically, I celebrated the victory listening to German music and songs. Across the street, some GIs tested their German weapons until a drunken second lieutenant stuck his head out of the window and shouted, "I'll have you court-martialed if you don't stop that god-damned shooting."

Sergeant Scott and I sat and philosophized, deciding how we would solve the problems of the world. We had played our roles as "Liberators of Europe;" now it was up to us to do more—to win the peace. Few of us realized that this was a more complicated task than winning the war. The average GI may have been more aware of the political problems of Europe than his father had been in World War I, but he fought the war mainly to get back to the "good ole USA," which he considered a secure shelter from the war-torn and hungry world. He often did not realize that America could still learn a great deal from the old country, and that our contribution to world peace needed to be more than a loaf of bread or the prestige of the American dollar or the generosity of the American soldier. We were still a young country—a country with thousands of opportunities. Many of the Europeans looked on us as if we were immature little children who read the funnies, played around a good deal, and never took life very seriously. It is true that, in the fields of art, politics, philosophy, and general culture, we had much to learn from the European countries. One might say that we had a more extroverted culture than most of these European nations. It might also be said that, in spite of all our economic wealth, the average American had a more materialistic philosophy than the average European, even though the European had been more materially deprived.

While the Europeans had a very distorted picture of life in America, described by their own press and by Hollywood, they nevertheless had come to realize that there was a good deal more to the average Yankee than they had originally believed. The uniformed GI was not always the best ambassador the American people could have sent abroad; yet, in spite of his occasional misconduct, the Europeans soon recognized many admirable qualities of the American people in the behavior of the GI.

My European friends were particularly impressed with our basic democratic attitude. They were amazed to see our enlisted men talk back to their superiors (within some definite limits!) They liked our easy-going and commonsense way of dealing with others. We agreed that there is no other country where the democratic attitude is imbedded in the hearts of the people to the extent it is in America.

While the Englishman, Frenchmen, Germans, and Italians were separated from each other by language and political, economic, and cultural barriers, the ethnically diverse Americans lived together relatively peacefully, listened to the same radio programs, and read the same papers. This was a powerful demonstration to those who believed the various European nationalities could never cooperate on any basis.

The European was impressed with the generosity of the average American soldier. True, the abundance of supplies made it easy to be generous; yet, the American was often seen to share his last rations with a hungry child. He was generous with his time, and he was always willing to talk and listen to anyone on an equal basis.

Most GIs had many meaningful experiences in Europe that they were unlikely to forget. They had become aware of some of the needs and problems that existed in Europe. In time, would the American soldier forget these problems, along with his unpleasant experiences? Would he crawl back into his isolationist's hole believing that Europe, a safe distance of three thousand miles away, was irrelevant? The Sergeant and I agreed that future world peace depended on America's whole-hearted participation in worldwide cooperation between nations. We would have to be educated for this by our schools and the press, including radio; we would have to be educated to become world citizens.

One Sunday while in Munich, I decided to go to the only Protestant church that had not been damaged in the war. I was the only American who attended the service, and I happened to sit next to the wall on which the names of the German war dead had been inscribed. Judging by the number of names listed, the congregation must have suffered a very large number of casualties.

The text for the morning's service was taken from Luke XVI, the story of Lazarus and the rich man. The worst thing a preacher could do, I thought to myself, is compare Lazarus with Germany and the rich man with America. Five minutes later, he did just that. He described Germany's miserable state, comparing it with the fate of the poor beggar, Lazarus. He felt it was a pity to see all those beautiful German automobiles lying by the roadside (most of these were actually military vehicles, or automobiles stolen from the French), while the Americans were sitting smugly in their speedies (jeeps), racing irresponsibly through the streets. He thought that it was wrong to judge Germany at this time; God had already taken care of that (he never explained how). Besides, he thought, Germany had been punished enough already. He also heartily condemned the fact that the plaintiff and the judge (the Allies) were the same person. Not one prayer was offered for the enemy or for the peoples of the world. The minister spoke of brotherly love, but apparently this love extended only as far as the German border. At the end of his sermon, he again talked about "das arme Deutschland " (poor Germany), while the ladies pulled out their handkerchiefs and started to cry. Since I was the only American present, I felt very self-conscious. After such a nationalistic sermon, however, I could muster little sympathy for "das arme Deutschland." And so I sat there for a while. The beauty of the churches I had seen, the goodness of many people I had known, the horror of war and of man's cruelty passed before me. I don't now remember how or when it happened, but I became aware that I was no longer interested in becoming a minister.

* * *

I was able to get a furlough to England where I hoped to see Al's mother and brother. I wrote to my mother before leaving Germany.

July, 1945

Dear Mom,
I am now stationed in Heidelberg. This is not as nice as Bad Wimpfen, since we are not as independent and isolated. Fortunately I am working with a very nice officer. Last week we went into the British sector, all the way up to Minden. Saw Kassel, which is really destroyed (everything from the Wilhelmshöhe to the Opera house).
Well, dear, my correspondence may be quite irregular from now on. I'll try to keep up the good works, though that

doesn't give you any excuses at all not to write. Right now I'm a wee bit worried about your literary absence.

PS: Where did you get the idea that the Russians in many ways are more cultural than the Americans? Let's take it easy there. However, the world appreciates your favorable attitude toward our Bolshevik ally.

From London, I wrote to her again:

August 14, 1945, London

Dear Mom,

This may, by chance, turn out to be a fairly long letter. Right now, I am sitting in the Red Cross Club on Piccadilli Circus in London, sweating out a plane for the continent. I am tired and weary. The first news of the Japanese willingness to accept the armistice has come through. I could cry with joy as well as with ill-forboding. Downstairs, London traffic is squeaking, honking, and rattling by.

Well, the furlough came through and I might as well give you a brief outline of how things happened. On the evening of the fifth in the courtyard of the Heidelberg Schloss I heard a very lovely all-Beethoven concert. Das kann man den Deutschen schon lassen. The Germans certainly know something about music.

Next morning I went to an airstrip at Mannheim. This was to be another "famous first" for me. In three hours and ten minutes we were to be in London. Everything went fine, except when we encountered very nasty weather over the channel. Even when we hit England, the storm persisted. Instead of being "dipped" down, we began to see wheat fields and villages first on the left side and then again on the right. Three fellows became sick and T.L.F. [me] set a precedent by being the first one. The plane was weaving from left to right. As this was my first plane ride, I got very tense and my digestive system began to work overtime, especially in the direction of my throat. I knew I might throw up. There was no regurgitation bag or bucket. Behind every seat in these C-47s is a window that cannot be opened, but has a rubber plug

SHEILA

that can be pulled out. I was dizzy and desperate, so I headed for the plug, which was big enough for my mouth to fit in. Any moment my German breakfast would be catapulting into the hole. Unfortunately, there was a tremendous gush of air into the plane. As I tried to feed the British countryside, the half-digested food was sprayed all over the inside of the plane, over my uniform and the uniforms of the other GIs. No one got angry, and after the most violent eruptions, I got a GI towel from my pack and wiped off the other soldiers.

As soon as I got into London proper I called up Larry [a college roommate] who is stationed there. L is still the "delightful old chap" he was, as they say in England, only he has become more reserved, or should I say "shy"? Next morning I visited the London art gallery which is still fairly empty. One of the guards told me that it'll take another two years before all the art treasures will have reached the home loft. The English painting school was quite well represented there, yet the very ones of their pictures I liked were those of Turner's. There were two very nice El Greco's, many altar paintings, and quite a good representation of the Dutch school.

This was quite a week. The news of the atom bomb struck me with very mixed feelings. Finally we are able to obliterate the whole human race if we want to. Perhaps some Chinese or Buddhist priest living at the foot of the Himalayas will survive the next war.

On the seventh I drove out to Croxly Green to meet my pen-friend Sheila. I had never met her in person before. I had only received the most amazing (interesting) letters from her. It was a blind date. She had asked me to come and I had got a room across the street from her. My landlady treated me as if I was her own son. At eight o'clock her daughter would come tiptoeing into the room, waking me up with a "spot of tea." In the evening I'd find a glass of milk and a tart standing by my bedside. Sheila was okay, but her boyfriend later sort of spoiled our fun by insisting that she go

ALFRED: THE BRITISH SOLDIER
WE RESCUED IN THE ALPS

out with him. I never met him, but he was frightfully jealous of her, going to the extent of crying when she let him down. Although the war has hardened me somewhat in this respect, my heart is still tender and I was a bit mad.

I also saw the man Alfred we rescued in Val d'Isère. He is amazingly well. He has his whole left hand, the thumb on his right hand, and one can hardly tell by his walk that he has two artificial legs.

Saturday I was alone, so I

went to St. Albans to see the famous cathedral and the only Roman amphitheater in England. The foundation of the cathedral was made out of the stones of the ancient Roman road and the largest part of the edifice dates back to 1077. One of the largest buildings I've ever seen; yet, I wouldn't say that it is one of the most beautiful of England's cathedrals. The strongly Norman influence makes it look heavy, almost like a fortress—and I don't mean "a mighty fortress is our God." That afternoon I saw a nice homemade sign over the entrance of an English home; flags were stuck all over the place. On the sign it said: "Welcome Home"... that sign struck me to the core. And with Japan slowly making up her mind to give up, perhaps I might be home sooner than planned.

Sunday I went to Oxford. The whole visit started out in a rather odd fashion: the train stopped for twenty minutes right by a cemetery just outside of Oxford—what an ill omen. My whole visit to Mammschen left me sad and I shall pass on my impression to you. The old lady was delighted to see me, but she has aged. Caring for Anni (her daughter) until the very last has taken it out of her. Hugo (her son) is still there and that's about all one wants to say about him. Mentally Mammschen is as alert as ever. In fact, she has some rather good ideas in politics and she certainly sizes up people fairly well. The liveliness she had just before Anni's death has somewhat disappeared. She has high blood pressure and frequent nosebleeds. With great effort she does her duties in the house. Hugo is as helpful as he can be. He still looks for "steady" garden work. He knits and crochets potholders, dishrags, and shopping bags, and helps around the house. He is terribly worried about earning his own subsistence... M. told me that Spatz writes every Sunday, Al about once a month and Lottie, when she does write, sends a very nice

VJ DAY AT PICCADILLY SQUARE - AUGUST 8TH

letter. You should get busy and write her once a week ... her only pleasure ... she certainly deserves it. In America your worries are different, you have enough to eat to get along, you have friends. Certainly Mammschen gives one the impression of having reached the end. Several months ago you apparently sent her many very nice parcels. M. hates to ask for stuff. Now that she cannot stand in line anymore the groceries are being sent to her. She told me she can manage, yet, almost by "third degree" interrogation, I found out that she badly wants some rice, cheese, and any kind of fats. Rationing in England is not only persisting, but in some respects is getting worse. I understand rationing will be finished in the USA soon.

    I saw the consul in London about the visa for M. No visas are being granted at this time. The new regulations should arrive here in two - three weeks, and I understand it'll be easier to get one. Yet M. will have to reapply since everything will be handled in London. Then, I went to see the doctor about Hugo, and it looks hopeless. Personally, I don't think Hugo is a burden on society. The doctor tells me that because he has such a low I.Q. and cannot take care of himself, he will not get a visa. I object to this. The Americans are fond of numbers and they force each individual into a category even if he doesn't fit it. The doctor (a colonel) admitted that H. was a borderline case. I wrote M. that she had two choices: go to the US by herself and provide for H. in England (with our help) or stay in England, receive more material and financial assistance from America, and still provide for H. It certainly looks bad for the old lady. Now that things are handled in London, your help and Spatzchens's will be of less use. I took some pictures of her. I'll send them to you and to Spatz. Now I have to report to London airport every morning at 8:00 am. Today all the planes to Germany were grounded. We have to stick around the office all day. This is certainly an anti-climax to a fairly nice furlough. The English—that is the common run of them—are okay. To the German, they seem conceited and reserved; to me, they are just like their homes: a bit off the road, surrounded by trees and shrubbery, but when you come in, you are welcomed with a spot of tea, and I certainly feel at home with them. They are quiet and gentle; and they never step all over you. Of course, I'm talking about the nicer English. If I could only stay here a little longer! I've never been as homesick, as eager to settle down and work, as I have during the past week here.

Last night victory news with Japan was announced. American soldiers in London went wild. The noise was so loud that I couldn't sleep for two hours.

Well, we'll all have to stand by now. I signed up for the duration and six months, and as far as points are concerned, I am not among those with the lowest score. I don't want to go back to Germany!

Goodbye dear, give my very best to Al and Chris.
Believe me, I am terribly eager to come home.
Take two big V-kisses from,
Tom

I returned to my team in Germany from my furlough in London. Going home and planning for the future had become an important theme of discussion for me, and among many GIs. I shared my thoughts and feelings in a letter to my mother:

September 17, 1945, Heidelberg

Dear Mom,

Right now I am in suspense. The point system is quite messed up; I might be sent home tomorrow or two months from now. This week all German-speaking personnel were frozen. After several changes they finally decided to let those people who had eighty-five points as of VJ-Day go. I have eighty points right now. Lucky for me, I am going to receive another medal which will give me five more points as of VJ-Day. Anyway, I figure on being home by Christmas, unless I sign up with some university, the Red Cross, or UNRRA,

and on that score I am unpredictable. To tell you the truth, I am terribly anxious to get home, but on the other hand, I am quite afraid of civilian life in the States.

FOLLIES BERGERE, PARIS

Not only do I see a wee bit of darkness for the post-war period, but I also have great fears about my own abilities.

Last Saturday I received a note from the office of the commanding officer of the Seventh Army (a lieutenant general) to the effect that my application for temporary duty in Berlin [in hopes of seeing my father whom I had not seen for seven years] was unfavorably considered. "Was kann der kleine Mann da tun?" was his response. [What can the little man do there?] Today I shall go to the Army headquarters in Frankfurt and try to arrange something there.

Last week I gave two lectures in the Army educational program. My mind is certainly in a rotten state right now.

You may wonder why I continue in ink. Well, this morning I was suddenly told that I might leave for the States this afternoon. So I sent home all my personal belongings including that super typewriter. This suspense is killing me...

The last two weeks I spent a good deal of my time on the road doing an average of two-hundred miles per day, which is quite a bit for Europe.

Last week I got myself a jeep and drove to Wiesbaden. I stayed at the house of a very good friend of mine. Sunday we went hiking in the Taunus ... remember our little trip with Hans in the good old days? Anyway, I had a very good time, in spite of the fact that the physical effort was simply too much for me.

I AM LEAVING FOR THE STATES TODAY! SEPT 20, 1945.

Finally we received orders that we would be going through Paris to a point of embarkation. From Paris I wrote again:

Sept 22, 1945, Paris

Dear Mom,

In all probability, I'll leave Paris tomorrow for a replacement depot. From there we'll go to a Port of Embarkation, and then by boat to the States. I haven't the faintest idea when I'll get to Portland. At any rate, it would be nice if you got the whole family together. There might be a chance that I arrive by plane. Whether I'll get a discharge right away or a furlough first, I don't know. But I'm a high point man (85 points, and I should soon become a civilian). Two days ago I was awarded the Bronze star for "liberating the files of all SS non-commissioned and commissioned officers." That means an additional five points, which is important.

Now, as to my plans for the future: I have been worrying about it for the last few months. It'll certainly not be very easy for me to adjust. Since I feel I don't know anything at all, I'll have to go back to school for at least one year. For the past two years, I have been thinking about studying social work in the same field as Warry [a friend who was the county welfare director]. There is a good school in Chicago. I doubt seriously whether I could start tout de suite. Might be a cagey idea to get a job until January while oiling my rusty mind. I'd simply love to go with the family somewhere for a few days. I hope you can take time out to get me straightened out.

All this uncertainty makes me feel somewhat pessimistic. I've seen too many French, English, and German soldiers return to civilian life, and I envied few of them.

I am still quite disappointed that I couldn't see Father, especially after I saw the Russian movie Fall of Berlin *last night. Anyway, my lieutenant, my last officer, a swell fel-*

low, is going to go to Berlin as soon as he can make the arrangements. I gave him two big boxes of rations, a lot of cigars, and a few odds and ends, and four-thousand reichsmark and pictures of the family. If Father is still alive, this packet should be some consolation to him. I gave the lieutenant three addresses, so we should hear something of him. Also, one of us ought to be able to return to Europe by air. I'm glad to be back in Paris. I had hoped to get a furlough to go to the beach, but apparently they want to ship me home in a hurry.

A bientôt ... je Vous embrasse.

Tom

Sept. 27, 1945, near Thienville, France

Dear Mom,

Might as well write, there's nothing else to do. We left Paris last Sunday. Had a grand time while I was there. My application for a furlough in France was immediately rejected. I had my first ride in a boxcar—forty men or eight horses [a term used in WWI]. We spent about twenty hours in this wagon. Perhaps they are trying to make hobos out of us. [These were the same box cars in which the Jews had been transported to the concentration camps, but for us it was a happy journey.]

Now I'm in a replacement depot, literally sweating it out. They're trying to put a bad aftertaste of the army into us. I wish I could give you more exact information as to my arrival. We will probably leave here on about the fourth of October. From there we will proceed to Le Havre or to Marseille. The former trip takes approximately one day, or at the most, three. At this staging area, one stays anywhere from three to seven days. The majority of troops are said to cross the Atlantic in overcrowded Liberty ships. This takes about twelve days. Thus, all things being equal, I should arrive in the States around the twenty-fifth of October. From the East coast they might ship me directly to Fort Lewis, Washington. Well, you should know the army by now and it has not changed. If I'm lucky, I will be home in the first week of November. Whether I'll be civilian or a soldier, I don't know. You can be sure, though, that when I am home I will be there!

I should like to ask you to do me a big favor. Perhaps Chris can do it for me. I should like to have some bulletins of the country's best schools of social work. The one in Chicago is said to be very good. Perhaps the Reed sociology professor will know. I am told it's best to arrange these things as soon as possible in order to derive the most benefit from the GI bill. According to the bill, the government will pay my tuition for three years and give me $50 a month for subsistence during the same period. Although this is not quite enough money, it is nevertheless an excellent deal. I probably won't be going to school all these three years. One builds dream castles in the air which are constantly overshadowed by the clouds of inability, frustration, misplacement, and what-have-you.

But whatever happens, we are all terribly looking forward to coming home to the folks, to have that party, to sit down at the table without standing in line for half an hour, to sleep between clean sheets, to—okay, so I am a materialist.

My love to all of you,
Tom

ON THE WAY HOME IN A BOXCAR
(PRIVATE ALTMAN, ME, AND JUNIOR-SGT. ON LEFT UNKNOWN)

Coming "Home"

On the way home, by chance, I met some of my old team from the Alps and we rode together in boxcars. My return to the US was laden with mixed emotions. I had had a rich experience in the war, and I knew what I had done was important. I had grown from a youth into a man. I felt I was truly becoming an American, yet I knew there was much for me to do to make peace with the Germans and to acknowledge and appreciate that part of me that was German. This was a task that lay before me.

I remembered my first trip across the Atlantic at the age of 16—a naive, if hopeful, refugee traveling to a strange land. This time I was returning home as a US citizen, jammed into a troop ship as one of thousands of American soldiers. They had given their extreme efforts in a war, and now they were eager to take their place in a peaceful future for America, and for the world.

Shortly before we embarked for the States, I had come across a timely quotation from Shakespeare's Anthony and Cleopatra Act IV, Scene 15, Line 64:

40 AND 8 (40 SOLDIERS OR
EIGHT HORSES) MY OLD TEAM

SOLDIERS MEDAL (LEFT) FOR RESCUING ALFRED
THE BRONZE STAR (RIGHT) FOR CAPTURING SS
PERSONNEL FILES

GAMBLING ABOARD SHIP

MARSELLE HARBOR ON THE WAY HOME

"OFFICER'S COUNTRY"

O! wither'd is the garland of the war,
The soldier's pole is fall'n: young boys and girls
Are level now with men; the odds is gone,
And there is nothing left remarkable
Beneath the visiting moon —

HOME AT LAST WITH FAMILY
CHRIS, AL, MOM AND ME

Epilogue

My mother Lottie continued an active social and artistic life. She and Al built their dream house in a small forest with a magnificent view of four snow-capped mountains. She remained in her beloved house until she died May 14, 1990, shortly before her ninetieth birthday.

Al enjoyed an active professional life, going to the office and caring for his patients until the day of his death in 1973. He was deeply mourned by his patients.

Max, my father, remained in Berlin during the war. He was bombed out three times, and then moved in with his life partner Lena on the Kurfürstendamm. In 1949, when the situation was desperate in Germany, I was able to bring him to this country, where he worked first as a houseman in a girl's dormitory at Northwestern University near Chicago. Later, as his English improved, he was able to get a good engineering job with Procon, an oil refining company, where he remained until retirement. He was in this country for eighteen years. He then returned to Germany and to Lena where he enjoyed walking the Kurfürstendamm and smoking and drinking in the cafés. I saw him many times during that period. He died in 1978 of lung cancer.

My brother Chris studied with Anna Freud in London and teaches at the University of California in Los Angeles. He was able to follow the dream he wrote about in his letter, and for many years has headed a project assisting at-risk mothers and babies to thrive. He has three sons with his English-born wife, Sally.

Lottie's mother (my grandmother), Maria Johanna, died sometime during World War II, and my mother heard about it much later.

Bernhard, my mother's brother, went through World War I unharmed and joined the family firm, which had profited immensely from war contracts. Times were very bad for the firm after the first war until Hitler came, and then they again did very well. Bernhard became a fervent Nazi, but when the Russians came in World War II, he lost everything and had to flee. After the war we sent him some packages, but then lost track of him.

Al's daughter, Hannah, my stepsister, remains a good friend. We talk on the phone (sometimes in French) several times a week. She lives in Baltimore and has two sons, as well as two grandchildren.

Christof Drexel, the painter friend of my mother's, was put on Hitler's "decadent art" list, but he withdrew into the Bavarian Alps where he continued painting. After the war, I visited him several times in Munich where he was painting character portraits that he hoped would be used by psychotherapists for projections—an idea he had originally developed with Carl Jung. He lived into his nineties and phoned Lottie the night before he died.

Ilse Frank, my mother and Al's friend (and my dancing teacher), is still painting and selling her works today in Hamburg. She has a life-partner, another painter, and is still a beautiful woman with great style. She recently celebrated her ninetieth birthday. She painted a beautiful portrait of my mother, and visited her here in the USA. I see her often when I visit Germany, and she has come to see me there, sometimes taking bus rides of many hours to do so.

Cora Schröeder, who was Jewish (her husband was not), stayed in Germany. During the war, she remained hidden in an attic. Neighbors and friends shared their ration coupons with her husband, Hanning. After the war, she continued an active life filled with music, and promoted her husband's works. I stayed in touch with her and visited several times. She died in 1997 at the age of ninety-seven, four days after my last visit.

The Edelsteins, Al's sister and brother-in-law, moved to the University of California in Berkeley, where Ludwig was one of the non-signers of the loyalty oath (loyalty to the US required of all state employees during the McCarthy era). Consequently, he had to leave and returned to Johns Hopkins. I saw them often when they were in California. They lived comfortable and active lives, involved with the academic community, until they were quite old.

Hans Tremmel married Friedl in Berlin and they had two children as well as several grandchildren. My mother and I kept in touch with them, and I visited him and his beloved Schreber garden (the small plot of land some apartment dwellers had nearby). I was with him shortly before he died.

Mount St. Helens, near where Chris and I camped, erupted in 1980, changing the landscape and spewing ashes as far away as the Levy house in Portland. Harry Truman, the old mountain guide and recluse, refused to leave and was lost in the devastation.

In 1966, I returned to Eichkamp with my own family, and visited a former neighbor who had remained in touch with my mother. I asked about my high school friends. "Where is Andrew?" I asked.

"Gefallen," she replied (meaning fallen in battle).
"And Pete?"
"Auch gefallen," she replied.
One by one, I asked, "And Jurgen?"
"Klaus?"
"Horst?"
"Dietrich?"
I listed them all, and to each she replied, "Gefallen."

Pastor Niemoeller was arrested and sent to jail in July, 1937, a few days after my confirmation. He was found not guilty by the courts, but Hitler then had him arrested as his own personal prisoner. He was in Sachsenhausen concentration camp in solitary confinement from 1938-41, when he was transferred to Dachau (the concentration camp). Shortly before the liberation of Dachau, he was sent to another camp, where he remained until the end of the war. I saw him again in 1947 when he visited Seattle. He had become a very influential, respected leader, and a member of the World Council of Churches. His writing and preaching became increasingly important, and politically, he turned more and more to the left. He died in 1984 at the age of 92— vital until the end.

I arrived home from the war in October, 1945. In December I began work at Multnomah County Welfare Department where I met many former Reed College students who were working there. Among them was one who became my wife. We attended graduate school in social work, both getting our masters degrees, and raised three children. I worked mostly in Corrections until I retired in 1977, and my wife Delphine and I then taught and gave workshops in group dynamics and counseling in Europe, particularly in Germany.

TOM & DELPHINE